NICCOLÒ

NICCOLÒ'S SMILE

A Biography of Machiavelli

MAURIZIO VIROLI

Translated from the Italian by Antony Shugaar

HILL AND WANG

A division of Farrar, Straus and Giroux

New York

Hill and Wang
A division of Farrar, Straus and Giroux
18 West 18th Street, New York 10011

Library of Congress Cataloging-in-Publication Data
Viroli, Maurizio.
    [Sorriso di Niccolò. English]
    Niccolò's smile: a biography of Machiavelli / Maurizio Viroli ;
translated from the Italian by Antony Shugaar.—1st American ed.
        p. cm.
    Includes bibliographical references and index.
    ISBN 0-374-52800-4 (pbk.)
    1. Machiavelli, Niccolò, 1469–1527.   2. Florence (Italy)—Politics
and government—1421–1737.   3. Statesmen—Italy—Florence—
Biography.   4. Intellectuals—Italy—Florence—Biography.
5. Authors, Italian—16th century—Biography.   I. Title.

DG738.14.M2 V74 2000
945'.5106'092—dc21
[B]

                                                    00-029380

Designed by Jonathan D. Lippincott

www.fsgbooks.com

3   5   7   9   10   8   6   4

In Memory of Pier Paolo D'Attorre,
Mayor of Ravenna

Contents

Author's Note

I did not write this biography in hopes of outdoing—in richness or in precision of historical information and documentation—those scholars who have explored the life of Machiavelli before me, foremost among them Roberto Ridolfi. His great work on Machiavelli remains an unrivaled classic; it has been my chief guide. What I have tried to do here is to recount the same stories in a new way, to focus on aspects that were previously overlooked, and here and there to revise accepted views.

I have always been fascinated by Machiavelli—by his political thinking and writing, but especially by the way in which he laughed about life and other people. I wrote these pages in an attempt to understand the meaning of his smile, a smile that emerges from his letters, from his works, and from certain portraits of him. I believe that his smile represents a great understanding of life, even deeper than his political thought.

The reader will find some fairly strong language in the letters by Machiavelli and his correspondents and in documents of the period, expressions that other biographers have edited or cut. I have left them intact. I have kept in-text citations to a minimum and have indicated the sources of quoted materials with abbreviations, as listed below. The translations I have used are mostly from the English-language editions listed here, with some minor modifications and adjustments I have chosen to make myself.

D (followed by book and chapter numbers)
  Discorsi sopra la prima deca di Tito Livio, in Niccolò Machiavelli, *Opere,* vol. 1, ed. Corrado Vivanti (Turin: Einaudi-Gallimard, 1997). *Discourses on Livy,* trans. Harvey C. Mansfield

and Nathan Tarcov (Chicago: University of Chicago Press, 1996).

G (followed by book and page numbers)
Francesco Guicciardini, *Storia d'Italia,* in *Opere,* vols. 2–3, ed. Emanuella Lugnani Scavano (Turin: UTET, 1970). *History of Italy,* trans. Sidney Alexander (New York: Macmillan, 1972).

IF (followed by book and chapter numbers)
Istorie Fiorentine, in Niccolò Machiavelli, *Opere,* vol. 2, ed. Alessandro Montevecchi (Turin: UTET, 1986). *Florentine Histories,* trans. Laura F. Banfield and Harvey C. Mansfield (Princeton, N.J.: Princeton University Press, 1990).

L (followed by page number)
Lettere, in Niccolò Machiavelli, *Opere,* vol. 3, ed. Franco Gaeta (Turin: UTET, 1984). Personal letters from and to Machiavelli are translated in James B. Atkinson and David Sices, *Machiavelli and His Friends* (De Kalb: Northern Illinois University Press, 1996).

LC (followed by page number)
Niccolò Machiavelli, *Legazioni e Commissarie,* 3 vols., ed. Sergio Bertelli (Milan: Feltrinelli, 1964).

O (followed by page number)
Niccolò Machiavelli, *Opere,* vol. 1, ed. Corrado Vivanti (Turin: Einaudi-Gallimard, 1997).

P (followed by chapter number)
Niccolò Machiavelli, *De Principatibus,* ed. Giorgio Inglese (Rome: Istituto Storico per il Medio Evo, 1994). *The Prince,* trans. Harvey Mansfield (Chicago: University of Chicago Press, 1998).

R (followed by page number)
  Roberto Ridolfi, *Vita di Niccolò Machiavelli,* 3d ed. (Florence: Sansoni, 1969).

SL (followed by page number)
  Scritti letterari, in Niccolò Machiavelli, *Opere,* vol. 4, ed. Luigi Blasucci (Turin: UTET, 1989).

Chronology of Historical Events

in Italy, 1494–1527

1494 The French king Charles VIII marches into Italy, laying claim to the throne of the Kingdom of Naples. In Milan, Ludovico il Moro (the Moor) takes the throne from his nephew Gian Galeazzo II Sforza. In Florence, Piero de' Medici is dethroned and a Republic is established. Pisa secedes from the dominions of Florence.

1495 Charles VIII enters Naples. An anti-French league is formed (Ludovico il Moro, the pope, Venice, Spain, and the Holy Roman Empire); after fighting the league's hostile forces at the Battle of Fornovo, King Charles barely manages to take his army back to France.

1498 Charles VIII dies. In Florence, Savonarola is executed.

1499 The new king of France, Louis XII, forms an alliance with Venice, Pope Alexander VI, and Florence against Ludovico il Moro. The pope's son Cesare Borgia, Duke Valentino, begins to build his personal dominion with conquests in Romagna.

1500 Ludovico il Moro is captured by the French after their victory at Novara with Swiss reinforcements. The Treaty of Granada calls for the partition of southern Italy between France and Spain, but it remains a dead letter.

1502 In Florence, the office of gonfalonier for life is established.

1503 Pope Alexander VI dies; the Valentino's dominion collapses. After the very brief pontificate of Pius III, Giuliano della Rovere is elected Pope Julius II. The war between France and Spain ends with a Spanish victory at the Battle of Garigliano.

1504 With the armistice of Lyons, Naples is ceded to Spain.

1506 Pope Julius II declares war on Bologna.

1508 Pope Julius II establishes the League of Cambrai (Spain, France, the Holy Roman Empire, and the duchies of Savoy, Ferrara, and Mantua) against Venice.

1509 Venice is defeated at Agnadello. Pisa surrenders and submits once again to Florentine rule.

1511 The Holy League (the pope, Venice, Spain, England, the Swiss, and the Holy Roman Empire) is founded against the French king Louis XII, who in turn calls a council in Pisa to overthrow the pope.

1512 Although victorious in the Battle of Ravenna, the French are forced to withdraw from Italy following the Swiss invasion of Lombardy. In Milan, Massimiliano Sforza, son of Ludovico il Moro, reclaims the throne. In Florence, following the Sack of Prato, Medici power is restored.

1513 Pope Julius II dies, and Giovanni de' Medici is elected Pope Leo X. The French, defeated by the Swiss, are forced to abandon Milan.

1515 The new king of France, François I, defeats the Swiss at Marignano and reconquers Milan and its territories. Pope Leo X renounces his claims to Parma and Piacenza.

1516 With the Treaty of Noyon, the king of Spain and future emperor Charles V (elected in 1519) recognizes French claims to the duchy of Milan, while King François I renounces his claims to the Kingdom of Naples, which remains Spanish.

1521 The first war between Emperor Charles V and King François I begins with the invasion of Milanese territory by imperial armies. Pope Leo X dies.

1522 Adrian Florensz Boeyens is elected Pope Adrian VI. The French are defeated at Bicocca.

1523 After the death of Adrian VI, Giulio de' Medici is elected Pope Clement VII.

1524 François I reconquers Milan.

1525 François I is defeated and taken prisoner in the Battle of Pavia.

1526 With the Treaty of Madrid, François I cedes Milan to Spain and again renounces his claims to Naples; he returns to France and establishes the League of Cognac with the pope, Venice, Sforza, Genoa, and Florence. The Spanish occupy Milan.

1527 Spanish and German soldiers in the service of Emperor Charles V sack Rome. In Florence, the Medici are overthrown, and the Republic is restored.

NICCOLÒ'S SMILE

one

The Mask and the Face

According to legend, just before his death on 21 June 1527, Niccolò Machiavelli told the faithful friends who had stayed with him to the very end about a dream he had had, a dream that over the centuries became renowned as "Machiavelli's dream."

In his dream, he had seen a band of poorly dressed men, ragged and miserable in appearance. He asked them who they were. They replied, "We are the saintly and the blessed; we are on our way to Heaven." Then he saw a crowd of solemnly attired men, noble and grave in appearance, speaking seriously of important political matters. In their midst he recognized the great philosophers and historians of antiquity who had written fundamental works on politics and the state, such as Plato, Plutarch, and Tacitus. Again, he asked them who they were and where they were going. "We are the damned of Hell" was their answer. After telling his friends of his dream, Machiavelli remarked that he would be far happier in Hell, where he could discuss politics with the great men of the ancient world, than in Heaven, where he would languish in boredom among the blessed and the saintly.

This dream of Machiavelli's is reminiscent of another, Scipio's famous dream that Cicero describes in his treatise on the republic. Scipio the Elder, according to Cicero, appeared to his nephew Scipio Aemilianus in a dream and told him, "All those who have preserved, aided, or enlarged their fatherland have a special place prepared for them in the heavens where they may enjoy an eternal life of happiness. For nothing of all that is done on earth is more pleasing to that supreme God who rules the whole universe than the assemblies and gatherings of men associated in justice, which are called states. Their rulers and preservers come from that place [the Milky Way], and to that place they return."

Machiavelli, who was surely familiar with Scipio's dream, offered on his deathbed his own version of the story, but with a different moral. In his dream, the great men who founded, wisely governed, and reformed republics—by deed or thought—received no reward of eternal happiness in the brightest place in the universe, as in the ancient dream, but were banished to Hell, because to have done the great achievements that made them immortal they had contravened the standards of Christian morality. In Machiavelli's burlesque, with Hell more desirable and more interesting than Heaven, he meant to reiterate the message of the ancient dream—that true statesmen are like gods and deserve everlasting glory—and at the same time to ridicule the Christian Heaven and Hell.

We cannot know for certain whether this tale of Machiavelli's dream is pure invention or not, but I mention it because it strikes me as the best way of introducing the man whose life and ideas are set forth here. In this story of the dream, we find every facet of Niccolò Machiavelli's personality: mischievous; irreverent; gifted with an exceedingly subtle intelligence; unconcerned about questions of soul, afterlife, or sin; fascinated by practical affairs and great men. To his way of thinking, the greatest men were princes and the rulers of republics: men who gave good laws to their people, who led their people out of slavery and into a state of liberty—

men like Moses. Greatness lay in the affairs and achievements of states and governments, in decisions that affected the lives and destinies of the masses. Greatness lay, in short, Machiavelli thought, in politics. It is hardly surprising that on his deathbed he said he would prefer to spend eternity in Hell with great politicians than in Heaven with saints.

If there is anything strange in this story, it is that he should have found the strength to jest in his last days. By the time he died, Niccolò had become a saddened, disappointed, resigned man. He was almost sixty years old. His face was tired; his lips were twisted with bitterness; his eyes had lost the intelligent, mocking, ironic expression that appears in surviving portraits from the prime of his life. His gaze was lost in the middle distance; his thoughts turned to the past. He no longer stood tall and confident as he had when meeting princes, popes, kings, and emperors; he was stooped with fatigue—too much travel, riding day and night, too many reckless races against time, too many tattered hopes, too many unattained dreams. Above all, too much stupidity, malice, and cruelty from his many enemies.

All his life, Machiavelli spared no effort to persuade the powerful men of Italy to free the country from foreign domination, from the outrages of invading and occupying armies. Then, just a few weeks before his death, Italy's tragedy was consummated in a final, appalling act. On 6 May 1527, an army composed of Spanish infantry and a company of fearsome foot soldiers commanded by Duke Charles of Bourbon stormed the walls of Rome. The Eternal City was defended by nothing more than a pathetic rabble of poorly armed paupers recruited from the household stables of cardinals and high prelates, from workshops and taverns. The pope, who had disbanded his army just a few months before, quickly took refuge in the papal fortress, the Castel Sant'Angelo. After a few hours of fighting, Rome fell to the Spanish infantry and the lansquenets. The Spaniards were bloody-minded and greedy for loot, the Germans were fervent Protestants and thirsted for blood, plunder, and revenge on the detested Roman Catholics, and together they perpetrated the Sack of Rome.

Machiavelli had foretold how the powerful of Italy could avoid such a tragedy. No one had listened to him. What was left, then, but to laugh and tell the story of his dream? Still, his smile did nothing to warm his heart or lighten its burden of care; if he laughed, it was to keep from weeping. His laughter concealed, but did nothing to lessen, his indignation at the injustice and absurdity of a world in which rulers were helpless to protect their subjects from violence, humiliation, and hunger; a world in which those who might govern wisely, who could rein in humanity's ambition and savagery with stable institutions, fair laws, and well-trained armies, were inevitably overlooked when they were poor or of low birth or lacked influential friends.

Such had been the lot of Niccolò Machiavelli: "I was born in poverty and at an early age learned how to endure hardship rather than flourish." That did not mean he had ever gone hungry, though at times he had had to settle for rough fare. When he said he was born in poverty, he meant he had not been born to a prominent, well-to-do family and therefore could not have hoped to be elected to public office or to make a fortune in business. Family ties and friendships with influential people determined everything. Those who had neither could only watch from the sidelines, however talented or knowledgeable they might be. For those without power in Florence, "there isn't even a dog who will bark in your face," as Machiavelli wrote in *The Mandrake (La mandragola)*, his finest theatrical piece, composed in 1518.

True, the Machiavelli were a venerable old Florentine family whose members had held high offices in the city government, but Niccolò's father, Bernardo di Niccolò di Buoninsegna, belonged to an impoverished and humble branch of the family. With the meager revenues of his landholdings, he could barely eke out a living for his wife, Bartolomea de' Nelli; his daughters, Primavera and Margherita; and his two sons, Niccolò, born on 3 May 1469, and Totto, born in 1475.

Bernardo held a law degree but, unlike most of the lawyers and notaries in Florence, earned very little from his profession. Yet he must have been respected for his intelligence, for Bartolomeo Scala, a secretary of the Republic and a great humanist, included him among the participants in a dialogue on justice and the law that he wrote in 1483. Bernardo genuinely loved books; at considerable sacrifice, he assembled a small personal library that included books by Greek and Roman philosophers—especially Aristotle and Cicero—works of the great masters of rhetoric, and volumes of Italian history. Sometimes he could only borrow them, or rent them for barter, paying with produce from his lands. On one occasion, in order to obtain a copy of an upcoming edition of Livy's *History of Rome,* an important but expensive book, Bernardo agreed to compile an index of place-names in it for the Florentine publisher Niccolò della Magna. The task was exacting and dull and took nine months, but in exchange he was allowed to keep the book. Thanks to his father's patient labor, the young Niccolò was able to read and reread at his leisure the Roman historian's account of the political and military achievements that transformed a small city into a free, powerful republic. As a grown man, Niccolò used Livy's book as the basis for *Discorsi sopra la prima deca di Tito Livio* (referred to henceforth as the *Discourses*), his most important work, which contains the whole of his political thought and, in particular, his ideas about how a great and free republic is built.

Niccolò was very close to his father. To judge from surviving documents, Bernardo and Niccolò were more like two friends than like father and son; like friends, they traded pranks and jokes. Once, when Niccolò was barely scraping by in Florence, Bernardo sent him from the countryside a fat goose. In thanks, Niccolò sent him a sonnet that ended with these grateful words: "O dear Bernardo, ducks and geese/You will have bought—yet eaten none of these."

Bernardo and Niccolò shared a cheerful nature and a love of company, a fondness for lively conversation and biting repartee. A few years after Bernardo's death in May 1500, a monk from the

church of Santa Croce told Niccolò that several dead bodies had
been secretly buried in the Machiavelli family chapel there. To the
monk's amazement, Niccolò replied, "Well, let them be, for my
father was a great lover of conversation, and the more there are to
keep him company, the more pleased he will be" (R, 56). Bernardo
had been unable to give him wealth or power, but Niccolò loved
him all the same, indeed, perhaps for that very reason felt a special
fondness for him, free from the deference and fear often inspired in
sons by a rich and powerful father.

A few years before his father's death, on 11 October 1496 Niccolò lost his mother. Sadly, we know almost nothing about
Madonna Bartolomea. We have neither letters nor other written
accounts to tell us what she was like or how she felt about her husband and children. As it has with so many others, especially
women, the destructive power of time has deprived us of documents and memories about her—a loss we must accept. And what
time did not destroy, prejudice did: the prejudice of those who
considered the life of Bartolomea de' Nelli not worth even a page
in a diary or a line in a letter. We know only that she was a well-
read woman who wrote poems and religious lauds. Perhaps it was
from her that Niccolò acquired his poetic gift—his gift, that is, of
looking at life and the world with the eyes of a poet and of writing "divine prose," as a great and demanding critic of Italian litera-
ture once put it.

Bernardo and Bartolomea could not afford illustrious tutors
who might make learned humanists of their children. They gave
Niccolò and Totto a good education, however, including a good
understanding of Latin, grammar, and the use of the abacus, as well
as—to judge from the books that circulated in the house—a familiarity with rhetoric, the art of writing and speaking eloquently so
as to convince, persuade, and move a reader or listener. When he
was about forty-five, Niccolò described his education in a letter to
a friend; he wrote that fortune had so shaped him that he knew
nothing about making silk or wool and nothing about profit and

loss. He was unfamiliar, therefore, with the manual skills involved in processing wool and silk, for which Florentines were famous, and equally unfamiliar with banking and trade, the other arts in which Florentines excelled.

Later in life, Machiavelli enriched the body of knowledge he had acquired as a child with other important studies. He read the Latin poets, Virgil foremost and then those he called the "lesser" poets who wrote about love—Tibullus and Ovid. Special mention should be made of Lucretius and *De rerum natura*, the great poem describing the origins of nature—the seas, plants, and animals— and the condition of man, which Niccolò not only read but diligently copied, perhaps to improve his Latin but, more likely, to have a copy to read and reread when he liked. He was especially attracted to Lucretius, whose majestic and disconsolate verses declare that man is far from being master of the universe, as he pridefully and vainly believes, but is, rather, the victim of nature and of fortune. Man is born naked and bawling; his voice fills the air. Alone among the animals of creation, he is capable of astonishing cruelty toward those of his kind, and yet no other creature has such an enormous desire to live or such a thirst for—and need of—the eternal and the infinite.

Machiavelli went on to read the ancient philosophers and, especially, historians: Thucydides, who told of the war between Sparta and Athens that tore Greece apart; Plutarch, who told of the lives of the great statesmen, generals, and lawmakers of ancient Greece and Rome; Tacitus, who recounted the corruption and perfidy of Tiberius, Caligula, and Nero; and above all, the work by Livy that his father had earned with so much hard labor and had proudly taken to the bookbinder (leaving as a deposit against payment "three flasks of vermilion wine and a flask of vinegar"). These readings engendered in Niccolò two great passions: love of antiquity and love of history. In the ancient Greek and Roman heroes, he saw examples of immense virtue, courage, and wisdom, overshadowing the corruption, baseness, and idiocy of modern times;

history allowed him to understand humanity's passions, hopes, and errors, and by reading about what had happened in the past, he grasped the meaning of what was happening in the present, because—he said—the same passions and desires are to be found in every city and every people.

Among modern writers, he chiefly loved Dante, followed by Petrarch and Boccaccio. For Machiavelli, Dante was a master of style and wisdom; he strove to imitate Dante's style in poetry and would often quote him from memory both in his books and in letters to friends. Boccaccio inspired in him a cheerful, puckish, irreverent view of life, which made him—to the everlasting delight of his friends—always quick with a witticism, a joke, a funny story. He was never offensive, never cutting; there was always an understanding of human weakness, his own first and foremost.

Most people, then and now, prefer to call attention to their own virtues; Niccolò enjoyed emphasizing his vices, at times going so far as to claim ones he did not possess. He was renowned in Florence as a political writer, playwright, and historian, of course, but also for his general lack of subservience, for his unsurpassed witticisms, for the stories he told and the pranks he played. His friends dubbed him "il Machia," a nickname that connoted his witty, irreverent nature.

Guided by teachers both classical and contemporary, Niccolò formed a distinctly personal conception of life—a rich blend of generosity, enthusiasm for great deeds, intense passions, comprehension of the fragility of life, and a love of beauty that sprang in part from a deep understanding of life's harshness and human malice. What he did not learn from books, he learned in the streets and squares, the public benches, churches, and taverns of Florence, a unique school of life, magnificent and harsh. Practically speaking, Florence forced him to live a life worth the telling.

TWO

Events That Left Their Mark

Florence at the end of the fifteenth century was magnificent and miserable. The beauty of its churches, its public and private buildings, its street and squares; the skill and industry of its citizens; the verve of its artistic and intellectual life—all these factors made Florence almost unrivaled in Italy. Venice alone could compete.

And yet Florence's splendor was undermined by the weakness of its political institutions, capable for only brief periods of preserving the peace and ensuring justice and security to its citizens. Under the clear Tuscan sky, in the fine air of Florence, human passions—whether foul or noble—took on a special intensity. The city's squares and streets were often the setting for ferocious battles among warring factions, each striving to win sway over Florence. Those battles left the streets red with blood, blood that cried out for yet more blood.

In the great palazzi, the wealth of the leading families nourished their arrogance and encouraged a steady decline in morals. At the same time, the lack of a trained standing army meant that Florence's liberty was in constant danger. To defend themselves and to

preserve their dominion over the other cities of Tuscany, the Florentines relied on the services of mercenary generals and soldiers of
fortune. These armed hirelings worked for the highest bidder, and
when the enemies of Florence offered more money, they freely
accepted. No more trustworthy was the protection of the king of
France, Florence's traditional ally: France saw Florentine independence as nothing more than a means to reduce the power of Spain
in Italy. When the French king no longer wished to, or no longer
could, protect the Florentines, he quickly abandoned them to their
fate, as we shall see.

Florence inspired both love and hate—love of its beauty and
elegance, hate of its lack of political wisdom and the despicable
selfishness of too many of its citizens. Machiavelli shared these
clashing emotions, which lasted all his life and dictated his thoughts
and actions.

Machiavelli's Florence was wealthy. The city's workshops pro-
duced woolens and silks that were exported far and wide. Its
bankers were adept at investing and reinvesting the wealth that
accrued from manufacture and trade. With money and skillful
diplomacy, Florence had built a broad dominion that included such
leading cities and military strongholds as Pisa, Livorno, Arezzo, and
Pistoia. From the cities and countryside that Florence ruled with a
view primarily to its own profit, the city took on new riches and
enhanced prestige in the eyes of the other powers of the Italian
peninsula. There was a price to pay, however: the threatened or
actual revolt of now one, now another subject city, open warfare,
the vast expense of preserving power.

The eminent families of Florence contributed greatly to those
wars, for they were at the core, for better or worse, of the city's
political life. Above all, the Medici left a deep and lasting mark on
the history and life of the city. These immensely wealthy, cunning,
and determined bankers built a vast and enduring system of power
in Florence based on a network of friendships and alliances
patiently assembled over time by means of an astute policy of

favors and patronage. The Medici would help some merchants set up trade or survive financial setbacks; they would lend other families the money for dowries so that they could marry off daughters with decorum and profit; to yet others they offered assistance in resolving problems with the law or the tax collector. In this way, the Medici became true lords of the city, though they never tired of proclaiming themselves citizens "like any other," and Florence continued to preserve the appearance of a free republic.

The power of the Medici became virtually absolute from 1434 on, after Cosimo de' Medici the Elder returned triumphantly from an exile to which he had been banished by his enemies. In short order, Cosimo impoverished or banished all those who, through either wealth or influence, might obstruct his plans. He was ready and willing to break laws and violate ethics in order to have his way. In response to those who criticized his unscrupulous behavior and accused him of loving "himself more than his fatherland and this world more than the next," he would say that "states cannot be held with paternosters [rosaries] in hand." That is, those who wish to preserve and expand political power cannot always respect the principles of Christian morality. If someone told him that his methods were ruining Florence, he would respond, "Better to ruin a city than to lose it." In his eyes, the Medici's interests were more important than the city's well-being. Yet when Cosimo died in Florence in 1464, vastly rich and greatly honored, the citizenry mourned him as a great Florentine, and he was solemnly proclaimed the Father of his Country.

Cosimo the Elder was succeeded at the head of the Medici regime by his son Piero. Piero was sickly and could not meet the demands of state; he died in 1469, survived by two sons, Lorenzo and Giuliano. Young though they were, they quickly displayed the qualities needed to continue the work of their grandfather and further strengthen the Medici's power. Lorenzo, in particular, established his reputation by waging war on the city of Volterra, in the face of disapproval from Florence's leading citizens, to settle a dis-

pute over the ownership and operation of some alum mines. The
war ended in a Florentine victory in 1472. Breaking through
Volterra's weak defenses, Florentine troops under the command of
Astorre Gianni sacked, burned, and looted, sparing neither women
nor the elderly. In Florence, news of the victory was met with
jubilation, and Lorenzo reinforced his sway over the city.

His growing power triggered resentment and jealousy among
the other leading Florentine families, especially the Pazzi, who felt
he had gravely and repeatedly mortified them. The Pazzi family
was headed by Iacopo, but it was Iacopo's nephew Francesco who
first plotted to assassinate Lorenzo and Giuliano in revenge for
their offenses against his family and to destroy the Medici's power
in Florence. The archbishop of Pisa, Francesco Cardinal Salviati,
joined the conspiracy out of a similar hatred for the Medici and so,
at first, did Giovan Battista da Montesecco, a condottiere of Pope
Sixtus IV, who in turn looked favorably on the conspiracy.

After several delays, the conspirators decided to carry out their
plan on Sunday 26 April 1478 in the church of Santa Reparata,
while the cardinal of Florence was saying Mass. At the precise
moment when the cardinal elevated the consecrated host, the conspirators drew their concealed daggers and lunged at Giuliano and
Lorenzo. Giuliano was stabbed to death by Bernardo Bandini and
Francesco dei Pazzi; Lorenzo escaped his attackers and took refuge
in the sacristy. Realizing the conspirators had failed to murder both
Medici, Archbishop Salviati unsuccessfully tried to occupy the
Palazzo Vecchio—the old fortified palace that was the seat of the
Florentine government. But he was captured and, dressed in his
priestly garb, hanged from a window of the palace. The family
elder, Iacopo dei Pazzi, appeared at the head of a band of about a
hundred armed men and tried in the name of liberty to raise a
revolt of the Florentine people against the tyranny of the Medici.
His appeal was ignored, and he fled for his life toward Romagna;
captured along the road, he, too, was hanged. He was buried in the
Pazzi family tomb, but later he was excommunicated and his

corpse exhumed, to be reburied outside the city walls in unconsecrated ground. As if that were not enough, his corpse was exhumed yet again, dragged naked through the streets of Florence with the noose that had been used to hang him, and finally tossed into the river Arno.

When these events were taking place in Florence, Niccolò Machiavelli was nine years old. Even if he did not see Archbishop Cardinal Salviati hanged from the windows of the Palazzo Vecchio, or the limbs of the defeated and murdered Pazzi raised high on the points of lances or dragged through the streets, he certainly heard people talking about these events for years afterward, accounts that made a profound impression on him. Many years later, writing about the Pazzi conspiracy and specifically about the failed attempt to instigate a popular revolt, he observed that when a ruler is powerful and lavish with favors, as the Medici were, the populace is deaf to appeals in the name of liberty, especially if it has never experienced liberty. He also noted, in connection with the horrible destiny of Iacopo dei Pazzi, that even the wealthiest and most powerful man can meet a miserable fate, through recklessness, excessive ambition, or simply a cruel whim of fortune.

After thwarting the Pazzi conspiracy, Lorenzo de' Medici found himself facing a far greater and more dangerous threat to his power and to Florence's independence. Pope Sixtus IV, who had actively supported the conspiracy, struck an alliance with the king of Naples, Ferdinand of Aragon, and declared war on Florence. Without a real army, with only limited assistance from the duke of Milan, and with no help whatever from the Venetians, Florence had little chance of withstanding the wrath of the pope and his allies (as it had a century before, during the War of the Eight Saints). It was Lorenzo in person who undertook the only diplomatic initiative that could free Florence from its terrible dilemma. After painstaking and secret groundwork, Lorenzo traveled to Naples in December 1479 to negotiate a peace with King Ferdinand. With a signed treaty in hand, he returned to Florence in

March 1480, acclaimed as the savior of his homeland and honored
as the true lord of the city.

Now that war had been averted, the Florence in which young
Niccolò was growing up returned to its peacetime vices. Young
people—especially the friends of the Medici, by now the city's
unrivaled rulers—cared for little else but "to appear splendid in
their dress and to be clever and smart in their speech," and whoever was best at offending and wounding with words "was wiser
and more esteemed," as Machiavelli recalled many years later (IF,
VII, 28).

In the end, it was a Dominican friar, Girolamo Savonarola, who
raised a powerful and prophetic voice to condemn the spreading
corruption. Savonarola came to Florence in the summer of 1489
and began to hold philosophy lessons for the novices in the garden
of the monastery of San Marco, near a damask-rose bush. As the
days passed, his reputation brought a growing number of listeners
to the monastery; his audience urged him to transform his lessons
into full-fledged sermons preached to the entire city.

Savonarola ascended the pulpit of San Marco on 1 August and
began preaching about the Apocalypse; he made prophecies to
which he would return over and over in the following years: the
Church will be scourged; then it will be reformed, and soon;
finally, a flood tide will pour over Italy. His fame grew steadily, and
during Lent of 1491, Savonarola preached in the cathedral of Santa
Maria del Fiore, the only church in Florence large enough to
accommodate the crowds that came to hear him. Within the walls
of that lovely church, he reiterated his accusations of corruption
against the clergy. We often hear, said Savonarola, that blessed is a
house that has many priests, but the time will come when the
opposite is said. With equal severity, he denounced the greed and
injustice of the wealthy, who forced the poor to pay usurious rates
for borrowed money.

Savonarola used his harshest words against tyrants who rule
cities; the citizens who heard his sermon on 6 April 1491 immedi-

ately understood that his target was Lorenzo the Magnificent. To Savonarola, all good and all evil in a city derived from its chief; in him responsibility for even small sins was great, because if he would cleave to the right path, the entire city would become righteous. Tyrants are incorrigible—because of their pride, because they love adulation, because they are unwilling to return the booty they have plundered. They give bad officials free rein; they yield to flattery; they disregard the needs of the very poor; they do not criticize the rich; they expect farmers and the laboring poor to work for them; they allow their officials to expect the same; they fix elections; and, increasingly, they try the people's patience.

Niccolò, then in his early twenties, certainly heard Savonarola's sermons. Unlike many of his fellow Florentines, however, he was not swept away by the friar's eloquence. He was not persuaded that the cause of Italy's ills was the sins of the Italians; even less did he believe that by fasting, praying, and abstaining from the pleasures of the flesh, gaming, and dance the Florentines could placate the wrath of God and establish peace and harmony anew.

He did agree with Savonarola, however, that the sins of a people have their roots in the behavior of princes. He recognized Savonarola's profound moral integrity and vast knowledge and recognized that he had used them to persuade the people of Florence, who were "neither rude nor ignorant," that he was inspired directly by God. Niccolò did believe that Savonarola, lies and mistakes aside, had the gift of prophecy, the ability to interpret those ominous signs which foreshadow remarkable events. For this reason and for Savonarola's great moral rectitude, Niccolò always spoke of him with respect, though he was never one of his followers.

The first signs of the great changes and great ills awaiting Florence and Italy appeared in the spring of 1492. A bolt of lightning struck the dome of the church of Santa Reparata, tumbling large stones down near the Medici family home. A comet appeared in the sky, and wolves were heard howling. In the church of Santa Maria Novella, a madwoman cried out that an ox with flaming horns was burning the city. A number of lions were heard fighting, and one especially handsome lion was found dead. These were omens, Savonarola told his many listeners, of the impending death of Lorenzo the Magnificent.

Lorenzo did in fact die on 6 April 1492. His gravest error lay in having made Florence subservient; it is said that even on his deathbed, as he confessed his sins to none other than Savonarola, he refused to restore the city's liberty, in particular the liberty to select which citizens would govern and the liberty to debate and approve laws in public council. Still, Lorenzo had crafted a fragile yet wonderful political equilibrium among the five leading states of Italy— the Republic of Florence, the Kingdom of Naples far to the south, the duchy of Milan in the north, the Republic of Venice on the Adriatic, and the papal states centered in Rome. Through his prudence, he had prevented the ambitions of any one power from disturbing the peace in Italy or opening the gates to foreign ambitions.

With Lorenzo dead, no one else could—or would—continue his policies. The Italian princes who went to Florence to attend his splendid funeral were right to mourn his death. Machiavelli wrote in *Florentine Histories,* composed around 1525, that once Lorenzo was out of the way, "those bad seeds began to grow which soon— since the one who knew how to eliminate them was not alive— ruined and are still ruining Italy."

THREE

The Birth of the Republic and
the Death of the Prophet

On the day a lightning bolt struck the dome of Santa Reparata, Savonarola said, "Behold the sword of God on earth, swift and sudden." And the scourge really did arrive. Summoned and financed by Ludovico Sforza, duke of Milan, the French king Charles VIII marched into Italy in 1494 to lay a claim of French sovereignty on the Kingdom of Naples, then ruled by Alfonso II of Aragon. King Charles led an army of forty thousand men, far superior in numbers and discipline to any force ever fielded by an Italian ruler.

With Charles and his army, there came into Italy, in the words of the great Florentine historian Francesco Guicciardini, "a flame and a plague" that resulted in changes of political regime and methods of rule, profoundly altering the old balance of power among the Italian states. Before his arrival, each of the five leading states in Italy was concerned chiefly with keeping any of the others from becoming too powerful; the slightest attempt at expansion on the part of any of the five was immediately blocked. If war finally ensued, the progress of Italian arms was so slow, and the use of artillery so primitive, that it took an entire summer to reduce a

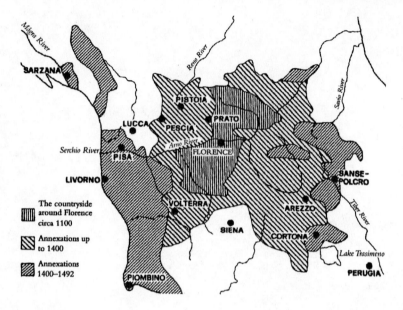

castle, and—to quote Guicciardini again—"battles ended with little or almost no killing at all."

The arrival of the French army like a sudden tempest threw
Italian politics into turmoil. No prince or ruler paid attention to
the general interests of Italy; driven by fear, each looked to his self-
interest. No one lifted a finger to prevent the conquest of a neigh-
boring state. War became exceedingly violent, far more violent
than in the past; the use of increasingly effective artillery meant
that a city could be stormed in days, even hours. War and politics
were rapid and harsh.

In hopes of shoring up his shaky regime, Piero de' Medici, son
and heir of Lorenzo, called on the French king in his camp at
Sarzana, near the Gulf of La Spezia. To win favor, Piero ceded control of the fortresses of Sarzana, Sarzanello, Pietrasanta, and
Ripafratta, which connected the river Po with Tuscany, and the
additional fortresses of Pisa and Livorno. These were all crucial to

Florence's power and security, for they guarded the approaches to the Republic's northern frontier and the coastline on the west.

Indignation swept the city. Even the Florentines most closely allied to the Medici began to question Piero's conduct; he had already squandered much goodwill with his insolent manners. Chronicles of the time report that when Piero Capponi, one of Florence's leading citizens, delivered a memorable speech before the Great Council, it marked the outbreak of open rebellion by the elite and the people of Florence against Piero and his entourage.

Piero de' Medici's faults, Capponi said, were many and serious. He failed to work with the duke of Milan and the king of Naples to prevent the French king's march into Italy; he failed to consult with the wisest and most experienced citizens; indeed, the more dangerous the situation became, the more he tended to operate in secret. But his most serious misconduct was to hand over Florence's fortresses to King Charles as if they were "old scrap iron" when they were the eyes and ears of Florentine rule, conquered by "our forefathers" with "much blood, effort, and expense." Capponi ended by exhorting his listeners to raise as many armed men as possible from the countryside, adding them to the soldiers already present in the city; he also urged them to send a delegation of six eminent citizens, including Savonarola, to King Charles, to convey to him that the will of the city was not the same as that of the Medici.

When Piero de' Medici returned to Florence on 8 November 1494, he quickly detected the chill in the air and the general hostility toward him. In a last-ditch maneuver, he tried to enter the Palazzo Vecchio with a squadron of armed men. The Signori—the city government's elected representatives—barred the doors and summoned the populace to help. The Piazza della Signoria in front of the palace filled with armed men, and Piero, protected by his own soldiers, was forced to take shelter in his family palace. Shortly thereafter, he was declared a rebel and an outlaw with a price on his head (ten thousand florins alive or four thousand florins dead). Fearing he might lose his life as he had his power, Piero fled north toward Bologna.

His flight marked the end of a Medici regime that had lasted for exactly sixty years. There was, however, no time to celebrate the city's newly regained liberty. King Charles was at the gates, and the Florentines knew full well that his army was waiting for a chance to storm the city, ravage its people, and loot its wealth.

A delegation led by Savonarola dissuaded the king from his plan to sack Florence by promising a sizable cash payment and full support of his scheme to subjugate the Kingdom of Naples. The city further agreed to house the king and some of his troops. King Charles sent emissaries to mark on the doors of various houses the names of the French gentlemen who would be lodging in each, so that in the end "the whole city was marked." Referring to this episode, which he certainly witnessed, Machiavelli wrote, "Charles the king of France was enabled to seize Italy with sticks of chalk." The king had conquered Italy without having to fight, to the enormous shame of all Italians and in particular the princes who had led Italy to such humiliation.

Charles VIII made his entry into Florence on 17 November 1494. Chroniclers described it as the most "magnificent and honorable and lovely thing" that had happened in Florence in a long time. Young men from the city's leading families along with respected citizens and high magistrates attired in their finest garments all turned out to greet the king and pay him homage.

The entry of the king's army into Florence was magnificent and lavish. The royal procession was led by seven thousand Swiss soldiers, forming seven square formations around twenty-five flags: they marched in such perfect order and so silently, according to the chroniclers, that the only sounds to be heard were the beating drums and trilling pipes. They were followed by seven hundred men-at-arms riding richly caparisoned horses, five hundred mounted archers, and more than a thousand archers on foot. To the watching Florentines,

Italy in 1494

these archers seemed truly savage creatures in both appearance and
demeanor. Following them were the royal guard, made up of the
tallest soldiers ever seen, so fierce-looking that the Florentines shiv-
ered as one. Last of all came the king himself, dressed entirely in
white, including his headgear, with a drawn sword in his hand.

No matter how spectacular the procession, there was no getting
around the fact that this was the army of a foreign power commanded by a king who had come to Florence determined to have
either gold or plunder. The general sense of wonder soon deterio-
rated into mistrust and hatred. Once the great king had dismounted and could be seen up close, he proved to be a short, pale
man with fuzzy red hair, blue eyes, an enormous nose and mouth,
skinny legs, and feet shod in slippers that resembled the hooves of
horses or oxen. This choleric and injudicious king was ably manip-
ulated by two high churchmen, the bishops of Brescia and Saint-
Malo. The king's arrogance, his soldiers' high-handedness, and
above all his demand that the Medici return to Florence all profoundly angered the Florentines. And during a heated negotiation,
Piero Capponi warned King Charles and his advisers that the city
might well revolt, using these famous words: "Most Christian
prince, we shall ring our bells, you may sound your trumpets, and
we shall show you how this people is armed."

Aside from the occasional skirmish, combat was avoided.
Charles signed a pact of alliance with Florence and solemnly swore
on the altar of Santa Reparata to respect the terms of the treaty.
No letters or writings by Niccolò Machiavelli survive to tell what
he thought or how he felt during that winter of 1494. But we can
be sure that the sight of those French barbarians offered lodging
and treated like lords offended him and led him to ponder the
faults of the Florentine governors, who had failed to spare the city
this great shame. In all likelihood, he was among those in the
church of Santa Reparata who heard the king swear eternal
friendship with Florence, but it is unlikely he believed those words.

Once King Charles finally left Florence, the Florentines set to work rebuilding the state from the rubble the Medici had left. United in their opposition to Piero de' Medici, the citizens who had led the rebellion and governed Florence during the French occupation were divided as to what form to give their new political institutions. A few wanted nothing more than to limit the Medici's power and to establish an oligarchy ruled by the city's old social and political elite; others wanted to give Florence a genuine popular government in which the power to legislate and to appoint magistrates would be entrusted to a broad proportion of the citizenry.

Siding in favor of the latter were Girolamo Savonarola and Paoloantonio Soderini, a citizen of great repute who had served for many years as the Florentine envoy to the Republic of Venice, which many considered an outstanding example of a state with a good political constitution. With all his authority and eloquence, Savonarola preached from the pulpit of San Marco that in order to ward off tyranny and corruption, Florence had to adopt a "universal and civil way of living" and institutions based on the rule of law and the participation of the citizenry in the exercise of sovereign power, that is, the power to legislate and to appoint magistrates.

The core of Florence's new Republic was the Consiglio Maggiore (also called the Consiglio Grande; I shall refer to it here as the Great Council), established on 22–23 December 1494 at Savonarola's recommendation. Requirements for membership in the Great Council were that one be at least twenty-nine years of age, that one not be on the list of citizens who owed back taxes, and that one's father, grandfather, or great-grandfather had been a *seduto* or a *veduto*. The *seduti* and *veduti* were Florentine citizens eligible to hold the three most important offices in the old Republic—the Signoria, or lords; the Sedici Gonfalonieri di Compagnia, or sixteen gonfaloniers*; and the Dodici Buoni Uomini, or twelve good men.

---

*Florence was divided administratively into sixteen neighborhoods, *gonfaloni*, each of which had a company of soldiers, *compagnia*. The gonfaloniers were in command of these companies.

The distinction between them was that *seduti* had been nominated and actually elected to one of those offices, while *veduti* had been only nominated but not elected, either because they already held the office in question or because they owed back taxes. If one was a *seduto* or *veduto,* one belonged to the so-called *reggimento,* which in modern terms meant one belonged to the ruling class of Florence.

Even though the Great Council established in 1494 was the broadest based such assembly in the city's history (it had some three thousand members), it was still composed of men from Florence's ruling class. It was the Great Council's responsibility to appoint all magistrates, choosing from a list of names drawn up by lot, and to pass or reject the laws proposed by the Signoria. Lastly, it was the Great Council's job to elect a smaller council, the Council of Eighty, whose members had to be at least forty years old; the Council of Eighty was charged with advising the Signoria and appointing ambassadors and commissioners of the Florentine government in the cities and territories under Florentine rule.

To the Republic of Florence, then, Savonarola was a spiritual and political father. But the Great Council was his final triumph. The very same republic that the Dominican friar had conceived and worked to create—and in the face of so much suspicion and hostility—failed to protect him from the hatred of the Roman Curia, a hatred engendered by his many fiery denunciations of the corruption in the Roman Catholic Church. On 15 May 1498, the Signoria authorized the interrogation and torture of Savonarola in the presence of the papal envoy, Francesco Cardinal Romolino, and the general of the Dominican order. On 23 May, Savonarola was condemned to death on a charge of heresy. The following morning, he was hanged in the Piazza della Signoria. His body was then burned and the ashes cast into the river Arno, lest they be gathered and revered as relics.

Niccolò Machiavelli was twenty-nine years old at the time. He had never been a follower of the friar (a *piagnone,* literally "weeper," as his followers were called). Years later, he described

Savonarola as an "unarmed prophet" and added that, like all unarmed prophets, he was defeated because he could rely only on the power of his words to keep his followers united and ensure that they did not abandon him when he most needed their help.

With his sermons, Savonarola had persuaded the Florentines that he was speaking in God's name, indeed that his words were divine commandments. The Florentines were hardly simpletons, Machiavelli observed, and some of the finest minds in Florence were fervent admirers of the friar. Still, all his prophetic powers, eloquence, and integrity were inadequate to protect him from the hatred of corrupt men, and especially from the hatred of the profoundly corrupt papal court.

In Machiavelli's view, Savonarola had made a number of grave political mistakes. For instance, when in 1497 five eminent Florentines with close ties to the Medici (Bernardo del Nero, Niccolò Ridolfi, Giannozzo Pucci, Lorenzo Tornabuoni, and Giovanni Cambi) were sentenced to die for conspiring to bring down the Republic and asked that their sentence be appealed to the Great Council, as a new law allowed, and when the Signoria refused them, Savonarola did nothing to defend them, even though it was he who had worked to enact this new law and who had encouraged its passage. To the contrary, chroniclers recorded, Savonarola sent two monks to Domenico Bartoli, the city's chief magistrate, to say that the Lord God intended the five to be executed.

Those most strongly opposed to giving the five condemned men the right to appeal to the Great Council were Savonarola's followers, foremost among them Francesco Valori. Piero de' Medici is already approaching the city, the Savonarola men said; he is already in Siena; any delay in moving against his friends may be fatal to the liberty of Florence. Others, in contrast, believed that the law allowing for appeals to the Great Council was intended to prevent injustices against individual citizens; according to the law, the true ruler of the city was the people themselves, expressing their will through the Great Council; therefore, if the five con-

demned men were really guilty of heinous crimes, the Great
Council would recognize that and confirm the death sentences.

The question whether or not to allow the five condemned men
to make their appeal split the city. The Palazzo Vecchio, according
to contemporary accounts, became a "mine, indeed, a cavern of
fury," where angry men clashed, weapons in hand. When the five
were finally put to death, the city calmed down, and Savonarola's
supporters had, or at least seemed to have, the upper hand. In reality,
as Machiavelli later wrote, the fact that the friar had neither
endorsed their right to appeal nor condemned their execution
"harmed his reputation" more than any other action. Rather than a
prophet driven by a devotion to the city's best interests, Savonarola
now appeared to many as "ambitious and partisan." This victory of
Savonarola and his supporters was actually a first step toward ruin.

Savonarola's death coincided with the beginning of Machiavelli's
life of public service. On 28 May 1498, four days after Savonarola
was executed, the Council of Eighty nominated Niccolò as secretary of the Second Chancery, which handled matters relating to
the dominions and foreign affairs of Florence. The appointment
was confirmed by the Great Council on 19 June. Niccolò emerges
from the shadows.

Machiavelli was an obscure young man with no experience in
politics, but the important events he had witnessed or heard about
from eyewitnesses had left their mark on him: the corpses of the
Pazzi dragged through the streets of Florence; hanged bodies dan-
gling from the windows of the Palazzo Vecchio; the entry of King
Charles and the evident weakness of Florence and the other Italian
states; the acrid smell of the funeral pyre as Savonarola's body
burned in the Piazza della Signoria; the heated discussions about
the death sentence for the five illustrious citizens accused of conspiracy. When he climbed the steps of the Palazzo Vecchio to take
office, he was already familiar with the harsh side of politics.

FOUR

A Very Special Secretary

How and why the Council of Eighty and the Great Council of the Republic of Florence chose a little-known young man—who had no political experience, was neither a notary nor a doctor of law, and had shown no special literary distinction—remains a mystery. Surely one factor must have been that both in the councils and in the Signoria the majority were opponents of Savonarola, and we know that Machiavelli was not a supporter of the friar from a letter he wrote on 9 March 1498 to Ricciardo Becchi, the Florentine ambassador to the Holy See.

At Becchi's request, young Niccolò went to the monastery of San Marco on 1 and 2 March to hear Savonarola preach; he reported on what he heard with great precision. It is not hard to guess that Savonarola's prophecies of terrifying catastrophes befalling his enemies made Machiavelli smile rather than tremble. The friar's points of view, he wrote to Becchi, are "quite effective" to "those not examining them closely," that is, to those who do not analyze them coolly. He ends his letter with a phrase that shows how little stock he put in Savonarola: "In my judgment, he acts in

accordance with the times and colors his lies accordingly."
Savonarola, adapting to the times, presented his lies in such a manner as to make them credible.

Machiavelli's election as chief of the Second Chancery was in
part due to the support of Marcello Virgilio Adriani, secretary of
the First Chancery and effectively first secretary of the Republic.
By time-honored tradition, the secretary of the First Chancery,
also known as the chancellor, was a scholar of renown (the humanists Coluccio Salutati and Leonardo Bruni had earlier been chancellors). Adriani himself had been a professor in the Studio
Fiorentino, the original core of the University of Florence, and
was a man of great learning. Machiavelli was of lower rank, and
the difference was evident in their respective salaries: 330 small
florins (worth less than gold florins) for Adriani; 192 for Machiavelli.

This did not mean that Machiavelli's job was simply to carry
out orders. As chief of the Second Chancery and secretary of the
Ten of Liberty and Peace (referred to henceforth as the Ten), a
commission that oversaw military matters and therefore also foreign affairs, he had assistants such as Agostino Vespucci, Andrea di
Romolo, and the good Biagio Buonaccorsi, who became a close
friend and admirer. With their help, Machiavelli was entrusted with
keeping the Signoria and the Ten informed on military and political problems so that they could make appropriate and timely decisions. Whereas the politicians in the Signoria and the Ten held
office for just a few months, the secretaries and their assistants held
their posts for years and therefore had an important function in the
institutional life of the Florentine Republic.

Machiavelli was thus an executive, as we would say nowadays.
He was a highly unusual chief, however, who knew how to trans-
form his subordinates into friends and how to turn the Second
Chancery into a "gang," even if rivalries and jealousies were not
uncommon. These abilities are evident in his subordinates' letters.
While Machiavelli was on a mission to the court of the king of

France, Agostino Vespucci wrote to him from Florence (in Latin) in October 1500: "I read your entire letter to Signor Marcello [Adriani], two other chancellors, and Biagio [Buonaccorsi], who are all seized by a marvelous desire to see you. For when your amusing, witty, and pleasant conversation echoes about our ears, it relieves, cheers, and refreshes us, who are exhausted and flagging from constant work. There are very many other things as well that urge your return, but more face-to-face."

The members of the Chancery were similar in their outlook, education, and political beliefs and therefore inclined to band together. Niccolò was the core of the group—with his lively curiosity, his witticisms that brought gales of laughter, and his uncommon vitality. He played this role his whole life: "Now that you are not here, nothing is heard of either gambling or taverns or any other trivia . . . Someone to bring the band together is always lacking because you are not here." These words written by Filippo de' Nerli, a Florentine aristocrat, in September 1525 were addressed to an elderly Machiavelli, yet the sentiments are much the same as those his Chancery colleagues expressed twenty-five years earlier.

It was one thing to take orders from "grave and haughty" men like Marcello Adriani and quite another to take orders from someone who, like Machiavelli, was always preoccupied with great matters of politics, loved to travel, and cared nothing for the petty jealousies, bickering, and rivalries that thrived daily within the walls of the Chancery. Machiavelli's subordinates often found they had to work doubly hard to make up for their boss's absence, and they were vulnerable without his protection. Of course they complained, but not behind his back, as commonly happens with bosses who are feared or disliked; instead, they spoke directly to him in the words and tone of equals. "So you see," Agostino Vespucci wrote on 14 October 1502, "where that spirit of yours, so eager for riding, wandering, and roaming about, has gotten us. Blame yourself and not others if anything adverse happens. I wish that no one but you were standing by me and was my superior in the

Chancery, although you attempt and dare all the things for which that most poisonous viper attacks me, pursues me, and cuts me to bits, about which that terrible man, worthless and contentious, gives me orders. But that is water under the bridge. Biagio likewise . . . blabbers on, reviles you with insults, damning and cursing you, says and cares for nothing, reckoning all things worthless."

In fact, Biagio Buonaccorsi's letters to Machiavelli feature a fine array of imprecations and colorful terms. He criticized Niccolò for failing to write to him during the missions that kept him from Florence for such long periods, but the outbursts reveal great admiration and also a hint of envy of this friend who so outstripped him in his understanding of politics and in the lively wit of his sharp tongue and pen.

Buonaccorsi was not the only one to scold Machiavelli for forgetting his friends as soon as he went beyond the walls of Florence. Others also accused him of indifference and recalcitrance in doing and repaying favors and kindnesses—from which one might conclude that Niccolò was hard-hearted, if not actually stingy with his time and affection. But such a judgment clashes sharply with the many reports and documents attesting to his being the delight of everyone in the Chancery and the one who held together the gang of friends.

The truth is that when Machiavelli was on a mission for the Republic, he immersed himself entirely in political matters. For that reason, he seldom wrote to his friends and paid little attention to news about them or to everyday operations of the Chancery—exceptions always being made, of course, for spicy stories. He was not cut out for the exchange of favors typical of daily office life. When Machiavelli asked the Signoria for a special indemnity, Biagio wrote to tell him that his request might be denied because the Signori say that "you are a blockhead, and you have never done a kindness for them." To protect his friend from such a reputation, Biagio took the liberty of doing some favors for the Signori "at Niccolò's expense and despite his wishes," telling him that if he was not happy with this approach, he could go to the devil, because that was how things should be done.

Let us now leave the walls of the Chancery and follow Machiavelli in his missions for the Ten of Liberty and Peace. He loved to ride long distances and see broader horizons than those of everyday Florentine life and politics. The legations and missions with which the Ten entrusted him were, however, neither easy nor comfortable. Even in the simplest cases, he had to use great eloquence, always employ the proper tone and take the proper tack, keep his eyes wide open, and above all understand what sort of men he was dealing with.

Consider the instructions the Ten gave him for his first mission, in March 1499, to Jacopo IV d'Appiano, lord of Piombino, the ancient port town on the Ligurian coast, near the island of Elba. He was to go to Jacopo, tell him he could not have the increase in pay he had requested for his soldiers, who were fighting for Florence in the war against Pisa, and enlist another forty men-at-arms. Child's play, perhaps, but one had to convey the bad news in words that nonetheless persuaded the lord of Piombino that Florence was well disposed to him, keeping the discussion in "broad and very general terms." If Jacopo became resentful, then Machiavelli was to speak to him affectionately and persuade him to be patient. In short, he was to reject the request without breaking off an alliance useful to Florence.

The secretary's job became especially difficult when he had to deal with important figures, politically experienced and cunning, as he did on his second mission, to the court of Caterina Sforza Riario. When he met her in July 1499 at her castle in Forlì—an important town on the road to Ravenna, northwest of Florence— Caterina was thirty-six, and she must have been renowned as a beauty: Buonaccorsi wrote to Machiavelli on 19 July asking his friend to send him, by return mail and nicely rolled up so that it would not be spoiled by folding, a portrait on a sheet of paper "of Her Majesty's head."

Machiavelli presented himself, once again using the finest words in his repertory; he had to persuade Caterina to accept the renewal of the contract for her son Ottaviano Riario to fight for Florence in the reconquest of Pisa without the increase in salary she was demanding. Caterina replied that she had always liked Florentine words but was less impressed with Florentine deeds and that she wished Florence to give her concrete recognition of her past services, especially her having put her own state at risk by siding against the powerful Venetians when they attacked Florence from the mountains of the Casentino, north of the city.

Sadly, we shall never know what Machiavelli felt and thought when the lovely Caterina spoke those words to him. We do know, from a letter written by Buonaccorsi, that she honored the young secretary and was "happy to see" him. For his part, Machiavelli reported very carefully to the Signoria on Caterina's views and demands. His official dispatches suggest he was trying to persuade his superiors to accept her requests. He insisted repeatedly, in fact, that she would lose face if she agreed to have Ottaviano fight for Florence at a lower rate of pay than the duke of Milan was offering. In a letter of 19 July 1499, he explained that if Florence wanted to preserve Caterina's friendship, it should do so through deeds, not words—first paying its old debts and then offering more generous conditions for the use of her son's troops. At the conclusion of his letter, he added that if the members of the Signoria were to do these things, they would win Caterina's friendship, for she was exceedingly friendly to Florence, as he could see every day from many "clearly evident signs."

Aside from her friendliness, Caterina's self-interest pushed her toward Florence. The new king of France, Louis XII, was about to attack the duchy of Milan, ruled by her uncle Ludovico Sforza (il Moro). Quite soon, as Caterina knew, she would lose the support of this powerful duke, just as a terrible menace was looming on the far horizon—that of Cesare Borgia, the duke of Romagna and son of Pope Alexander VI. Nonetheless, Caterina was always concerned about "matters of honor," which she held "above all things," Machiavelli wrote. She wanted terms that in the eyes of her uncle and everyone else would preserve her honor and her reputation. Her behavior here undoubtedly prompted Machiavelli's admiration; he was keenly aware that those who rule states cannot afford to lose either honor or reputation. The two negotiators had divergent interests, though: Caterina wanted Florence to make a formal commitment to protect her; Florence, and its representative, Machiavelli, wanted only her son's soldiers, a little gunpowder, and the happy resolution of a few minor incidents involving Florentine citizens in lands ruled by Caterina. All the same, they understood and respected each other. Certainly, Machiavelli admired Caterina's beauty and intelligence and her determination in defending her honor; but he was also touched by the streak of maternal tenderness revealed when the lady of Forlì asked her first secretary, Antonio Baldraccani, to convey to Machiavelli her apologies for being unable to receive him: she was indisposed and "in very poor spirits" about the serious illness of her son the future Giovanni delle Bande Nere.

At one point during the negotiations, Machiavelli felt certain he had persuaded Caterina to settle for a verbal promise of help and to abandon her request for a written commitment. Then came a brusque about-face. On the morning of 24 July, Caterina informed Machiavelli that her honor demanded a written commitment from Florence to defend her state and that he should not be surprised at her change of position because "the more things are discussed, the better they are understood." Machiavelli was both greatly surprised and hurt, and he made this clear in words and actions—a strange reaction for a man who knew how to conceal his true feelings and feign others when he wished to do so. Perhaps he was irritated because he had already written to the Signoria of Caterina's presumed agreement, and therefore the new decision somewhat undermined his reputation. Or perhaps it was simply that after many respectful, understanding, and happy conversations, the about-face could not but hurt him, personally and diplomatically.

In any case, Caterina remained without the protection of Florence, which did not lift a finger when Cesare Borgia (known as the Valentino) laid siege to Forlì. She rejected the terms offered for surrender and retreated for her last stand into the fortress and citadel with all the soldiers, artillery, and provisions she could raise. But, Guicciardini recounts, "as she was the only one of manly spirit, among so many defenders of womanly spirit, the [fortress and citadel] were soon stormed by the Valentino, through the cowardice of the captains manning them" (G, IV, 13). Once the fortress had been taken, the Valentino held Caterina in her rooms for two weeks and then sent her off as a prisoner of the pope in Rome, to Castel Sant'Angelo.

Machiavelli laconically mentioned the end of Caterina's rule over Forlì in his *Decennale Primo (First Decennial)*, a history of Italy from 1494 to 1504 in verse. There the Valentino "made himself master of Imola and Forlì,/and abducted a woman with her children." He spoke of her again in the *Discourses*, telling in his own manner a story that had been circulating for some time about her great courage in 1488 against the men who had killed her husband, Count Girolamo Riario. Some conspirators from Forlì, Machiavelli wrote,

killed Count Girolamo, their lord, and took his wife and small children. Since they did not see how they could be secure if they did not become masters of the fortress, and the castellan was not willing to cede it to them, Madonna Caterina (so the countess was called) promised the conspirators that if they let her enter it, she would deliver it over to them and they could keep her children with them as hostages. With this pledge they let her enter. As soon as she was within, she stood on the walls and berated them for the death of her husband and threatened them with every kind of revenge. And to show that she did not worry about her children, she showed them her genitals, saying she still had the means to make more of them. (*D,* III, 6)

(This same episode, differently worded, also appears in *Florentine Histories.*)

Machiavelli also mentioned Caterina in his *Art of War,* when he described how she defended the fortress of Forlì against Cesare Borgia, "who had led there the army of the king of France." Machiavelli's words are full of admiration: "So the badly structured fortress and the incapacity of its commander brought shame upon the countess's bold undertaking. She would have had the spirit to await an army, as neither the king of Naples nor the duke of Milan had done. And though her efforts did not turn out well, nonetheless she earned the esteem her valor deserved" (*O,* 671).

His memory of this countess whom he met on one of his first missions remained vivid over the years, and with his accounts of her deeds, he introduced her into legend, making her live forever.

FIVE

Broader Horizons

On the way back from Forlì, as he was crossing the mountain passes of the Apennines, Niccolò Machiavelli must have thought long and hard about the countess and the grim fate that awaited her. As he drew nearer to Florence, his thoughts may have shifted to the problems of the Republic, notably the nasty question of Pisa, a veritable thorn in the side of the Florentine government. Florence had lost Pisa in 1494, when Piero de' Medici had ceded it to the French king Charles along with the fortresses of Livorno, Sarzana, Sarzanello, Pietrasanta, and Ripafratta.

King Charles had solemnly promised to give back Pisa and the other fortresses as soon as he completed his conquest of the Kingdom of Naples. But these were the promises of a king and, moreover, a French king. It would take strength to enforce the agreement, and strength is what Florence lacked. The French quickly forgot their promises: they did not give back Livorno until September 1499; they sold Sarzana to Genoa for thirty thousand ducats; they gave Pietrasanta to Lucca and Montepulciano, whose fortress King Charles himself had seized, to Siena. And to complete the disaster, the commander of the citadel of Pisa ignored his king's orders to return the fortress to Florence and instead sold it to the Pisans themselves for twenty thousand ducats.

Once it became clear that there was no real hope of France's returning Pisa, Florence would have to retake it, with kindness or by force, as Machiavelli wrote to the Signoria in a memo drawn up between late May and early June 1499. It was necessary to reconquer Pisa, Machiavelli explained, in order to "preserve the liberty of Florence." It was vain to hope that the city might return voluntarily under the Florentine yoke; Pisans hated Florentines and their dominion more than anything on earth. It was equally unlikely that someone might become lord of Pisa and then offer to hand it over to the Florentines, for the obvious reason that anyone strong enough to conquer Pisa would also be strong enough to keep it.

The only remaining option was to take Pisa by force. Convinced of the necessity of this path, the Signori committed themselves to preparing a military campaign. They collected money, hired troops, and entrusted the command to one of the most valiant condottieri of the time, the Roman baron Paolo Vitelli. "Our campaign in Pisa," Biagio wrote to Machiavelli on 27 July 1499, "is going better and better." The Signori worked day and night to make sure that everything was in a state of readiness, and everyone in Florence thought Pisa was as good as reconquered.

The Florentines' hopes were short-lived, however. After infuriating dithering, Vitelli finally attacked the walls of Pisa. The artillery shattered a broad stretch, opening a breach for a decisive infantry attack. It seemed a question of days, even hours. But inexplicably, Vitelli failed to order an infantry assault, giving the Pisans breathing room to reorganize their forces and restore their morale. Deaf to the Signoria's pleas and threats, he let days pass in inactivity, and, finally, at the beginning of September, when his troops were already being decimated by the malaria lurking around Pisa, he broke camp.

The disappointment stung. The Florentines had thought Pisa

was theirs, and instead, after wasting an enormous amount of money, they were back where they started. The city's wrath descended on Vitelli. He was accused of having been bribed by the duke of Milan to withhold the attack. He was arrested, interrogated, and tortured, but Vitelli refused to confess. Whether he remained silent out of pride or cunning or because he really was innocent we cannot say. No evidence was found against him, but he was sentenced to death all the same and beheaded on 1 October 1499.

Before the death sentence was handed down, there were lengthy debates in the Palazzo Vecchio and throughout the city as to whether Vitelli should be judged according to ordinary jurisprudence or whether the seriousness of his crime deserved an exemplary punishment. Niccolò Machiavelli certainly listened to those fiery debates and heard the opinions both of those who believed it was necessary to respect the principle of justice and of those who thought the normal body of law should be set aside to make way for the greater interests of the state, which meant sending Vitelli to his death even though his guilt had not been proven.

A similar case had occurred two years earlier, as we have seen, when the five eminent Florentines had been put to death on charges of plotting against the Republic, a decision Machiavelli was to condemn years later as a serious political error. At this point, however, Machiavelli was in the Palazzo Vecchio and spoke directly for the Republic. When a chancellor from Lucca criticized the decision to put Vitelli to death, he replied with cutting words: If you wish to continue offending us, at least do so in a manner that makes you less ridiculous. Vitelli has caused no end of harm and trouble to Florence, and it matters little whether the cause was corruption or incompetence. He deserves "no end of punishment."

A few years later, in 1504, Machiavelli commented on the death of Vitelli with these verses:

shortly following the rude deception
you took full revenge, by putting to death
the one who caused such harm.

Here he speaks of "revenge," not of justice. He knew perfectly well, as did his Florentine readers, that these are two very different things. He said no more, however. As secretary, he was duty-bound to silence, and he observed the duty scrupulously.

With Vitelli beheaded, the Pisan dilemma still awaited solution. Stubbornly, the Florentines tried to regain Pisa with French help, taking advantage of the presence in Italy of King Louis XII, who had come to conquer Milan and Naples. Of course, his help was expensive: the Florentines would have to pay fifty thousand gold scudi to hire five thousand Swiss infantrymen, and they would have to pay the expenses of five thousand men-at-arms whom the French would use in their conquest of the Kingdom of Naples; and finally, they would be obliged to arm and provision an occupation force in the duchy of Milan. In sum, the Florentines were to put up lots of money; the French were to hire troops for their own conquest of the Kingdom of Naples and promise to make the Swiss infantry available (under French command) for Florence's reconquest of Pisa.

The questionable wisdom of this agreement became evident as soon as it was put into effect. The troops, painstakingly assembled in Piacenza, at first refused to march to Pisa; after setting off, they halted along the way to extort money from and plunder Bologna and other cities in Emilia. Once they reached the district of Lunigiana, between Liguria and Tuscany, they launched an attack on Marquess Alberigo, an ally of Florence, and dethroned him. And when they entered Pisan territory, these hordes of mercenary soldiers began plundering the countryside; only after the greatest reluctance were they finally persuaded to set up a few cannons and start firing at Pisa's city walls. The crowning touch to this glorious campaign came when Swiss and Gascon troops mutinied, furious at the scanty and inferior provisions of wine and foodstuffs the Florentines had furnished. A few companies of soldiers, under the command of Hugh of Beaumont, abandoned the field entirely, while others took prisoner the Florentine Luca degli Albizzi, the official representative of the Republic paying for the campaign.

This tawdry affair reflected poorly on both the French, greedy and deceitful, and the Florentines, timid and indecisive. Once again, Machiavelli describes the situation for us, in verse, as if it were before our eyes:

And as soon as [Beaumont's men] *stood face-to-face with the Pisans,*
thrown into confusion and panic,
they failed to rise to the occasion,
instead fleeing in disarray, blushing
with violent shame. (SL, 305)

In the wake of this unfortunate imbroglio, the Signoria sent Machiavelli, accompanied by Francesco della Casa, to the court of King Louis XII. Machiavelli, who had witnessed the events at the siege of Pisa, was particularly well qualified to answer the French charges against his city. He could argue persuasively that responsibility for the fiasco lay entirely with the French, especially the inept Beaumont, who had been unable to impose even the slightest discipline on the soldiers under his command.

Machiavelli and della Casa reached the King's court in Lyons on 26 July 1500, "exhausted but determined." Niccolò immediately saw that there was quite a difference between serving as the representative, or *oratore,* of a greater power, as he had done with Caterina Sforza, and being a small republic's envoy to the most powerful king in Christendom. It was clear from the way important men at the court treated him; for example, the cardinal of Rouen answered the Florentine envoys' points by saying they were "all words, and showed a lack of faith in our wisdom"; then he complained loudly, so everyone could hear, of his deep dissatisfaction with Florence; and finally, to underline his contempt, he simply leaped onto his horse "and rode off to enjoy himself" (LC, 120).

Matters did not improve when Machiavelli and della Casa spoke with the king. Here in Lyons, everyone is blinded by their sense of power, the two envoys explained to the Signoria back in Florence. They consider only their own immediate interests; they respect only those who are armed or willing to give money. And since Florence is unwilling to pay France and has no army of its own, they hold you in no consideration whatsoever and insist you are entirely to blame for the failure in Pisa.

If Machiavelli's political satisfactions in France were few and far between, his material satisfactions were even scantier. With the limited funds budgeted by the Republic, he could not even cover his expenses. In order to follow the court, hire horses, send dispatches, and pay for board and lodging, he had to spend his own money. Thanks to his brother Totto's insistence, in August his salary was increased, but throughout the mission in France, no money reached him from Florence except for fifty scudi Totto managed to get to him via Florentine merchants working in Lyons.

Machiavelli had set out with a heavy heart because of the death of his father on 10 May 1500, and during his mission in France, his sister Primavera also died. He had been very close to his good-hearted and unfortunate father, and he may have been close to Primavera too, considering he was to name one of his daughters after her. Understandable tension shows in a letter to the Signori of 25 October, in which he requests permission to return to Florence because he was "running out of resources, in more ways than one" (LC, 184). He was certainly referring to his expenses in France and his need to settle matters left open by his father's death. But perhaps he was also thinking of his soul.

While he was running out of resources in more ways than one, he was also gaining greatly in many other ways. Living in proximity to a great monarch for the first time, Machiavelli learned how a real court operates. The first thing that became clear was that to accomplish anything at court, you need influential friends, and friends of this sort can be had with money. All of the *oratori* of the Italian states were trying to win the king's friendship by choosing protectors. Florence should do the same, he wrote to the Signori on 26 August, because a reasonable claim alone is not enough.

Instead, the Republic expected Machiavelli and della Casa, two penniless nobodies, to placate the wrath and moderate the demands of the French court. From 14 September on, Machiavelli had to get by on his own, because della Casa fell ill and went to Paris for medical care. The harder Machiavelli worked to explain that Florence had been bled white by the expenses of the Pisan campaign—and that it was unfair to demand that it pay for soldiers who had not even fought on its behalf—the more strenuously the French insisted that if they did not soon receive the thirty-eight thousand florins that were due, the king would begin to consider Florence an enemy.

Back in Florence, no one seemed to understand how serious the situation had become. Not only did the Signori continue to waver on paying the thirty-eight thousand florins, but they waited an inordinate time, until 11 October, before announcing that Pier Francesco Tosinghi was to set off from Florence with the rank of ambassador—and therefore with the authority, which Machiavelli lacked, to sign a formal treaty.

That same day, Machiavelli reported to Florence that when he had informed the cardinal of Rouen that the ambassador was on his way and would settle the question of the money due, the cardinal had replied, "When the ambassadors get here, we shall already be dead, but others will die before us" (*LC*, 168). A few hours later, he demanded that Machiavelli tell Florence that France wanted an answer immediately and that Florence must pay the money one way or another, either as friends or as enemies.

Machiavelli could do nothing but accept the bill the French

had drawn up—without objecting, because that would have wors-
ened the situation—and enclose it with his letter. He wished the
letter could fly to Florence as swiftly as a bird, but he did not have
the money to pay for a courier: "I will pray God to help me," he
wrote, "and what little money I find, I will spend all on this." He
ended his letter with these words: "It would be urgent to tell the
oratori to fly here" and to "make all haste" (*LC*, 173).

Caught between French threats and Florentine delays, saddened
by deaths in his family, Niccolò nonetheless now gave an early
demonstration of his remarkably penetrating understanding of politics. Indeed, he—penniless envoy of a minor republic—ventured
to impart a lesson to no less a personage than the cardinal of
Rouen, who had told him Italians understood nothing of war.
That may be, Niccolò retorted, but you French understand nothing of statecraft. He explained that if King Louis truly wished to
conquer part of Italy, then he should follow the example of past
kings: history teaches us, Machiavelli told the cardinal, that to succeed in taking possession of a foreign nation with different customs,
languages, and traditions, it is necessary to weaken its powerful
men, treat the subjects well, preserve friendships, and above all
beware of other powers with authority equal to your own that also
wish to conquer. In the present context, the French king should
first and foremost protect the Italian states friendly to him—Florence, Genoa, Ferrara, Bologna, Mantua, and Forlì. He should then
do everything he can to diminish the power of the pope and of
Venice and above all make absolutely certain that Spain—equal if
not superior in power to France—was kept from expanding its
dominion in Italy.

The cardinal, Niccolò reported in a letter of 21 November
1500, listened "patiently" and answered that His Majesty the King
was "exceedingly prudent": his "ears were long but his credence
was short"; he listened to everyone but believed only "that which
he touched with his own hand and saw to be true" (*LC*, 205). As if
to say: the king knows his own business.

Events proved that King Louis did not know his business well, however, since he did exactly the opposite of what Machiavelli advised and failed miserably in his plans for expansion in Italy. As soon as he had retaken Milan, he began to help the pope expand the papal dominions in Romagna with troops commanded by Cesare Borgia; in so doing, the French king alienated the small states that had placed themselves under his protection. Then, with the Treaty of Granada (11 November 1500), he agreed to split the Kingdom of Naples with King Ferdinand of Spain, thereby introducing an exceedingly dangerous rival into Italy.

If Machiavelli felt any satisfaction in giving a lesson in politics to the cardinal of Rouen, it was a small victory, perhaps his only one, during his difficult days in French territory. When he finally received a letter of 12 December in which the Signoria gave him permission to return, he did not dally. He mounted his horse immediately and set off for Florence. Still, his experience in France had been important. It had given him a chance to study the politics of a major court up close; in the letters he wrote, we see some of the earliest instances of how the mechanisms of his intelligence continued to function even amid grief and tribulations.

SIX

A Furious Wife and an Unsettling Duke

After returning to Florence on 14 January 1501, Machiavelli plunged into the business of the Chancery and took up his old habits: dining, wining, and roguery with his friends, who were happy—Biagio happiest of all—to see him back. Without a doubt, he paid more than one call on a lovely lady of Ponte alle Grazie who awaited him, in the licentious words of Andrea di Romolo, "with open figs." That winter, however, he began to think about marriage. After his father's death, only his brother, Totto, remained at home; the house must have begun to seem cold, empty, and silent, and Niccolò loved neither silence, nor solitude, nor tranquillity. In August or thereabouts, he married Marietta Corsini, who came from roughly the same social background that he did, an obligatory consideration in Florence at the time.

Even as a married man, Niccolò never gave up his yen for women and romance, and Florentines knew this about him, especially since he did nothing to conceal it. More than the infidelities—and his wife may not even have known of them or, if she did, may have cared little—what bothered Marietta were his long

absences, about which she complained to his friends. "Madonna
Marietta wrote to me via her brother to ask when you will be
back," Biagio wrote Niccolò in mid-October 1502, a little more
than a year after the wedding. "She says she does not want to write,
and she is making a big fuss." Niccolò had promised her that he
would be away from Florence for no more than eight days, but he
had been gone for ten and would not return until 23 January 1503!

Marietta lost her temper; she resolved not to write Niccolò
another word. Niccolò disliked the silence and asked Biagio to
intervene, explaining to his young wife in a letter that, since he was
on a mission for the Republic, it was not up to him when he
returned to Florence. Marietta would not listen to reason:
"Madonna Marietta is angry," Biagio reported on 26 November,
"and does not want to write to you. I cannot do anything else."

Two months later, when Niccolò still had not returned, Marietta, furious, openly rued the day she had married this reckless fool,
who seemed to enjoy nothing so much as traveling the world. Biagio reported again: "Madonna Marietta is cursing God, and she
feels she has thrown away both her body and her possessions."
Worrisome words: not only was she renouncing God, in whose
name she had vowed to marry Niccolò, but she was declaring that
that scoundrel was neglecting her and had not yet paid—or had
paid only part of—the stipulated dowry. About the first complaint,
Niccolò could do little until he returned; about the second, he
could at least take care of the debt and to a degree placate Marietta's wrath. His wise friend Biagio exhorted him to take this step:
"For your own sake, arrange for her to have her dowry like other
women, otherwise we won't hear the end of it" (*L, 162*).

Besides asking Biagio to act as emissary and peacemaker, Niccolò tried to cheer up Marietta with jokes and witticisms, making
fun of her outbursts. Marietta herself refers to this tactic, in her
only surviving letter—a lovely one from a year later: "You make
fun of me, but you are not right to . . . You know how happy I am
when you are not down there" (*L, 182*).

From this letter emerges a portrait of a young woman in love, sincerely worried about the perils that threaten her faraway husband. She also finds a way, through a description of their newborn son, of telling Niccolò she considers him handsome: "For now the baby is well, he looks like you: he is white as snow, but his head looks like black velvet, and he is hairy like you. Since he looks like you, he seems beautiful to me. And he is so lively he seems to have been in the world for a year; he opened his eyes when he was scarcely born and filled the whole house with noise" (*L*, 182–83).

She wants more letters from Niccolò. Since his departure for Rome—and it had been a month now—she has received only three. (Actually, that's a fair number.) Niccolò, too, wanted letters from her and feared that her silence was a sign of anger, as it had been the year before. "Do not be surprised if I have not written you," Marietta reassured him, "because I have not been able to, since I had a fever up to now" (*L*, 182).

It is a pity that more letters from Marietta have not survived. They might have allowed us to form a better idea of her personality, perhaps showing that she was more than a good housewife and mother, which is all Machiavelli's biographers have told us. Niccolò did not consider her a great love, much less *the* great love of his life; but she was his wife, his companion, and she was anything but submissive and passive. She stated her views, called the shots as she saw them, and was not taken in or placated by the jokes and endearments that her rascally husband foisted on her in an attempt to get out of his latest fix. With a little imagination, we can envision the couple quarreling—Marietta with arms akimbo, Niccolò with his eyes downcast, mumbling excuses.

Marietta's desire for more time with Niccolò—and the similar wish of his friends—conflicted with the demands of his office. Just two weeks after his return from France, he was in Pistoia, a city on the far side of the Apennines, northwest of Florence, and then under Florentine rule. A longtime rivalry between the powerful Panciatichi and Cancellieri families there had degenerated into open civil war, with killing, looting, and burning. At all costs, peace must be made and the flames contained, lest foreign armies be tempted to intervene.

Brief though it had been (and his other two missions in July and October 1501 were similarly brief), this visit to Pistoia offered Machiavelli a chance to ponder the causes and consequences of factional infighting. He realized the sheer folly of the principle, accepted for time out of mind by Florentine rulers, that the most effective way of dominating Pistoia was to foment rivalry between the factions and then step in as peacemaker. In reality, the factional struggle threatened to bring an enemy prince or condottiere— summoned by one of the warring parties—right into the heart of Florence's dominion. It was essential, as Machiavelli wrote in a memoir composed for the Signoria, to do everything possible to "prohibit, quench, and eliminate both factions" (O, 10).

In the case of Pistoia, the foreign power that might intervene was close at hand and lethal. This was Cesare Borgia, known as Duke Valentino, who had already conquered Rimini and Pesaro on the Adriatic coast, and, on the way to Bologna, Imola, Faenza, and Forlì, and who had encouraged rebellion against Florentine rule in Arezzo and the Valdichiana. True, he had claimed that the rebellion had been not his doing but the work of the condottiere Vitellozzo Vitelli, who wished to avenge the death of his brother Paolo. But Vitellozzo Vitelli was a partisan of Borgia's and signed his Arezzo dispatches "from the papal camp," as if he were acting in the name and on behalf of the pope and his son the general. Add to all this that on 3 September 1501 the long arms of the duke seized Piombino and in June of the following year were to take Urbino as well, and it is easy to understand that Florence was in mortal danger. On all sides, it was surrounded by a powerful, cunning, unscrupulous enemy who was supported by the pope and the king of France and who wished above all to end its republican government.

To settle accounts with Florence, Duke Valentino asked the Signoria to send two authoritative *oratori* to negotiate with him in

Urbino. The Signori chose to send the illustrious Francesco Soderini, bishop of Volterra and brother of the gonfalonier Pier Soderini, and Niccolò Machiavelli, who had evidently won the confidence of his superiors in his earlier missions.

Along the way, at Pontassieve, just outside Florence, the two men learned from a monk that Urbino had been taken; in those days, this was one way news traveled. That very evening, 22 June 1502, they wrote to Florence to warn the Signoria that Borgia was exceedingly crafty, remarkably quick to strike, with fortune on his side. With such a man, one had to keep one's eyes wide open lest one meet the fate of Guidobaldo da Montefeltro, the dethroned duke of Urbino, "whose death was reported before his illness was" (*LC*, 264).

Once they arrived in Urbino, the Valentino received them at night (two hours after the evening Angelus bell rang) in the magnificent, newly conquered ducal palace. He was in the company of only a few associates, and the doors were locked and closely guarded, clearly indicating how little he trusted anyone, even his own men. It was hard not to be impressed by this twenty-seven-year-old condottiere, his fierce intelligent face framed by long black hair and illuminated fitfully by torchlight. Over the course of just a few months, he had eliminated—by deceit or violence or both—the vicious and arrogant small-time tyrants of Romagna. It was even said that he had ordered the murder of his elder brother, the duke of Gandía, in 1497.

He was a man to treat with caution, and the two envoys wanted the Florentine rulers to be aware of this: they sent back a description of the duke worth more than any portrait. The report was signed by Francesco Soderini, but both style and vocabulary were Machiavelli's: "This lord is most splendid and magnificent and is so vigorous in military matters that there is no undertaking so great that it does not seem a minor thing to him, and he never ceases from seeking glory or enlarging his state, and he fears no effort or danger: he arrives in a place before it has been noticed that he set out from another; his soldiers love him; he has recruited the best men in Italy: and all of this makes him victorious and formidable, to which we should add that he is perpetually lucky" (LC, 267–68).

With the two Florentine emissaries, the Valentino wasted no time. He told them right off that he wished to be a friend to Florence, but if Florence did not want his friendship, he was ready to use all necessary means to ensure that the Republic could do him no harm. Whatever he did, he said, "I will be forgiven by God and men": whether God forgave him was of little importance and his fellow men even less so, because he knew that a winner is always forgiven. Your republic, he added, borders my territories for long stretches, and I want to be absolutely certain I have nothing to fear from you.

Then he unsheathed his threats: Last year, if I had so desired, I could easily have restored the Medici to power; I could have imposed harsh rule upon you; I could have humiliated you all. I did not do so. But listen carefully and remember my words: I don't in the least like this republican government of yours; I do not trust it. Either change it or give me the thirty-six thousand ducats you promised me a year ago; show me that you are truly on my side, because talk is cheap. I don't want to be left guessing. If you don't want me as a friend, you will soon see what it is like to have me as an enemy (LC, 261–63).

These harsh words offended the two Florentines. Most offensive was the duke's appraisal of the government of which they were so proud. They answered him tit for tat: Florence has the best possible governance, and if we are satisfied with it, everyone must be satisfied with it. They wished to make it very clear that they had not come to be insulted and threatened. Faced with their indignation, the duke burst out laughing: "Did you come here thinking I wanted to justify myself to you" for what Vitellozzo Vitelli did at Arezzo? Certainly, Vitellozzo is one of my men, but I know nothing about what happened at Arezzo. I am not in the least sorry that you lost Arezzo and Valdichiana; indeed, I am delighted, and I hope that Vitellozzo continues his work. And if you expect any favors from me, put that far from your minds, because "not only have you not deserved them, you have deserved quite the opposite" (*LC, 263*).

At that point, the Florentine emissaries played the only card they had left, the king of France. They reminded Borgia that the king had signed a three-year treaty of alliance with Florence, pledging—in exchange for a large payment—to protect the city from any attack. The duke didn't bat an eye, answering, master of subtle deceit that he was: "I know better than you what the king has in mind; you will be deceived." And he said no more.

The next day Borgia had his trusted henchmen Giulio and Paolo Orsini tell the two Florentines that he would be a fool to act in this way without the consent of King Louis. We have so many soldiers and so much artillery that even if the French troops do arrive, you can be sure they will fight with us against you. If we decide to attack your city, we can ride forty miles a day and be outside your walls long before you can do anything to defend yourselves.

Perhaps Borgia was just talking big; perhaps in fact he actually needed Florence's friendship, which would explain why he was trying to obtain it—at times by promising the city greater and more certain help than the distant and unreliable king of France, at others by threatening to become an implacable enemy. Machiavelli and Soderini knew that the king of France was hardly trustworthy and that the Valentino was close at hand and disposed of no fewer than sixteen thousand well-trained and well-armed soldiers. There was nothing they could do but hurry back to Florence to gain a little time and ask the Signoria for instructions. It was, rightly, Machiavelli who rode ahead, better suited than Francesco Soderini to gallop at full speed. And as he pressed on to Florence, urging his horse along, the duke's mocking laughter echoed in his ears, far more menacing than his terrible words.

The Signoria had no interest in making an alliance with the Valentino. So the unfortunate Soderini was forced to manage as best he could in the face of his hail of demands. Yet truth to tell, Borgia was becoming more tractable and pliant with each passing day, and instead of thundering and threatening, he was working to persuade the Florentines that an alliance was in their best interests. He insisted that their sole reliance on French protection concealed a latent but evident peril: if French assistance was inadequate, the city would be vulnerable; if French assistance was lavish, Florence would incur enormous obligations. Rather than raising his voice, Borgia now relied on the implicit argument that he alone, with his authority and his weapons, could bridle the ambitions of his allies Vitellozzo Vitelli and the Orsini family, both sworn enemies of Florence.

Francesco Soderini was entirely in favor of him—out of fear, perhaps, or because he believed that the alliance was best for Florence. He wrote in his letters that Borgia spoke from the heart and wanted nothing more than that the terms agreed to at Campi be respected. In his last letter from Urbino, he recounted that when he had read the duke the letter in which the Signoria reiterated for the umpteenth time that Florence did not wish an alliance, he had seen him "change completely." The duke's face for an instant had betrayed disappointment. Perhaps it was precisely at that moment, as he saw his last hope for an understanding with Florence evaporate, that he conceived the remarkable plan which, just a few months later, was to astonish one and all, including Machiavelli, who was in the Palazzo Vecchio mulling over what he had seen and heard during his brief stay at the Valentino's court.

seven

The Great Theater of Politics

Little more than three months had passed, time spent by and large
on Chancery business (aside from three trips to Arezzo to oversee
that city's return to Florentine rule), when Machiavelli found himself in Duke Valentino's presence once again, this time on his own,
at Imola. Fortune seemed to enjoy bringing this remarkable pair
together: Borgia, master of the art of simulation, supremely skilled
in the use of both weapons and words; and Machiavelli the political observer, unrivaled in his ability to peer behind masks, glimps-
ing the true state of things in the slightest facial expression or
careless turn of phrase.

The Valentino and Machiavelli staged an enthralling game of
cat and mouse—first on the Via Emilia, the main road between
Bologna and Rimini, in Imola and then in Cesena, and again on
the road to Siena. It dragged on until 20 January 1503, when
Machiavelli turned over to Iacopo Salviati the task of monitoring
Borgia's activity. It is certainly worth our while to retrace the steps
of that game, as described by Machiavelli himself in letters that
prompted the admiration of everyone who read them in Florence.

Niccolò reached Imola on 7 October 1502 and was still in his
traveling clothes when the duke received him "lovingly" and spoke
to him at length, explaining that he desired nothing on earth so
much as friendship with Florence. This was a very different duke
from the one who had greeted Machiavelli and Soderini a few
months before in Urbino. There were no threats, only words of
respect and admiration for Florence. The change in attitude was
due, as Machiavelli knew, to the fact that the duke needed friendship with Florence now more than ever, though he was already
hatching a scheme to solve his problems on his own.

Those problems concerned the very same condottieri and
small-time tyrants whom he had used to build his dominion in
Romagna, as well as others who feared they might end up like
Guidobaldo da Montefeltro. Realizing that by helping Borgia they
were digging their own graves, Paolo and Giambattista Orsini,
Vitellozzo Vitelli, Oliverotto Eufreducci da Fermo, Giampaolo
Baglioni, Ottaviano Fregoso (representing the dethroned duke of
Urbino), and Antonio da Venafro (for Pandolfo Petrucci of Siena)
agreed to meet on 8 and 9 October at the Castello della Magione,
near Lake Trasimeno. The agenda of the meeting was to devise a
mutually satisfactory plan to overthrow the Valentino. Just a few
days before, on 5 October, the fortress of Urbino had rebelled
against the duke, an act that some said was done in the name of
Venice, others in the name of the Vitelli and the two Orsini brothers.

It appeared, then, that the duke's state was on the brink of dis-
solution, yet the face he showed Machiavelli betrayed neither resignation nor fear. He displayed, on the contrary, enormous
confidence. He wanted to convey the impression that he was perfectly in control of the situation. The conference of my enemies at
Magione, he told Niccolò, is a "congress of losers" (LC, 341).
(That opinion coincided with the view of the Venetian ambassador to the papal court, who observed that, by setting themselves
against the Valentino, the conspirators had taken a *tossego a termine,*
a poison with a delayed effect.) The conspirators were now living

on borrowed time, the duke explained to Machiavelli; those fools have chosen the wrong moment to attack me. With the king of France in Italy and my father, Pope Alexander VI, not only alive but hale and hearty, I can count on strength far superior to theirs. Losing Urbino doesn't bother me, since I remember precisely how to conquer its fortress.

The duke was working to persuade Machiavelli and the Florentines that he would emerge triumphant from the impending clash with those miserable little tyrants and that it was therefore in Florence's best interest to throw in its lot with him rather than waiting to see how matters turned out. Vitellozzo Vitelli and the others, he added, are as much your enemies as they are mine. After the conquest of Faenza, Vitelli threw himself at my feet, begging me to lead the army to the walls of Florence. I refused him and even refused to give refuge to Piero de' Medici.

Machiavelli wanted to know more about the alliance the duke had in mind and about his plans against the "losers" of the Magione. He tried to winkle information out of him, he reported, draw him out into the open, get him to talk. But the duke evaded the trap; he "skirted the matter" and left him empty-handed. A few days later, he summoned Machiavelli again and delightedly showed him a letter dated 4 October from Monsignor Giovanni Ferreri, bishop of Arles and papal *oratore* to the king of France; in it, the monsignor informed Borgia that both the king and the cardinal of Rouen were extremely well intentioned toward him and had ordered three hundred lancers under the command of Monsignor de Lanques sent to him. Borgia even showed Machiavelli the bishop's signature as proof that the letter was authentic and that the king of France was on his side. He added: "Now you see, Secretary, that this letter is written in answer to the question I asked about attacking Bologna, and you see how vigorous it is; imagine what I can get to defend myself from those men, the greater part of whom His Majesty the King believes are his violent enemies, because they have always tried to move chessmen in Italy for his injury. Believe me that this thing is to my advantage, and the Vitelli cannot reveal themselves at an hour when it will damage me less, nor can I . . . wish for a thing that will be more useful to me; because I shall know this time against whom I have to protect myself, and I shall recognize my friends" (LC, 345).

That the duke would emerge victorious Machiavelli had understood from the very first day, and he told him so, on 19 November—not to flatter Borgia, but to show that he, too, knew how to evaluate the situation. I told him, he wrote Florence, "I had always thought of him as the winner, and if the first day I had written down what I thought, and now he should read it, it would seem to him a prophecy" (LC, 446). Machiavelli had come to this conclusion through a subtle chain of reasoning that flew in the face of common sense: the duke would win in the end, he thought, because he "was alone" and faced many enemies. His strength lay precisely in his apparent weakness. Alone, he could act quickly and decisively; his enemies, divided by hostility and mistrust, would never be able to agree on an effective course of action.

The letters Machiavelli sent the Signoria in mid-October show unequivocally that he had quickly grasped two facts: that the duke would soon be rid of his enemies, and that an alliance with him was in the Republic's interest. Borgia, he wrote to the Signori on 13 October from Imola, is "highly reputed, very fortunate, and accustomed to winning" (LC, 357). As compared with a year ago, when the Republic signed an agreement with him calling for a mercenary contract, the duke had grown in both dominion and power, while Florence had become weaker. To renew the agreement, then, would redound more greatly to your honor than to his.

In Florence, however, they thought differently. The Signori preferred to let events play out, hoping the duke and his enemies would slaughter each other. They ignored Machiavelli's veiled warning: if you insist on remaining neutral, the victor in the end will owe you nothing and may consider you an enemy. Instead, Florence laughed at him, as his friend Biagio reported in a 15

November letter: "Niccolò, you are going to be let down, because you thought you were going to conclude something there that would please His Lordship." You are "an asshole," he added, if you think we want to make a deal with the Valentino.

Besides making fun of his political views, Biagio kept Niccolò up to date on important events in Florence. He assured him that Lorenzo di Giacomino would soon deliver the wine he had purchased and said Niccolò had been a fool to agree to a price of five ducats: "you are going to be ruined by it," he noted in jest. He also informed him that in a quarrel over cards, Andrea di Romolo had hurled a wooden shoe at Antonio della Valle, hurting him in the kidney, and the two were on the outs, snarling at each other. In time, they would make peace, but first Antonio would have to convalesce and heal. Finally, after updating Niccolò about Marietta's anger, Biagio told him that his new long, high-necked outfit (*l'uchettone*), which Niccolò probably planned to show off in the duke's presence, was ready. In your absence, Biagio wrote, I had it made to my measure. I hope it fits you well; if not, "go scratch your ass" (*L*, 129–31). A true friend.

In the same tone—indeed, telling him to go to the devil with his incessant requests—Biagio told him that in all of Florence there was not a copy to be found of Plutarch's *Parallel Lives*, which Niccolò had asked be sent to him at Imola. He would have to write to Venice, and wait. It is clear why Machiavelli wanted this book. In his masterpiece, Plutarch describes and compares the great generals, lawmakers, and rulers of ancient Greece and Rome. Niccolò wanted to search through those ancient biographies for examples or episodes that might help him better understand the enigmatic prince whom he saw every day and whose every gesture and word he studied with care and zeal. He hoped the lives of the great men of antiquity might help him to decipher that inscrutable face.

More than once, Machiavelli confessed his and everyone's inability to divine the duke's intentions. The Signoria must realize, he wrote on 13 November, that "I am dealing with a prince who

manages things for himself" and it is therefore extremely difficult
to know what he means to do (*LC,* 427). On 26 December, when
his mission was coming to an end, he said this even more directly:
"As I have many times written to Your Lordships, this lord is very
secretive, and I do not believe that what he is going to do is known
to anybody but himself. And his chief secretaries have many times
asserted to me that he does not tell anything until he orders it, and
he orders it when necessity compels and when it is to be done and
not otherwise" (*LC,* 503).

On 26 December, the duke put his cards on the table, and he
did so spectacularly, in the style of a great political showman. That
morning, he had the corpse of his right-hand man, Ramiro de
Lorqua, left in the main square of Cesena, hacked into two pieces.
Next to the body he ordered a wooden wedge and a bloody knife
be left. Butchers used such wedges to split open the carcasses of
animals. The same fate had probably been visited upon Ramiro.

The duke intended this gesture as a sign that he had punished
his trusted henchman for some serious offense and, at the same
time, as a reassurance to his subjects, who had begun to resent his
lieutenant's harsh behavior. To Machiavelli, the macabre piece of
stagecraft had a more general meaning: "Messer Ramiro this
morning was found in two pieces on the public square, where he
still is; and all the people have been able to see him. Nobody feels
sure of the cause of his death, except that it has pleased the prince,
who shows that he can make and unmake men as he likes, according to their deserts" (*LC,* 503).

That gesture was also—though Machiavelli could not have
known this—a generous concession on the duke's part to his enemies, especially Paolo Orsini, who had put all the responsibility for
Urbino's rebellion against the duke Valentino on Ramiro's cruel
ways. Borgia's move, a few days earlier, to send away nearly all the
French troops was equally conciliatory, a decision that, Machiavelli
wrote, "has turned the brains of this court upside down" (*LC,* 495).

It was here that the duke's greatness lay. Just as he was coming
to terms with the rebellious leaders, especially the Vitelli and the

Orsini, he was also preparing a deadly trap for them. After leaving Ramiro's butchered corpse on the main square of Cesena, the Valentino marched with all his troops to Senigallia, where Vitellozzo Vitelli, Paolo Orsini, the duke of Gravina, and Oliverotto da Fermo awaited him, ready to hand over the keys to the city.

Let's listen now to the words of Machiavelli himself. In *Description of the Method Used by Duke Valentino in Killing Vitellozzo, Oliverotto da Fermo, and Others,* he left a most vivid, concise account of the diabolical duke's masterpiece:

> Vitellozzo, Paolo, and the duke of Gravina, riding mules, went to meet the duke, accompanied by a few cavalry. And Vitellozzo, unarmed, in a cloak lined with green, very disconsolate, as though he were aware of his coming death, caused some astonishment to those who knew the valor of the man and his past fortune. Moreover, it is said that when he left his soldiers to come to Senigallia to meet the duke, he as it were took his final leave from them; and from his officers he asked aid for his house and its fortune, and exhorted his nephews that not the fortune of their house but the capacity of their fathers and their uncles should be present in their minds.
>
> When these three then came into the presence of the duke and saluted him courteously, he welcomed them pleasantly and they, being quickly greeted, were placed between those to whom they were assigned. But when the duke saw that Liverotto was missing (he had remained with his soldiers at Senigallia and was waiting at the public square by his quarters near the river to keep them to the arrangement and to instruct them in it), he winked at Don Michele, to whom Liverotto had been entrusted, as a sign that he should take measures to ensure that Liverotto would not escape. So Don Michele rode on ahead and, when he reached Liverotto, he told him that it was not the right time to keep his soldiers in ranks outside their quarters, because

the space was needed by the duke's men; he advised him to
send the men to their quarters and to come with him to
meet the duke. And as soon as Liverotto had carried out this
order, the duke came up, and on seeing him spoke to him.
Liverotto, having paid his respects, joined the rest. And having entered Senigallia, all of them dismounted at the quarters of the duke and went with him into a private room,
where the duke made them prisoners. (*O*, 21)

On the night of 31 December 1502, the duke had Vitellozzo
and Oliverotto da Fermo strangled. On 18 January 1503 at Castel
della Pieve, the same fate was visited upon the duke of Gravina,
Francesco Orsini, and Paolo Orsini. The slow poison they had
quaffed at that ill-fated conference at the Magione several months
earlier had finally done its work. Borgia had planned to rid himself
of these tyrants as long ago as his meeting in Urbino in June with
Machiavelli and Francesco Soderini. That was why he had been
seeking the friendship of Florence, that was why he had been so
disappointed when Florence refused to help him: as he wrote, "This
is what I meant to say to Francesco Soderini when he came to
Urbino, but I could never rely on his ability to keep a secret, and
now that the opportunity has presented itself, I have made excellent use of it, and I have performed a great favor and service for
your lordships" (*LC*, 330).

The very evening of the massacre at Senigallia, Borgia summoned Machiavelli. He wanted once again to express his desire for
friendship with Florence: "He summoned me at seven in the
evening and with a most cheerful demeanor rejoiced in his success,
and said that he had referred to the coming events in our conversation the day before, but had concealed the specifics, which was
true" (*LC*, 507–8). Machiavelli was struck by the duke's deeds and
words and confessed as much to the Signori. He added, after listing
the duke's demands, that it would be wise to send as ambassador a
man of great prestige with the authority to make a formal treaty.

This time he was not disappointed. On 20 January, Iacopo Salviati arrived, and Niccolò could bid farewell to the duke, who was now besieging Siena, having already taken Città di Castello and Perugia.

Machiavelli set out for Florence filled with admiration for the duke. Ten years later, in *The Prince*, he explained the reasons for that admiration:

> Thus, if I summed up all the actions of the duke, I would not know how to reproach him; on the contrary, it seems to me he should be put forward, as I have done, to be imitated by all those who have risen to empire through fortune and by the arms of others. For with his great spirit and high intention, he could not have conducted himself otherwise . . . So whoever judges it necessary in his new principality to secure himself against enemies, to gain friends to himself, to conquer either by force or by fraud, to make himself loved and feared by the people, and followed and revered by the soldiers, to eliminate those who can or might offend you, to renew old orders through new modes, to be severe and pleasant, magnanimous and liberal, to eliminate an unfaithful military, to create a new one, to maintain friendships with kings and princes so that they must either benefit you with favor or be hesitant to offend you—can find no fresher examples than the actions of that man. (*P*, VII)

A forceful spirit, ambition to accomplish great things, swiftness and secrecy in decision making, military ability: Machiavelli had found in the duke all the qualities lacking in the Florentine Republic, qualities whose absence made it so weak that the slightest shock could bring it down. He had to convey this to its rulers. No sooner had he dismounted, on 23 January 1503, than he was hard at work.

EIGHT

History Teaches Those Who Wish to Learn

With the help of the king of France, good fortune, and a great deal of money, Florence had saved itself from Duke Valentino. But the problem of the city's political and military weakness remained unresolved, and Florence's liberty was greatly at risk.

On the morrow of the Arezzo rebellion, when the Florentines had felt the duke's hot breath at the back of their necks, the city had approved a major institutional reform to rectify one of the most serious faults in its constitution, namely, the lack of continuity and competence in governance, especially in foreign affairs. The Republic's highest offices were assigned by lottery, and the citizens named to those offices held them for a very short time. As a result, inexperienced men often found themselves facing knotty and dangerous problems of domestic and foreign policy. Then, once they had finally acquired some experience, they had to leave the Palazzo Vecchio, and new officeholders started over from scratch.

To address this defect, on 10 September 1502, the Florentines instituted the office of permanent gonfalonier, to which they elected Pier Soderini, the brother of the Francesco Soderini who had gone with Machiavelli to Urbino. With this move, the Republic gained a new dimension of political wisdom and improved its capacity to face and resolve critical situations. But there remained the matter of Florence's lack of a stable military force and—after the enormous outlay required to secure the French king's assistance—a grave financial crisis.

The new gonfalonier had the highest regard for Machiavelli— for his integrity, his intelligence, and his longtime friendliness toward the Soderini family. While Machiavelli was in Imola dealing with Duke Valentino, Soderini wrote to him on 14 November 1502, mincing no words, "We have found the city very disorganized in respect to money, allotments, and many other things . . . We hope very soon to work out something suitable, in order to be able to benefit both ourselves and others: up to now it has been the contrary" (L, 149).

Money was needed, and so the Great Council, the highest lawmaking body of the Republic, had to be persuaded to levy new taxes. With that aim, Niccolò wrote the introduction to a speech that the gonfalonier was scheduled to deliver to the citizenry. The text has an unassuming title, more like that of a confidential memo than of a literary composition: *Words to Be Spoken on the Law for Appropriating Money, after Giving a Little Introduction and Excuse.* But in fact, Machiavelli put into it everything he had learned in France and in his time with Cesare Borgia. It is a passionate, lucid composition, remarkable for its subtle political analysis, its persuasive power, and the evident love of liberty that pervades every line. It is worth rereading carefully.

Every city, whatever its form of government, Niccolò wrote, has always defended itself with "force combined with prudence." One without the other is not enough, because prudence without force is useless and force without prudence is insufficient to govern political matters and preserve a state. Force and prudence, then, are the "backbone" of all states past and future, and anyone who has studied the changes and collapses of realms and republics throughout history knows that they were caused by either lack of arms or lack of wisdom. With the establishment of the office of gonfalonier, Florence has assured a minimum supply of wisdom; now a supply of military force must be assured, too, for which new taxes are needed.

The reasoning was impeccable. Machiavelli knew, however, that the stingy and rather foolish Florentines might respond that they had the French king to protect them and that the danger posed by Borgia had passed, so there was no need to spend more money. Such an attitude, Machiavelli explained, was reckless "because every city, every state ought to consider as enemies all those who can hope to take possession of her territory and against whom she cannot defend herself." No state that lives at the discretion of another state has ever truly been secure.

After setting forth the general principle, he tried to strip the blinders from the eyes of his fellow citizens and show them Florence's real situation: You are unarmed, and your subjects neither love you nor fear you. Look around, beginning with Tuscany. You see Lucca, Siena, and Pisa, all cities that "are more eager for your death than for their own lives." Now look at Italy. You will see that everything revolves around the king of France, Venice, the pope, and Duke Valentino. As far as King Louis is concerned, it should already be clear that you can count on his protection only if you gain his respect and only if you can keep others in Italy from taking advantage of you. The Venetians have always been your enemies, and you still owe them 180,000 ducats: it would be better to spend the money making war on them than to give them the money to use for war against you. As for the pope and the Valentino, everyone knows they are scheming to take your lands. Do not forget that you still have no agreement with the Valentino, and even if you do make a deal, you must remember that laws, contracts, and agreements are guarantees of promises and obligations among ordinary citizens, but among princes only weapons ensure that promises are kept, and you have no weapons. Do not think you can always rely on the sword of the king of France, because you might not have time. The last few words were the same that Borgia's envoys had used with him in Imola. Now he was repeating them to the Florentines to persuade them to establish a real army.

Machiavelli was a master of rhetoric. He had studied the classics and knew that no amount of reasoning is as powerful as an example, a story, a narrative. He found a masterful story, which would surely touch the hearts of the citizens assembled in the Great Council. He harked back to the fall of Constantinople to the Turks in 1453. The emperor, Machiavelli wrote, summoned all the citizens to ask them for money and help against the terrible enemy drawing near. The citizenry "ridiculed him." Finally, the Turks laid siege to the city, and as soon as the citizens of Constantinople heard the cannonballs pounding against their walls and the cries of the Turkish soldiers, they ran wailing to the emperor, their pockets full of money. He spurned them with these words: "Go and die with this money, since you have not wished to live without it" (O, 15).

If you continue to act in this way, you will meet the same fate; and you know that when the Valentino marched on you with his troops you came close to that fate. I tell you, Machiavelli concluded, "Fortune does not change her decision when there is no change in procedure; and the heavens do not wish or are not able to support a city determined to fall. Such a fall I cannot believe in, when I see that you are free Florentines and that your liberty rests in your own hands. For that liberty I believe you will have such regard as those who are born free and hope to live free always have had" (O, 16).

We do not know whether Soderini or anyone else used this essay by Machiavelli to secure permission to levy new taxes. What we do know is that Soderini passed a law that imposed a tithe on real estate, including ecclesiastical properties.

There was also the matter of determining what policies to

adopt toward the towns and peoples subject to Florentine dominion. Florence was sometimes too kind, sometimes too harsh, but
always too slow in its decisions. Machiavelli weighed in on the
issue with another brief essay, *On the Method of Dealing with the
Rebellious Peoples of the Valdichiana,* written in July–August 1503. As
he had done in his earlier work on levying taxes, here he distilled
his observations and reflections on what he had witnessed in
Arezzo and other rebellious cities. Here, too, he availed himself of
historical examples as a source of political wisdom and held up
ancient republican Rome as a model for the rulers.

He began his essay by quoting from a lengthy speech by Furius
Camillus cited in Livy's *History of Rome.* From Camillus's speech,
he took the following principle: In dealing with peoples who had
mutinied, the ancient Romans used one of two methods—either
they tried to earn their trust by awarding them favors, or they punished them so severely that they could cause no more trouble. Any
"middle course" was considered "harmful."

Now, I have heard, Machiavelli continued, that "history should
guide our actions," especially the actions of princes, and that men
have always been driven by the same passions. If something was
true in antiquity, it may still be true today, so the best way of treating a rebellious people is still the method used by the ancient
Romans: either give them favors or punish them so severely that
they cannot rebel again. Yet in the case of Arezzo, Florence has
been following a "middle course." It punished the people by selling
their property and taking the city out of the hands of its magistrates,
which naturally caused the people of Arezzo to hate the Florentines more. At the same time, it left the city walls intact and failed
to send Florentines to live in Arezzo to keep an eye on it. As soon
as an occasion presents itself, it is safe to say, they will mutiny again;
as in the past, they will be a dangerous thorn in Florence's side.

The Valentino still poses a threat, Machiavelli observed. It is
likely he will once again lay hands on Arezzo. His plan has always
been to conquer the Tuscan states that border on states he already

holds. This is not a convenient time for him to attack you, but bear in mind that the duke and his father the pope are very skilled at exploiting opportunities, as I have seen with my own eyes at Senigallia. Moreover, if one also takes into account "the short span of life remaining to the pope," now well along in years, it is reasonable to expect that when an opportunity presents itself, the Valentino will try to make trouble for you (O, 22–26).

Machiavelli wrote these words as an exhortation to the Florentines not to lower their guard and to deal resolutely with the problem of their dominions' security. But the words were unwittingly prophetic: on 18 August 1503, Pope Alexander VI died of an attack of tertian fever. On 24 October, after a first departure had been planned and then canceled, Machiavelli set off for Rome to observe the papal conclave and to negotiate the hiring of new troops. He would thus have a chance to watch the complex diplomatic maneuvering that always surrounds the election of a new pontiff, and above all he would see with his own eyes the demise of Cesare Borgia, who had filled him with such admiration.

He found Borgia full of animation and hopeful of "achieving great things." Despite having lost many of the most important cities in his dominions—the Vitelli family had reconquered Città di Castello, Giampaolo Baglioni was back in Perugia, the Appiano family had returned to power in Piombino, the Montefeltro family in Urbino, the da Varano family in Camerino, Giovanni Sforza in Pesaro, while the Florentines were working to restore the Ordelaffi family in Forlì, and the Venetians were active in both Rimini and Forlì—he still controlled many Spanish cardinals and therefore many votes in the papal conclave. For that reason, as Machiavelli noted in a letter of 30 October, many cardinals were visiting him at Castel Sant'Angelo, and it was widely believed that the future pope would owe him a substantial debt of gratitude. The Valentino, meanwhile, was cheerfully trusting that the new pope would treat him well in appreciation of his Spanish votes. Machiavelli was doubtful, however, and he added a significant postscript to the same letter: it remains to be seen "whether the duke will succeed in winning the protection of the new pope, as he expects" (LC, 587).

The new pope was Giuliano della Rovere, cardinal of San Pietro in Vincula, who took the papal name of Julius II. Machiavelli was one of the first to learn of his election, directly from one of della Rovere's servants, during the night and early morning of 30 October–1 November. He wrote immediately to Florence, dispatching the news in the middle of the night, proud to report such an important development before it was public knowledge. The following morning, he sent a two-line message as confirmation: "In the name of the Lord I notify your Excellencies that this morning the cardinal of San Pietro in Vincula was elected the new pope. May God make him a useful leader of Christendom" (LC, 591).

Julius II owed his election to the votes of the cardinal of Rouen and the Spanish cardinals controlled by Borgia. Why on earth the latter had decided to help him—the Borgia family had once inflicted ten long years of exile on della Rovere—was a mystery. Even more mysterious was why the duke, who had never kept a promise in his life, now implicitly relied on an enemy's promises so much that he placed that enemy on the throne of the Church. The explanation of these mysteries lay in the fact that Cesare Borgia was politically a dead man, and, as Machiavelli wrote, he needed to come back to political life. But when the end is near, clarity of thought and determination begin to waver, and desperate decisions are made that only hasten one's fall. The Valentino was no exception to this rule.

Machiavelli's reports to Florence describe a duke who was "inconstant, irresolute, and timid and not standing firm in any decision"—the very same man who had once amazed friends and enemies with the confidence of his decisions and the rapidity with which he executed his plans. Perhaps this is his nature, Machiavelli commented, or perhaps the many blows of ill fortune have bewildered him, and so, "unaccustomed to receive them, his mind is confused" (LC, 631). Thus, on one day, he would hurl threats at

Machiavelli, saying, "in words filled with venom and passion," that he would deliver all of Florence's remaining possessions "into the hands of the Venetians" and that he would soon see the Florentine state lying in ruins and would laugh at the sight (*LC,* 607); and on another day, he would say there was no good to be had from digging up the past and it was time to think of their shared best interest, namely, to halt Venice in Romagna. For Venice had remained, unintentionally, the Valentino's sole ally, and both Pope Julius and Florence feared that Venice would expand in Romagna on the ruins of Borgia's state.

Unfortunately for the future of Italy, its two most important republics, Florence and Venice, were split by an intrinsic conflict of interests. Florence owed much, in truth, to the example set by Venice. Its Republic had followed the Venetian example when it established the Great Council in 1494, and Savonarola himself had preached sermons encouraging the Florentines to take Venice as a model, excepting only its unique institution of the doge, who served a life term. Not ten years later, Florence adapted, with the institution of lifelong gonfalonier, the Venetian scheme down to the last detail. Yet though Florence may have owed Venice a debt of gratitude, that did little to assuage Florentine resentment over its all-too-evident expansionist plans.

The king of France, Florence, and the pope now developed strategies to stop Venice that bypassed the Valentino. Now everyone wanted to get rid of him. Certainly the French did: God, said the cardinal of Rouen, "up to now has not left any sin unpunished, and he won't leave that fellow so" (*LC,* 607). Florence, too: it fell to Machiavelli to give the duke the sad news that the Signori would not give him safe-conduct through Florentine territory; near Castiglion Fiorentino, the Republic's soldiers disarmed the remains of Borgia's armies and captured Don Michele de Corella, the duke's trusted lieutenant. And more than anyone else, Pope Julius II: when he learned that Don Michele had been taken prisoner, he could not restrain his jubilation; as Machiavelli wrote, "the pope was overjoyed, more than words could say, and believed that the capture of this man offered an opportunity to uncover all the cruel thefts, murders, desecrations, and other countless evils that had been committed in the last eleven years in Rome against God and men" (*LC*, 702).

A few days before, the pope had ordered the arrest in Ostia of Duke Valentino himself, who was refusing to hand over the few fortresses he still controlled in Romagna. He ordered Borgia brought as a prisoner to Rome, in an effort to persuade him to relinquish the fortresses without bloodshed. It is not clear what will become of the duke, wrote Machiavelli on 2 December, but the general view is that it will not be a pretty end. Once he gave up the fortresses, his days were numbered: the duke, Machiavelli commented, is slipping gradually into the grave. In his last days, he wrote in the *First Decennial*, Borgia sought in others that pity which "he had never known himself," and he met the fate he deserved as a rebel against Christ.

nine

A Great Idea, Perhaps Too Great

While observing the demise of the Valentino, Machiavelli was also keeping an eye on Rome and on the Venetians' moves and working to persuade Pope Julius II to halt their expansion in Romagna. Instructions he received from the Ten were exceedingly clear: You are to speak to the pope, the cardinal of Rouen, and anyone else who can "warm up" His Holiness and make him see that Venice is a danger to everyone. Tell them that the Venetians have many soldiers, enjoy the support of the people of Romagna, and are masters in the art of rendering their subjects docile. For all these reasons, they could make themselves lords of Romagna quickly and easily.

The next day, 21 November 1503, the Ten sent him another letter presenting a different picture of the political situation and ordering Machiavelli to undertake new tasks. Here in Florence, they told him, we are beginning to suspect that the Venetians are advancing into Romagna with the pope's permission. Now, try to understand just what is happening, and provide us with a "subtle" analysis of the matter.

But even before he received these new instructions, Machiavelli had been studying the Venetian maneuvering with respect to the pope. In a letter of 20 November, he had explained to the Ten that a subtle game of pretense and seduction was being played in the papal court and that the development of the Venetian situation would be greatly influenced by the pope's character. Over the autumn in Rome, he had seen that emotions and moods count for a great deal in politics, as does the art of manipulating them both with words and ceremonies.

The Venetians, he wrote to the Ten, know that the pope is an "honorable and choleric" man, easily inflamed against anyone who might try to dishonor the Church during his pontificate, always quick to charge at enemies. Understanding him as they do, they are trying "to see whether they can lull him," flattering his attachment to the honor of the Church by presenting themselves as "obedient children" and conveying to him with much ceremony that their sole desire is to ensure that not only Romagna but the entire vast Venetian dominion obey him. Indeed, Machiavelli noted, they have sent *oratori* to declare their complete obedience, something they had never done in the past. The Venetians were now continually mouthing promises of obedience and declarations of loyalty in the Roman court; they told anyone who would listen that they wanted the pope as their father, protector, and defender. They were not ashamed to pretend to be the pope's servants, Niccolò concluded, in order to "turn him to their purposes" and "succeed in ruling over all the others" (*LC,* 655–56).

Before his eyes, a refined piece of political playacting was under way, with consummate actors delivering virtuoso performances of deceit, flattery, and seduction. Machiavelli not only saw it all but suggested to the Ten that, in order to hinder the Venetian plans, Florence, too, should make a great show of ceremonial humility with the pope, since it could not compete in power and wealth with the Republic of Saint Mark.

As for the other task—to understand whether the pope was hostile to the Venetians' expansion and would move to stop them or whether he secretly favored them—Machiavelli took days to resolve his doubts. On 24 November, he informed the Ten that he had discussed the question at length with the cardinal of Volterra, his friend Francesco Soderini, who, like the cardinal of Rouen, believed the latter hypothesis was wrong. The pope is too openly resentful of Venetian expansion in Romagna, Machiavelli added; and the cardinal of Rouen agreed. For the Venetians, Machiavelli predicted, the conquest of Faenza would thus be either the door that would open all of Italy to them or, more likely, the beginning of their final ruin.

Machiavelli presented this prediction as an opinion held generally in the court of Rome. That, however, was an old diplomat's trick. The prophecy was his and his alone and this time sprang not from his observation of the moods, deeds, and words of men but from his analysis of the forces at work in the Italian theater, where Venice, as a result of its expansionist ambitions, was now almost entirely isolated. But the prediction also sprang from his coldness—as a commoner and a Florentine—toward the aristocratic Venetian Republic, stingy in awarding citizenship rights, without its own army, and yet desirous of extending its dominion not only overseas—where Venice's nature and history pulled it—but also across the Italian mainland. Machiavelli's dark prophecy derived from his belief that in order to expand on the mainland, Venice would need a powerful non-mercenary army and the willingness to grant citizenship rights to the peoples it conquered. It had neither. When he wrote to Florence that the Venetians were shameless in playing the part of good children of the Church, he was not expressing a moral criticism, since he then advised the Ten to adopt the same tactic; rather, he was showing his disdain for the cheap and vulgar policy behind it.

On 4 December, Biagio Buonaccorsi informed Machiavelli that Raffaello Girolami and Matteo Strozzi were purchasing fine clothes and other sumptuous accessories for a trip to Rome as Florentine ambassadors to take part, with all due decorum, in the celebrations of the coronation of Pope Julius II. A few days later, a letter from the Ten arrived enjoining him to return to Florence at

once. This time, oddly enough, Machiavelli did not mount his
horse immediately and in fact did not leave until 18 December. He
claimed, cunning fellow, to be ill: "Your Excellencies command
that I leave with the cardinal of Rouen for Florence, and that once
I had left I should travel posthaste to be there before His Emi-
nence. The letter reached me yesterday, and the cardinal of Rouen
had already left, which would have obliged me to set out immediately, and this was difficult for me to do, as I am suffering from a
common sickness now infecting this city, resulting in coughing and
catarrh, which have so pounded the head and chest that a violent
agitation, such as riding posthaste, would have done me great
harm" (*LC,* 724). In all likelihood, Niccolò was having a high old
time in Rome, as his finest biographer has written, enjoying beautiful women and lavish dining and, in his spare time, reasoning with
Cardinal Soderini on matters of great importance about which he
cared deeply. But more of that later.

Yet in mid-November, he had taken fright because he had
come into contact with people infected with the plague, or so he
believed. He had written about it to Florence, to his brother, Totto,
and to others, including his brother-in-law Piero del Nero. Both
had tried to allay his fears. Totto told him that Florentine merchants in the Levant went "all the time" from Pera to Constantinople in the same boats used to transport the corpses of plague
victims, and though now and again one of those merchants died,
the cases were rare. Piero told him that he had spoken, eaten, and
slept with people infected with the plague so often that he should
have died twenty times over by now. The most interesting thing
about these letters is that both brother and brother-in-law accuse
Machiavelli, in veiled terms, of being overly fearful; both urge him
to "be a man." "Try to be a man," Piero wrote. "Keep your spirits
up," advised Totto, "because losing heart is something for children
or women."

Strange words. They suggest a Niccolò easily overcome by fear
and discouraged, unable to face danger, even a danger that was

scarcely impending. We shall soon see how things really stood. For now, let us imagine him enjoying the last few days of his Roman legation, dividing his time among exceedingly subtle interpretations of the grand theater of politics, beautiful women, taverns, and serious discussions of great matters with Francesco Cardinal Soderini.

The idea that Machiavelli was exploring with the cardinal was indeed a great one: to endow Florence once again with a militia that would allow the Republic to defend its independence and to live free from mercenaries' demands. It was a dream that had probably begun to take shape as early as 1500, at the time of the mercenary troops' mutiny in the camp outside Pisa, and had then grown while Machiavelli was in France, where he had had a chance to see the quality of an army whose core was formed by the king's subjects. In the *First Decennial*, Machiavelli put it clearly to his fellow Florentines:

> . . . *we only trust the prudent pilot*
> *Who knows the oars, the rigging, and the sails,*
> *But the road would be easy and quite short*
> *Should you once again open Mars's temple.*

You have established the office of gonfalonier for life; now you must establish a militia if you want to live securely.

The idea was received poorly in Florence. The gonfalonier, Pier Soderini, approved and supported it, but "leading citizens," that is, aristocrats, viewed it coolly and suspiciously, in some cases with outright hostility. Francesco Guicciardini summarized their misgivings when he said that Machiavelli's idea was considered "new and unusual" and added that the general populace of Florence also viewed the project dimly, at best.

Florence had once had a militia of citizens and subjects from the surrounding countryside, but those glorious times were two hundred years in the past. The Florentines—craftsmen, merchants, and bankers—had forgotten the military arts and lost their martial spirit. Moreover, the aristocrats feared (or claimed to fear) that Soderini, with Machiavelli's assistance, was planning to establish a militia in order to become a tyrant. Worries increased when it was learned that the commander of the new militia would be the exceedingly cruel Don Michele de Corella, the Valentino's former right-hand man. While Machiavelli was in Rome, rumors had spread that he was a fervent supporter of the Valentino, who was roundly despised in Florence; some had insinuated he was trying to win favors from Borgia. So of course tongues wagged when it was learned that the militia Machiavelli had encouraged would be commanded by the Valentino's "strangler," as Don Michele was called.

These difficulties did not discourage Machiavelli. Also, Cardinal Soderini urged him with affectionate words to keep at it. Criticism of the plan to have an ordinance establishing a militia, Soderini wrote from Rome on 29 May 1504, was wrongheaded, and it was a necessary, wise undertaking; nor was it right to be suspicious of a military force established not for someone's private interest but for the common good. Don't give up. One day it will bring you grace and glory.

Pier Soderini helped Machiavelli to extricate the plan from this impasse. He advised not submitting the proposal for the ordinance immediately to the Council of Eighty and the Great Council for formal approval and to begin in the meantime to organize militias in the countryside. Once they saw the new troops, the Florentines would agree there was nothing to fear, and perhaps they would begin to understand the usefulness of such a new and unusual undertaking.

And so Machiavelli leaped onto his horse and went off to recruit foot soldiers in the villages of the Mugello and Casentino valleys. In an essay on the ordinance, he explained on what basis he chose the men. The state of Florence, he explained, is divided into three parts: the city itself; the district, made up of the territories of subject cities (Arezzo, Sansepolcro, Cortona, Volterra, and Pistoia); and the countryside (*contado*). To introduce the militia into all three right away would create danger and confusion, because "great matters" must be prepared and managed slowly. In a province that has forgotten the use of arms, it is necessary to begin "with the easiest part," namely, establishing the infantry.

To arm infantry in the district, Machiavelli observed, would be very dangerous, because subjects there were not well disposed toward Florence and might, if they were armed and the city were not, gather around the larger towns and start rebellions that could be difficult to put down. As for Florence itself, clearly it was the place where cavalry and officers would be recruited; since that took longer and was more difficult than establishing an infantry, it was better to undertake it later. What was left, then, were country places like the Mugello and the Casentino, "full of men" but without fortified strongholds that might become hotbeds of revolt.

Reading Machiavelli's text, we can see that he had in mind a militia that would be efficient, powerful, and numerous yet at the same time disciplined and loyal to the Republic and its laws. For that reason, he emphasized that all its companies should have the same emblem, that of the Marzocco, or Florentine lion, so that all the men would see the public emblem (*segno pubblico*) and become loyal and steadfast defenders of this one symbol. For the same reason, he insisted on the need to establish the new militia in full compliance with the Republic's constitution, that is, with a law approved by the sovereign councils and overseen by a magistracy specially created for the purpose, able to punish or reward according to law.

A militia could do the city of Florence harm in only two ways: either by mutinying and joining forces with foreign troops or by becoming the tool of some powerful citizen or magistrate. The first danger was unlikely because, being scattered through the countryside, the soldiers could not assemble of their own initiative. And the second danger could be obviated by placing the soldiers under different public authorities: one to govern and train them, another to command them in wartime, and another still to reward and punish them.

Machiavelli thought the militiamen should assemble no more than ten or sixteen times a year and the rest of the time "go where they liked and mind their own affairs." When summoning them for drills, reviews, and combat, the magistrates would be required "not to take from home" those who had legitimate reasons for staying. Company commanders (the "banners") were to be recruited from places other than those from which the soldiers came—"people from Casentino for the Mugello, and for Casentino, people from the Mugello"—in order to prevent separate loyalties from forming between soldiers and commanders based on local interests. In other words, Machiavelli wanted a militia that would be loyal to the Republic alone.

Bit by bit, once the countryside had been consolidated, a militia could be formed in the city. That was the core of Niccolò's great project: to revive in Florence a militia of citizens, which he had read about in old history books and especially in the history of the exemplary Roman republic. When he writes about it, his prose becomes solemn and evocative: You will see what a difference there is between having your own citizens as soldiers by their own free choice and having them as soldiers because they are corrupt. Nowadays young men with poor morals who have grown up in bordellos become soldiers to escape paternal authority; tomorrow the soldiers will be young men who emerge from "honest schools and good educations" and who can bring "honor to themselves and to their homeland."

In giving form to the militia project, Machiavelli had taken into account the urban mood of the city of Florence and the specific character of Florentine history. But he was essentially inspired, as he had been when he wrote *Words to Be Spoken on the Law for Appropriating Money*, by the general principle—the fruit of study and reflection during his travels—that the foundation of any form of dominion is justice and arms. Florence, though, offered little justice, especially to its subjects, and lacked a standing army. To have one and the other, Machiavelli wrote, it is necessary to "make provisions for a militia, by public deliberation, in an orderly fashion, and maintain it" (O, 26–27).

With the benefit of hindsight, historians have realized that Machiavelli's militia had numerous defects. It was not clear how the companies were to be armed and organized; the foot soldiers were never assembled in numbers greater than three hundred and therefore never drilled in square formation, which required more men; the company commanders changed too often, making it impossible for them to develop ties of loyalty with their soldiers.

All these shortcomings were due to the Florentines' not trusting the soldiers they recruited. The Republic was insatiable in its demands for tribute from the inhabitants of the countryside but in exchange offered neither full-citizenship rights nor any real protection from the abuses of local lords or the raids of enemy armies. Florence was, in a word, unjust, as Machiavelli had written in his essay on the ordinance. This was the problem that needed solving if Florence was to have a secure and powerful militia. Machiavelli knew this but could not solve the problem himself.

A friend of Machiavelli's, Francesco Vettori, left us a significant document concerning the Florentines' opinion of the ordinance. Vettori recounts that once, as he was setting out for Germany, he stopped to rest not far from Barberino, a town north of Florence on the road to Bologna. He stayed at an inn run by one Anselmo di Ser Bartolo, a Florentine citizen, where, after he finished his meal, he heard a thunder of drums. He asked the innkeeper the reason for the noise and learned it was ordinance battalions. To pass the time and distract himself from the oppressive heat, Vettori chatted with the innkeeper, asking him whether he thought the new militia would do Florence good or ill.

The host replied with these words: "I have no doubt that these battalions, once they are armed and trained, may be very similar to those considered good infantry. But I do not know how secure we Florentines will be even then; nor do I know how well these armed, trained men will obey unarmed, untrained men. They are likely to think that having once been subjects, they could now become lords. And believe me, for I deal with them all day every day: they do not love us, and they have no reason to love us, because we tyrannize them, we do not rule them. And if we fear attacks from without, perhaps it would be better to pay men to fight for us every four or six years than to fear these fellows, who could turn against us every day. And if we can assemble them quickly, they can assemble themselves just as quickly to do us harm. And if we can use them to frighten our neighbors, we can frighten and harm ourselves."

All the same, on 15 February 1506, when Machiavelli had four hundred farmers from the Mugello parade, in good order, dressed in "white doublets, stockings with a white-and-red pattern, white caps and slippers, and iron breastplates," armed with lances or *scoppietti* (small firearms), the commoners hailed it as "the finest thing that had ever been ordered for the city of Florence."

While Machiavelli rejoiced twice over—as creator of the militia and as a commoner—the aristocrats looked out from their palaces with baleful eyes on those troops marching behind the standards of the Republic.

TEN

The Envoy of the Florentines and a Warrior Pope

The life of every person is composed of an infinite number of moments, states of mind, thoughts, and dreams—all of which vanish into the lightless, bottomless well of time. We can do nothing more than try to discover—through surviving letters, writings, documents, and recollections—some fragment of the life of the person whom we wish to rescue from oblivion. It is unfortunate but inevitable that what emerges often has a less-than-perfect plot and an ill-defined rhythm and pace. But even a brief moment of life snatched from the jaws of time is priceless.

At this point in the story of Niccolò's life, we may be ready to single out certain states of mind and thoughts and to explore them in detail. From the day he began to work on the militia project, Machiavelli was a happy man. From the Casentino, where he rode from one village to another enlisting infantry, he wrote "exceedingly cheerful letters." From the Mugello, he joked about the cold north wind. He conveyed to the Ten of Liberty and Peace that the greatest obstacle to overcome was the peasants' mistrust of the Republic. Young men, he told them, enlist willingly; some, however, fear I have come to carry out a census on which to base new taxes; others fear some trick. As soon as their fears are laid to rest, they will come running to enlist. He felt certain he would succeed: everyone here wants to help, and "I believe in it more than ever," if only we devote the diligence and wisdom required for so great and important an undertaking as that of "reforming a province" (*LC*, 927). That was what Machiavelli was doing: not enforcing a political or military decree but reshaping people's lives.

He believed this was a truly great undertaking; he was absorbed by the enterprise; it seized him, excited him, increased his physical and mental energy a hundredfold. He hurried from one village to the next, angry when weapons were delayed and "time was wasted." He was exceedingly strict in his choice of soldiers. He refused to compromise. He would not enlist men who demanded the Republic abrogate death penalties it had decreed for some of their townsfolk. Florence, he responded, did not wish to force anyone to serve under its flag, and that flag "must be all one color." He saw the creation of the militia as an opportunity to win recognition and glory, as Cardinal Soderini had said it would be. But he also felt he had found an idea that might save Italy from the grim destiny the stars seemed to have reserved for it.

That at this point in his life he believed Italy was the victim of a cruel destiny we know from the *First Decennial,* dating from November 1504. In the dedication to Alamanno Salviati, the aristocrat who wisely led Florence during the crisis with Cesare Borgia, Machiavelli wrote that Italy's travails over the decade of 1494–1504 were caused by fate, whose power is irresistible. Even more significantly, he began the poem with a reference to the stars as being hostile to Italy's well-being and ended it with an exhortation to the people of Florence to establish a militia.

Machiavelli believed the militia could mark the beginning of Italy's military rebirth, and thus the end of a barbarian domination that had originated under the influence of bad stars. He wanted to challenge the power of the stars. He went so far as to consult a

Paduan astrologer, Bartolomeo Vespucci, as to whether men could escape the influence of the heavens. The astrologer replied that Machiavelli's belief was "quite accurate," that people can change by taking advantage of various experiences life has offered them and especially by adapting to new circumstances. What was the institution of the militia but an effort by Florence and Italy to change, to adapt to and survive the new political and military situation that had developed when King Charles VIII came to Italy in 1494?

His friends, too, believed that the creation of the militia might well change the destiny of Italy. We can see this in a letter from Francesco Soderini of early March 1506. I am exceedingly pleased, the cardinal wrote, to learn from your latest letter that the organization of the militia is proceeding well, because this undertaking fully meets my hopes for the security and dignity of the fatherland. I cannot believe that foreign troops today are superior to our own, except inasmuch as our troops have for so long been lacking in adequate discipline. And he added a few words that must have filled Machiavelli's heart with joy: "You must get no small satisfaction from the fact that such a worthy thing should have been given its beginnings by your hands. Please persevere and bring it to the desired conclusion."

The same letter reveals that Machiavelli was lobbying the cardinal's brother, the gonfalonier Soderini, in favor of a more equitable treatment of city and countryside by the Republic. He knew that justice was crucial to the militia's success, and he did all he could to persuade the Republic's leaders on that point. Let us read the cardinal's words: "You write wisely that this idea requires justice above all, both in the city and in the countryside." I will do all I can to keep your words in mind, he added, because I, too, believe it is necessary to the proper completion of the task.

Machiavelli was aware of the resistance his project was likely to encounter, and he worried, especially when he could not be in Florence to oversee things in person. As soon as he reached Rome on a mission I shall shortly describe, he wrote back to ask how the ordinance was going. Biagio answered, knowing how happy Machiavelli would be to read his words, that Bastiano da Castiglione, the captain of recruits from the Valdarno, had prompted widespread admiration by announcing that he could assemble "seven hundred men in four hours," ready for orders. Good news such as this and the support of so many and such important friends led Machiavelli to believe that, in time, it would be possible to win over everyone. He said as much in a letter of 23 September to Antonio Giacomini Tebalducci, one of the Republic's finest military leaders, whom Machiavelli greatly admired. I mention this letter because Machiavelli so rarely used words expressing hope and optimism, and the occasions are worth treasuring.

At the end of the summer of 1506, he was forced to suspend work on his beloved militia to go back to the job of tracking the intricate, far less glorious maneuverings of Italian politics. The Ten of Liberty and Peace sent him this time to the court of Pope Julius II with the mission of stalling for time, a tactic he disliked but by this point must have mastered. Determined to regain full control over the territories of the papal states, Julius II, confident because of his French reinforcements, had left Rome and was marching on Perugia and Bologna to expel Giampaolo Baglioni from the former city and Giovanni Bentivoglio from the latter. He was demanding that Florence lend him the condottiere Marcantonio Colonna and his troops, all currently in the hire of the Republic, with which he intended to attack the Bentivoglio family.

The Florentines were hemming and hawing for various reasons, first and foremost because they needed both the troops and their general for use against Pisa. At the same time, it was important not to offend the fiery pope, who might otherwise fall into the welcoming arms of the Venetians, who had offered to help him take Bologna in exchange for recognition of their rights over Faenza and Rimini. So it was necessary to flatter the pope with pleasing words and promises and to stall for time and see how things developed.

To perform this mission, Machiavelli mounted his horse and

rode through the night and morning of 25–26 August 1506. He reached Nepi on the twenty-seventh but could not speak with the pope, as His Holiness was "withdrawn from business." (It is unlikely that he was immersed in spiritual matters and more likely that he was engaged in worldly amusements.) Machiavelli was given an audience the next day, at Civita Castellana, and he recited one of his well-turned little speeches to the pope, in accordance with the Ten's instructions.

In terms of political value, the legation did not amount to much. But Machiavelli was not about to turn up his nose at the chance to follow a pope who rode at the head of an army (Julius scorned the more customary sedan chair). This was a unique opportunity to study the actions of an unusual prince, who brandished a sword in one hand and the scepter of Saint Peter in the other. Machiavelli certainly trained his gaze and observed closely; on that legation, he found several important new tiles to add to the political mosaic he was gradually constructing, driven as he was by an insatiable passion for knowledge and a yearning to find grandeur and meaning in even the less elevated aspects of the world.

The first tile Machiavelli found concerned a matter dear to him: the cause and significance of human actions on the stage of politics. The event itself, as recounted by Machiavelli in a 13 September letter to the Ten, was unassuming: given confidence by a treaty signed with Giampaolo Baglioni, the pontiff entered "solemnly here into Perugia"; but it did not escape Machiavelli's watchful eye that the pope had left his troops outside the city gates, thus placing himself "at Giampaolo's discretion" instead of making sure that Giampaolo was at *his* discretion. Why did Baglioni not take advantage of this papal mistake?

One reason might be (Machiavelli was writing about it the very same day and therefore did not know how things would end) that he did it out of "his own good nature and decency" (*LC*, 979–80). Baglioni had decided not to defend his state with force, he added, and, taking the duke of Urbino's advice, preferred to follow the path of humility. Let's call it humility, which can be easily feigned; but to attribute "good nature and decency" to Baglioni was a bit much. Can it be that Machiavelli did not know whom he was dealing with here? That is especially hard to imagine since he had met the man in person in April the year before and had spoken with him at length.

This episode made a profound and lasting impression on Machiavelli. Years later, in the *Discourses,* he returned to it, offering a very different interpretation based entirely on the emotions dominating the souls of the two main actors, the pope and Baglioni. The pope, he wrote, entering Perugia unarmed and thus putting himself into his enemy's hands, was driven by that "fury" which so often guided his actions. Baglioni failed to take advantage of the pope's error—not because he was good or kind but because he was a coward. Indeed, Machiavelli explicitly states that at the time of these events, the most intelligent people in the pope's entourage all concurred that Baglioni's conscience had absolutely nothing to do with his failure to crush his enemy. A man of his type, who had murdered his own father and kept his sister as a concubine, was incapable of feeling pity. He failed to seize a remarkable opportunity to establish a legacy that would be forever admired and "eternally commemorated"—as the first who dared to show the priests how little respect was due to men who lived as they did and governed states as they did with so little wisdom. In short, Baglioni had missed an opportunity to perform a deed that would certainly have been evil but would have had a kind of "greatness," a deed that showed a sort of "generosity" or public-spirited ambition. Baglioni was bad, but he was incapable of either generosity or greatness; his evil was squalid (*D,* I, 27). Machiavelli's finely drawn and disquieting portrait of the passions that drive a prince, first sketched out in Perugia on that Sunday in 1506, derived from close, living contact with events and men.

That day another equally important idea first took form, an idea that was to be fully articulated in *The Prince.* Referring to

"ecclesiastic principalities"—that is, realms governed by the pope
or other high prelates—Machiavelli wrote that they were supported by the ancient orders of the Christian religion, orders so
powerful that they would sustain the principalities no matter how
these were governed. Because of the support of religion, ecclesiastic princes could behave however they wanted, neglecting to govern and protect their subjects, failings that would cost any other
prince his state (*P*, XI). What Machiavelli saw at Perugia was something similar. Giampaolo Baglioni, who did not hesitate to murder
his father and commit other infamous acts, was unwilling to order
his soldiers to hack to pieces the pope and the cardinals who
accompanied him. Thinking back on that episode, Machiavelli
concluded that what saved Pope Julius II was probably—aside from
Baglioni's cowardice—the special protection accorded by religion.

While some seeds from the events at Perugia were planted in
the fertile soil of his mind and germinated only much later, others
gave fruit almost immediately, and splendid fruit it was. The pope's
actions further confirmed what Machiavelli had long suspected
about how men behaved in the world—in particular, how different
forms of behavior, even diametrically opposed forms, may sometimes lead to exactly the same results.

Machiavelli set his thoughts down in a long letter to Giovan
Battista Soderini, the gonfalonier's nephew. He begins by admitting
that his last doubts as to the accuracy of his interpretation have
been swept away by "the actions of this pope and the effects of
those actions" (*L*, 241). Then he goes on to illustrate his thinking
with an example from ancient history. How can we explain the fact
that Hannibal won the admiration of the peoples of Italy through
perfidy, cruelty, and scorn for religion, while Scipio, in Spain,
achieved the same result with piety, faithfulness, and respect for
religion? Moreover, Lorenzo de' Medici preserved his power in
Florence by disarming the people, while Giovanni Bentivoglio
achieved the same result in Bologna by arming the people; similarly, Francesco Sforza in Milan and the duke of Urbino each pre-

served his state, one by building new fortresses, the other by destroying existing ones. The answer is this: men's success or failure depends on whether their talents and imagination—and thus their actions—are well or poorly suited to their times and to events. That is why different forms of behavior may give, in different places and times, the same results.

The problem lies in the fact that the nature of times and events changes, while men often fail to change their thoughts and actions. It therefore happens that the same person may have good luck for a while, and then bad luck. If men could understand the nature of their times and of events, and change their behavior accordingly, then it would be true that wise men command the stars and their destinies. But men are shortsighted and cannot change their natures or their behavior, and so the reverse almost always happens. "Fortune is fickle, controlling men and keeping them under her yoke." This was exactly the opposite of what Machiavelli had written two years earlier to the astrologer Bartolomeo Vespucci.

After Perugia, Machiavelli followed the pope on his march north to Bologna, the ultimate destination of his expedition. His thoughts, however, continued to dwell on the Florentine militia. In Cesena, on 5 October, after observing a parade of soldiers in the pope's service, he took advantage of the opportunity to praise the newly established militia to the Ten: "If your Excellencies were watching this infantry, they would feel no shame at their performance, nor would you be unimpressed" (LC, 1012). A little self-promotion never hurts. But the militia met with almost universal approval in any case, and on 6 December 1506 a new magistracy was established, the Nine Officials of the Ordinance and Militia of Florence, charged exclusively with overseeing military affairs. This was formal recognition that the militia was now an integral part of the institutions of the Republic of Florence. The chancellor of the new magistracy was, of course, Niccolò Machiavelli.

Amid all this appreciation and praise, there were those who looked on Machiavelli and his patron Soderini with unconcealed hatred. Nor were they negligible enemies; one was none other than Alamanno Salviati, to whom Machiavelli had dedicated the *First Decennial* and one of the leaders of the aristocratic opposition to Pier Soderini. Machiavelli had learned of this animosity in a letter of 6 October 1506 from Biagio: at dinner, in the presence of many young men, Salviati called you a "rascal" and hinted that, as a member of the Ten, he would do everything he could to prevent your reconfirmation as secretary.

We shall soon see the reasons for such hatred; and we shall also see that in the short run, Salviati's hostility had no serious consequences. Times were still good; glory still lay in the future, even though the horizon was beginning to darken with the first clouds of a terrifying storm.

ELEVEN

The Mission to the Emperor's Court and the Conquest of Pisa

To tell the truth, the hostility of Alamanno Salviati and the other *ottimati,* the aristocrats and nobles, did harm to Niccolò. In the spring of 1507, word began to spread that the Habsburg emperor Maximilian—who called himself the Roman Emperor–elect—was planning to march into Italy to expel the French from Lombardy and obtain the Holy Roman imperial crown from Pope Julius. Florence ran the risk of finding itself between a rock and a hard place: France on one side, the emperor on the other. The situation was made yet more complex by rivalry between the supporters of the gonfalonier Soderini and the aristocrats who opposed both him and government by the people. Soderini wanted to continue Florence's traditional pro-French policy (despite the terrible defeat that had been inflicted in 1503 on French forces at Garigliano by Spanish troops commanded by Gonzalvo de Cordova); his opponents favored a formal alliance with Maximilian.

Before making any decision, it was vital to know—and fast—whether Maximilian was about to march over the Alps and, if so,

how many and what sort of soldiers he had. It was a mission made
to order for Machiavelli; on 19 June, he was told to set off for the
imperial court in German territory—Todescheria, as the Florentines called it.

The party of the aristocrats weighed in against Machiavelli. In
unison, they cried out that one of the "well-born young men" of
Florence should be sent to the emperor's court, since they needed
practice in affairs of state and there was no need to send that
uppity commoner Machiavelli. So vehement were they that on 27
June the sought-after posting went to Francesco Vettori instead of
Machiavelli.

The rejection was dictated by political animosity toward
Soderini. But the justification was particularly arrogant: the prefer-
ence for a "well-born" young man from one of the families that
had always controlled Florence's city politics and especially foreign
policy. It mattered not at all that Machiavelli had already amply
proved his complete devotion to the Republic's best interests; it
mattered not at all that he had shown remarkable political skills and
understanding; he was not "well-born," so he needed to move
aside. It is difficult to imagine a more humiliating and offensive
attitude.

Machiavelli took it hard—all his work and sacrifice, the splendid reports that had astounded everyone: everything subordinated
to considerations of family and birth. He felt betrayed; he had discovered that men he had considered friends were his most vicious
enemies. He told his real friends how bitter his disappointment
was, though we can be sure he did not cry on their shoulders. One
of them, Filippo Casavecchia, wrote him a long letter on 30 July
1507, reminding him that history abounds with instances of
friendship that turn into fierce hatred: Marius and Sulla, Caesar and
Pompey, and, in Florence, Giuliano de' Medici and Francesco dei
Pazzi. He ended by urging Machiavelli to take consolation in the
thought that the victory of those who had kept him from Germany would be unimportant and short-lived.

The same day, another friend, Alessandro Nasi, began a letter with these words: "My good, and not unfortunate, Machiavelli . . ." He, too, encouraged him and urged him to cheer up, because in the end it was better for him to stay in Florence than to ride to Todescheria. The letter concluded with a few words that went straight to the heart of the problem: those who are of good spirit, attentive to both God and the common good, should be trusted, whether they "be rich or poor," of high social standing or not. But it was not so in Florence, and this was nothing more than a foreshadowing of what Machiavelli would ultimately suffer for the crime of having a generous soul and a free mind while enjoying neither wealth nor social standing.

Yet in the end, Machiavelli did go to Todescheria. Soderini could not rely on Vettori's letters; whether out of ignorance or for ulterior political motives, Vettori predicted Maximilian's imminent departure from Germany for Italy and greatly overstated the number and readiness of his troops. Using the excuse that someone was needed to give oral reports in case the letters were lost, Soderini sent his trusted Niccolò to the imperial court. Officially, Machiavelli was little more than a courier; in actuality, he was there to ensure that the letters sent to Florence did not offer grist for the mill of Soderini's enemies.

Machiavelli set out on 17 December 1507. He traveled across Lombardy, then to Savoy, Geneva, Bolzano, and Constance. In Lombardy, French guards searched him closely; he had destroyed any letters that might have revealed Florence's intention—however cautious and qualified—of helping to fund the emperor's march into Italy. In Geneva, he did his best to understand the sentiment of the Swiss communities and concluded they had little interest in helping the emperor fight the French. During his half day in Constance, he spoke with as many people as he could to get information about the real condition of the emperor's Italian project: in the city cathedral, he met two Milanese; then he visited Heinrich Isaac, a musician; lastly, he dined with the duke of Savoy's *oratore*, pestering him with so many questions that the diplomat finally burst out, "You want to learn in two hours what I have been unable to determine in many months!" (LC, 1065–66).

We should not think, however, that Machiavelli blindly trusted his acquaintances' words. He weighed every statement carefully, checking each against what he could see with his own eyes. This is clear in a letter he wrote on 17 January from Bolzano. After observing that Baron de Viry, who was generally considered "quite prudent," believed the emperor's enterprise would produce great effects "of either peace or war," he concluded by noting, "In many miles of countryside, I never met a single soldier or saw a single horse," adding that, between one imperial negotiation with the Swiss and the next, time was passing and money was dwindling.

When he reached Bolzano, he actually befriended Francesco Vettori, even though circumstances might easily have caused hostility and resentment. The two Florentines worked together and got along famously. They discussed matters and wrote letters in harmony (Machiavelli wrote and Vettori signed). Machiavelli may have been disappointed and offended that he had not been named oratore, but he was not a man to hold a grudge; he had too many other things to do: working to understand the political and military organization of a people he knew nothing about; analyzing the intentions of a highly secretive and indecisive emperor. In any event, Machiavelli and Vettori understood, admired, and respected each other.

Machiavelli's finest writings on his visit to Germany were composed immediately after his return to Florence, on 16 June 1508. He had left Innsbruck on 10 June; by the fourteenth, he was already in Bologna—a clear sign that he was fed up with Germans and Swiss and wanted to breathe the sharp clean air of Tuscany once again. No sooner had he unloaded his luggage than he set to work on Report about German Matters (Rapporto di cose della Magna), probably addressed to the Ten.

In Machiavelli's view, as we have seen, politics is the work of human beings, with their emotions, their temperaments, and their imaginations. Since this was so, he always did his best to understand the hearts of the princes he met, and he worked hard to explore their souls thoroughly, peering behind their masks and pretenses. Of the emperor Maximilian he wrote that "his easygoing good nature" is such that any member of his entourage could easily deceive him. A member of the court told Machiavelli that no one could deceive the emperor more than once, because he always knew when he had been deceived. But, Machiavelli replied, even if this were so after the fact, there were so many men and so many situations arising every day that the emperor might still be regularly deceived. We can imagine the courtier's feelings when he heard that answer. But then we already knew what a rascal Machiavelli was.

Let us continue with his report. "He has countless virtues," he observed. If Maximilian toughened his nature, he would be "a most perfect man," because he is an excellent leader, governs his land justly, willingly grants audiences, and is well liked. In short, if he could only change his nature, he would be a great prince and could achieve anything he set his hand to.

Unfortunately, it is difficult for a man to change his nature, and Maximilian was no exception; he remained a mediocre prince with enormous potential.

His imperial task was that much harder because, although he may have been emperor, his subjects were "free and wealthy." German communities enjoyed great independence; if Maximilian wanted soldiers, he first had to obtain the approval of local community authorities and then had to pay the soldiers well and on time. If pay was not forthcoming within thirty days, the soldiers went home, and the emperor could do nothing—neither plead nor threaten—to stop them. In addition, the communities sent soldiers only when they pleased and only for set terms. And so when soldiers from one community arrived, soldiers from another community were just heading home. Thus, the emperor had many soldiers in theory but very few in fact. With the few soldiers he did have, he had tried to force the hand of Venice, which had first declared its friendship, only to spurn him later; all the emperor obtained for his trouble was a painful defeat that cost him the whole of Friuli.

What struck Machiavelli most was Germany's excellent military organization and the wealth of its communities and free cities. To be precise, he was impressed that they were wealthy *because* the populace lived in poverty. The German people, he wrote, "live like paupers"; they do not build, they do not spend money on garments, their larders are usually bare; they are happy to have bread, meat, and "a stove to ward off the cold." At the very most, they spend "two florins every ten years" on clothing; the people worry not about the things they lack but only about the bare necessities, and "their needs are much more modest than our own." All these factors keep money from leaving the communities; instead, it accumulates in their common coffers.

It is unlikely that Machiavelli found the "rude" life that satisfied the Germans particularly attractive. He admired their liberty, as well as the "free liberty" of the Swiss—who refused to recognize distinctions of rank or class save that between citizens and elected magistrates—but not their "rudeness" (*O,* 79–81). He approved of the principle of encouraging frugality in order to enrich the coffers of the state, but the Swiss and Germans took it too far: bread, meat, and a fire seemed a little austere; life demanded other things, such as wine—good wine—and velvet garments (like the suit he had recently ordered, the material for which alone had cost four and a half ducats).

But the Florentines and Italians could learn a great deal from the Germans and Swiss in one area: military organization. Their practices, he wrote, are admirable. They keep their soldiers "armed and well trained," just as he wished to do with the new Florentine militia. Every city had great armories filled with weapons and munitions in perfect working order (this must have come to mind when he was forced to scrounge and scavenge for gunpowder dur-

ing the siege of Pisa). And they kept enough reserve stocks of food
and firewood to last for a year, should they fall under siege. They
might lead "rude" lives, but they were not likely to be enslaved, as
were the refined and arrogant Florentines, who lived comfortably
while their Republic begrudged its envoys the money to send dispatches.

Machiavelli's attention would return—more than once—to the
emperor Maximilian and the ways of the Swiss and the Germans.
Now, however, more urgent matters intruded. Worn out by the
long siege, Pisa was beginning to show signs of exhaustion. After
placating with gold the halfhearted protests of King Louis XII of
France and Ferdinand of Aragon, the Florentines began to glimpse
an end to the seemingly endless war and the long-desired reconquest of the city.

The militia had its first trial by fire in the siege operations. At
stake was not only its credibility with Florentines but also the reputation of Machiavelli himself, who had done so much to assemble
the troops. As was his habit, he plunged headlong into the project;
in supervising military operations and training his militia, he com-
muted tirelessly from one army to the other. So hard did he work,
and so great was the authority he had won, that at one point it
seemed he alone was overseeing siege operations in the name of
the Republic. Biagio Buonaccorsi, in a letter of February 1509,
went so far as to address him as "Your Magnificence, the Captain
General." It was in jest, but it gives us an idea of Machiavelli's role.

Such fame engendered, once again, jealousy and resentment. It
was necessary to write letters, flatter, placate. Biagio implored Niccolò to do so: "Do it, I pray you," he wrote on 21 February. But
Niccolò had neither the time nor the desire to flatter and placate.
He wanted to be in the middle of the action. When he learned
that the Ten intended to transfer him to a quieter camp near
Cascina, under the command of Niccolò Capponi, he wrote in

terms that convey how passionate he was about the Pisan enterprise: "I know that being stationed there would be less arduous and
dangerous, but if I had not wanted danger and hard work, I should
not have left Florence. So may it please Your Lordships to leave me
here in the field to work along with the commissioners [Alamanno
Salviati and Antonio da Filicaia] on matters that arise, for here I can
be of some use, but there I should not be doing any good and I
would die of despair" (R, 169).

He wanted to be where he could do some good and where his
intelligence and devotion could make a difference. In mid-March,
he went to Piombino to discuss the possibility of surrender with a
Pisan delegation. The Pisans refused to discuss things in detail and
expressed their disappointment that the Signoria had sent only "a
secretary" rather than two or three illustrious citizens; Machiavelli
immediately showed them that even if he did not have an impres-
sive surname, he knew how to conduct negotiations.

At first the Pisans waffled, then asked for assurances of the
safety of their citizens and their rural and urban property. They
proposed ceding jurisdiction over the countryside to Florence
while maintaining sovereignty over their city itself. Machiavelli
replied that they could rest assured that all inhabitants would be
perfectly safe, because the Signoria of Florence had no designs on
their lives or possessions or honor but desired only "their obedience." As for the idea of settling for jurisdiction over the countryside, he made it very clear that such a proposal could only be taken
in jest; Florence wanted "Pisa in hand, free with all its dominion."

He wanted the Pisans of both town and countryside to understand that they had no other choice than to surrender and to
pledge obedience to Florence, but he also wanted to persuade
them that they could rely on the Signoria's guarantees about the
safety of the populace. This was especially the case for the rural
component of the Pisan delegation. He raised his voice and threatened, then he tried to "move them" with well-chosen words: "I
addressed the country dwellers and said I was disappointed at their

simplicity, because they were playing a game they could not win, because if the Pisans were victorious, they would want them not as equals but as slaves, and they would be back working in their fields; on the other hand, if Pisa were stormed, which might happen at any hour, they would lose their possessions and their lives and everything" (LC, 1166–67). This attempt to divide the representatives of the city from those of the countryside was successful. The former were furious; the latter greatly admired Machiavelli's words. "We want peace, we want peace, ambassador," was their reply.

Peace arrived on 4 June 1509. The city's official surrender was signed by Florence's first secretary, Marcello Virgilio Adriani, and by Niccolò Machiavelli, who had overseen the entire undertaking, both military and diplomatic. Machiavelli even consulted an astrologer to know the most propitious time and day for the entry of the Florentine commissioners into Pisa. Make very sure, the astrologer responded, that they "by no means" enter before 12:30 on Thursday; if possible, they should enter just after one in the afternoon, "which will be a fortunate hour for us."

The commissioners entered Pisa on Friday 8 June. There was immense satisfaction, indeed enthusiasm, in Florence. The city was in a fever of celebration, and bonfires were burning everywhere, as Agostino Vespucci told Machiavelli. If I were not afraid of making you over-proud, he added, I would go so far as to say that you, with "your battalions," made this reconquest possible. "I swear to God, so great is the exultation we are having" that I would write an oration worthy of Cicero for you! A few days later, Filippo Casavecchia invited him to spend a few days as his guest, eating trout and drinking fine wine; he congratulated Machiavelli for the Pisan triumph. His words clearly show that everyone in Florence understood that much of the credit was due to Machiavelli: "I wish you a thousand benefits from the outstanding acquisition of that noble city"; it was truly safe to say that "your person was cause of it," without detracting in any way from the merit of the other "very noble commissioners." It is still best to be cautious, however, he added, because Machiavelli's ideas find favor only with the wise, who are few.

Casavecchia was right. Machiavelli had accomplished something magnificent for his city. His ideas made him seem something of a prophet, as Casavecchia had written. For those very reasons, he needed to be wary of the hostility of the many people who were anything but wise and of those who were mean-spirited, ambitious, and ungrateful. In all likelihood, he realized this himself. When and if he pondered his friend's words, he might have thought about changing *his* nature a bit, learning to flatter the powerful, as Biagio had begged him to do, to rein in his tongue, to work in the shadows, to stop striving for grandeur. But Machiavelli had said it himself: men can rarely change their nature; and so they remain slaves to Fortune, who turns the wheel at her pleasure, now this way and now that. Machiavelli had already reached his highest point on that wheel.

TWELVE

The Gathering Storm

A person who does good, who serves the public interest with total dedication and honesty, who tries to understand the problems of his country and find solutions to them—such a person should be esteemed and admired by his fellow citizens. Since people are largely envious and ignoble, however, the opposite is almost always the case: the harder a person works, honestly and intelligently, for the common good, the more his fellow citizens will look upon him with suspicion and venom, the more they will work to harm him, the more obstacles they will throw in his way. Honor and success accrue, instead, to those skilled at flattering, adulating, and serving the powerful.

Only six months after the reconquest of Pisa, and as the plaudits and praise died down, hostility toward Machiavelli began to emerge in ever clearer forms. Once again, Biagio Buonaccorsi alerted his friend to the danger. Eight days ago, he wrote on 28 December 1509, a man wearing a mask appeared before the magistrates to report that "since you were born of a father, etc., you can in no way exercise the office that you hold, etc."

The anonymous accuser was probably referring to the fact that Niccolò's father, Bernardo, had failed to pay his debt of back taxes to the commune, and therefore his children were barred from holding public office. Both the law and various precedents were on Machiavelli's side, as Biagio hastened to point out. Still, the matter was worrisome, because so many people in Florence were attacking Machiavelli, including the keepers of whorehouses, where Niccolò was evidently well known.

According to Biagio, Machiavelli's best course of action was to stay away until things had calmed down, leaving Biagio to manage in his absence. He offered this advice because he knew that if Machiavelli was in town, he would not do what was required in a case like this: coax and blandish. Instead, Biagio knew, he would hurt his own cause: "All men," said Biagio, "want to be recognized and honored and esteemed, even if their standing is clear, and it seems advisable to thank and solicit and then solicit again those who do you favors; how well you might be fitted for this I let you yourself judge" (L, 325–27).

True, Biagio tended to exaggerate dangers, but it is clear from his words how bad Machiavelli was at asking nicely and saying thank you properly, at least for things that were his by right and just deserts. And Biagio makes it equally clear how many people in Florence wished him ill and how "few people here" wished to help, to quote him again. Truly a handsome reward for his efforts to give Florence a militia and to win back Pisa.

While Biagio was writing this letter of alarm, Niccolò was on his way back to Florence from a mission to Mantua and Verona, where the Ten had sent him to deliver the second payment to the emperor Maximilian (due for the events at Pisa) and to keep an eye on the progress of the war that the emperor together with King Louis was waging against Venice. He was in good spirits; he was blithely indifferent to events in Florence. He had hopes of setting aside a little money—a rare, if not unique, state of affairs—and even "doing a little business" once he returned. He planned to build a chicken house, and he asked Luigi Guicciardini to inquire whether one Piero di Martino might be interested in running it for him.

While he was thinking about chickens, Machiavelli got himself into situations that did not redound to his honor, at least if we take him at his word. Luigi Guicciardini had written to him about an amorous escapade that had left Guicciardini with a burning desire to see a certain lovely lady once again. Machiavelli responded with a story of his own, a topsy-turvy reversal of his friend's account: Guicciardini was yearning for a repeat of his own experience, and Machiavelli had had an encounter in Verona that killed any future desires for quite some time; Guicciardini emerged from his tryst feeling glorious, whereas Machiavelli played the fool about having been, to use his words, a "naive prick."

But let us get to the facts. Blinded by "conjugal famine," Niccolò accepted the insistent invitation of an "old bawd" who did his laundry to sample some merchandise. The merchandise in question was a woman; when the customer arrived, she was sitting in a dark corner, her face half covered with a towel. Here I will let Niccolò tell the unappetizing tale; his details are appalling:

> I, shy fellow that I am, was absolutely terrified; still, to make a long story short, alone there with her in the dark (because the old bawd promptly left the room and shut the door), I fucked her one. Although I found her thighs flabby and her cunt damp—and her breath stank a bit—nevertheless, hopelessly horny, I went to her with it. Once I had done it, and feeling like taking a look at the merchandise, I took a piece of burning wood from the hearth in the room and lit a lamp that was above it; but the light was hardly lit before it almost fell out of my hands. Ugh! I nearly dropped dead on the spot, that woman was so ugly. The first thing I noticed about her was a tuft of hair, part white, part black—in other words, sort of whitish; although the crown of her head was

bald (thanks to the baldness one could make out a few lice promenading about), still a few, thin wisps of hair came down to her brow with their ends. In the center of her tiny, wrinkled head she had a fiery scar that made her seem as if she had been branded at the marketplace; at the end of each eyebrow toward her eyes there was a nosegay of nits; one eye looked up, the other down—and one was larger than the other; her tear ducts were full of rheum and she had no eyelashes. She had a turned-up nose stuck low down on her head and one of her nostrils was sliced open and full of snot. Her mouth resembled Lorenzo de' Medici's, but it was twisted to one side, and from that side drool was oozing, because, since she was toothless, she could not hold back her saliva. Her upper lip sported a longish but skimpy moustache. She had a long, pointy chin that twisted upward a bit; a slightly hairy dewlap dangled down to her Adam's apple. (L, 321–22)

Niccolò's was a subtle gambit: his friend had ecstatically described the beauty of the woman he had possessed; he replied with a description of his woman's appalling ugliness. He seemed to enjoy laughing at his boastful friend and at himself, thinking of himself, in reality and not in jest, in such a nightmarish circumstance. Now, whether the encounter ever took place, and lived up to his account, is quite another matter.

Aside from pursuing affairs of the heart (so to speak), Machiavelli was trying to follow the intricate twists and turns, the countless uncertainties, in the war against Venice. He arrived in Mantua on 15 November 1509 but at first did not gather much useful information. The marchesa Isabella d'Este, ruling in the absence of her husband, Francesco Gonzaga, a prisoner of the Venetians, did not receive Machiavelli until 18 November; she kept him waiting on that day not to punish or humiliate him but because she liked to sleep late and never gave audience before lunch. This was the sec-

ond time he had been received by a female ruler, his mission to the
court of Caterina Sforza in Forlì being the first. About Isabella
d'Este he said only that she treated him "with great humanity,"
providing him with what scanty and unreliable information she
had on the progress of military operations. Even less reliable was
the information he gathered from those in her court, where "liars
flourish, indeed rain from the sky" (*LC,* 1187).

To get better information, he went to Verona. Arriving on 21
November, he immediately saw that, if the aristocracy sided with
the emperor, the populace and the "lowest commoners" favored
Venice. The emperor's soldiers stole and plundered freely, he reported on 26 November, especially in the countryside, and so the
peasants, driven to starvation, were determined to take revenge or
die. They harbored a hatred for the Venetians' enemies as great as
that of the Jews for the Romans, he said, and they would sooner be
put to death than to deny their allegiance to Venice. One of them,
captured and brought to the bishop of Trent, the emperor's minis-
ter, said he was loyal to Saint Mark and wished to die loyal to Saint
Mark. Neither the chance to live nor the promise of other rewards
shook his resolve. The bishop had him hanged.

From these observations, Machiavelli derived—as was his
habit—important predictions and political analyses that he hastened to send to Florence. Concerning the likely progress of the
war, he noted that in the face of the people's widespread and
determined hostility, the emperor and the French king would do
all they could to complete military operations as soon as possible.
But the armies were commanded by two monarchs who, instead of
working together, "eye each other with suspicion." While Louis
"could wage war but would not," Maximilian "would like to but
cannot." Under these circumstances, it was safe to say that the lands
taken from the Venetians would soon fall back into the hands of
their longtime rulers (*LC,* 1195–99).

Perhaps the peasants' loyalty was due not solely to the cruelty
and harassment of the occupying armies but also to the fact that

Venetian rule was at least tolerable, more tolerable than Florentine rule. But Machiavelli did not consider this, focusing rather on the larger question of how states and domains are preserved. In this connection, he noted that the Venetians painted the emblem of Saint Mark in all the places they reconquered and that instead of being shown with a book, as was traditional, the lion of Saint Mark was shown with a sword. This was a sign, Niccolò commented on 7 December, that to preserve states, "study and books are insufficient" (*LC*, 1202).

Machiavelli was reiterating the refrain he had emphasized for years now: to preserve a state, subtle diplomatic maneuvering is not enough; adequate military force must be available. His words contained yet another lesson. The book Saint Mark holds in the traditional depiction is his Gospel. By replacing the Gospel with a sword, the Venetians demonstrated, in Machiavelli's view, that they understood this principle: in order to preserve a state, especially in war, one must set aside the principles of Christian morality.

These were his thoughts when he set off just after Christmas for Florence, arriving on 2 January 1510. The anonymous accusation concerning his father had been shelved, in part because Machiavelli could rely on the unconditional support of the gonfalonier Soderini. He spent the first few months of the new year on family matters, a few missions of minor importance, and new expeditions to recruit soldiers for his militia.

In the meantime, the Italian political barometer was dropping rapidly, and a terrible storm was about to hit Florence. Pope Julius II was determined to expel the French from Italy, and he was preparing to wage a war for that purpose. A papal victory would mean the end of Florentine liberty—not only because Florence would find itself entirely surrounded by papal dominions but also because the pope was allied with the Medici, who had never given up the idea of exiling Soderini, overthrowing the republican government, and returning to power. The danger was accentuated by the fact that the family was now headed by Giovanni Cardinal de' Medici,

who had been skillfully winning the sympathy of many Florentines, including those who had been enemies of his brother Piero,
by great displays of humanity and charity at the papal court. Still,
Florence could not take sides openly by sending troops to reinforce
France's royal army, though the king and, especially, his lieutenant
in Milan, Charles d'Amboise, had requested assistance. To comply
with such a request would make Florence vulnerable to the pope's
troops, and whereas the French soldiers were far away, the pope's
were dangerously close.

The only way out was to promote some sort of agreement
between the French king and the pope. The former had to be persuaded that it was against his best interests either to wage a full-
blown war or to strip Florence of its defenses. The stakes were
high, and the job difficult. It required someone familiar with the
French court who knew how to maneuver in that setting.

Our secretary was the only logical choice. He reached Lyons on
7 July 1510, bearing the usual letter of instructions from the Ten as
well as a personal letter from Pier Soderini that reveals the fundamental lines of Florence's foreign policy in this exceedingly delicate situation. You must tell the king, Soderini wrote, that I "have
no other wishes in life than three things: the honor of God, the
well-being of my homeland, and the prosperity and honor of his
Majesty the King of France." You must convey to him that the best
way of preserving his power in Italy is to weaken Venice and
maintain good relations with the emperor; above all, you must
explain that he must make every effort "not to break off relations
with the pope; because if the pope is not worth much as a friend,
as an enemy the pope can do great harm, because of the repute in
which the Church is held," and it is impossible to wage open war
against him without making everyone else your enemy (*LC*,
1227–28).

Such was the Italians' unity against foreign interlopers! The
self-proclaimed paladin of Italian liberty was Pope Julius II, who
told everyone who would listen that he intended to expel the

French barbarians with the help of the Venetians, the Spanish rulers of the Kingdom of Naples, and the Swiss. His plan won support in Italy and in Florence, but those with a more intimate knowledge of political realities, such as Francesco Guicciardini, did not allow themselves "to be blinded by the splendor of a name" and feared that the hot-blooded pope's enterprise would only make the foreign domination of Italy harsher and more complete.

The pope and Venice alone were not powerful enough to defeat France and Spain. It was far more likely that one of the latter would become absolute master of Italy, dominating even those few Italian states that had preserved their liberty. Until things improved, the best policy was to leave things as they were, with Spain ruling the Kingdom of Naples and France governing Milan, supporting now one, now the other, as events dictated.

Machiavelli held this opinion, and others in the French court were of the same view: "All are disappointed at this move by the pope, who seems to be trying to ruin Christendom and lay the foundations for the destruction of Italy," he wrote to Florence on 26 July. Even the papal envoy, Bishop Camillo Leonini, shared this opinion. Machiavelli spoke of him as "a truly respectable gentleman, both experienced and knowledgeable in affairs of state," ready to do all he could to make peace and ward off a war that promised to be bloody and brutal, especially for Italy's "poor commoners" and lesser principalities. In conversation with Leonini, Machiavelli glimpsed the possibility of a rapprochement between king and pope, and he lobbied for such a diplomatic initiative: by a "respected and eminent personage, I have been asked to urge Your Lordships to undertake this matter and to use all of your authority to persuade the pope with all the considerations you can sagely adduce; because the personage in question assures that such efforts would meet with a positive reception here" (LC, 1258).

Such an intervention had a good chance of success, Machiavelli explained, because the pope, after failing to take Genoa from the

French, had probably become humbler and more fearful, while King Louis, however deeply he may have resented the offense, knew that if he attacked the pope head-on, he would find "one and all" arrayed against him. Machiavelli therefore advised that Florence act as an "intermediator," even though he knew he was over-stepping the bounds of his office and begged pardon for it: "I have ventured to write the last section to Your Lordships because I feel it falls within my responsibilities to convey what I learn and what I am told in this court" (*LC,* 1258).

Machiavelli understood this was an excellent opportunity to escape a lethal trap, and he urged the Signori to seize it without delay, though delay was their favorite tactic, since they thought time would work in their favor. On 3 August, he wrote again in favor of a diplomatic initiative. Florence, as even the blind and the deaf knew, had everything to lose from open warfare between the king of France and the pope and everything to gain from a state of peace. If it were to persuade the two rivals to come to an agreement, the city would prevent a catastrophic war and earn the gratitude of both pope and king; if the pope should boycott the agreement, the king would still owe Florence a debt of gratitude and could easily blame the pope before all of Europe; the pope, on the other hand, could have no grounds for resentment if Florence, after attempting to make peace and receiving his refusal, waged war against him in alliance with the king. Once again he begged pardon for overstepping his office: "All of these considerations have led me to engage willingly in these maneuvers. If they chance to meet with the approval of Your Lordships, I am pleased; otherwise, I beg your pardon, because I could not judge things any differently than I have" (*LC,* 1273).

The attempted mediation failed in the course of a few weeks. Pope Julius II did not even listen to the Florentine ambassadors' proposals for a peace agreement. To the contrary, he flew into a rage and threatened them, as if they had committed some terrible affront. The unfortunate envoys could neither placate him nor persuade him to consider seriously the idea of peace. In his last audience with them, the pope actually said that while he was working to free Italy from the French, Florence was doing everything imaginable to hinder his plan: he would make them pay dearly for their obstructionism. The Florentine envoys had achieved nothing but the choleric pontiff's rage, but they could consider themselves lucky, compared with the unpleasant fate of the duke of Savoy's envoy: when he made overtures of peace, the pope accused him of espionage and had him clapped in irons and tortured.

The failure of the peace overtures was damaging to Florence. The Ten instructed Roberto Acciaiuoli, who was going to be permanent envoy to France, to point this out to King Louis. It was a defeat for Machiavelli as well; he had supported the initiative with enormous conviction. But he did not have lasting cause for regret: even if the effort had ended badly, it was still better than remaining neutral or, worse, putting off a decision, acting one day like friends of the king, the next like friends of the king's enemies.

Machiavelli explained this to the Florentine rulers with all his intelligence and passion. Yesterday morning, he wrote on 9 August from Blois, I spoke at length with the king about Italian affairs, and I clearly saw that he neither trusts you nor is likely to trust you until you declare openly in his favor, with your "arms in hand, side by side" with his troops. He added: "Your Lordships should believe, as a gospel truth, that if there is war between the pope and this king, it will be quite impossible to refrain from choosing one side over the other, forgetting all the various conflicting considerations." In the judgment of "those who wish your best interests," he wrote, using an old trick of diplomacy to conceal and amplify his own opinions, it is necessary that "Your Lordships take a decision now, well reasoned and carefully considered, without waiting for events to overwhelm you" (*LC*, 1282–83).

Unless a peace treaty is signed, and unless the king of England and the emperor do something to prevent him, King Louis will move into Italy with an army so large that marching to Rome will be like a walk in the park for them. Let us hope, Machiavelli wrote, that God removes the "diabolical spirit" that seems to have possessed the pope's body and that God keeps him from destroying Florence and himself, even though it would be desirable that "these priests taste the occasional bitter morsel in this lifetime" (*LC*, 1298). He simply could not bite his tongue: so great was his scorn for the enormously corrupt prelates who lived like princes, using religion as a tool to increase their power and wealth; so great was his hatred for Julius II, who, under the pretext of freeing Italy, was maneuvering to subjugate Florence to the Medici and Italy to the Spanish.

In the meantime, one had to help oneself, to make an immediate decision and stick to it: either peace, or else war alongside the king. To Machiavelli's mind, there were no other options. Of the two possibilities, peace was preferable. The proud French had to be persuaded that it was not wise to provoke a war with the pope and his allies, even less wise to demand that Florence send troops to Milan, since the papal armies might attack the city at any moment from every direction. He explained to Robertet, the king's treasurer, that the French could not wage open war against the pope without enormous risk: if they fought, they were unlikely to win; if they fought with a powerful ally, they would have to share Italy with that ally and then fight another, even more dangerous war. He explained all this before the Crown Council, emphasizing that the pope's armies surrounded Florentine territory and that if Florence sent its troops outside its borders, the city would become easy prey.

His words made the French dignitaries stiffen in indignation, but gradually he bent them to his point of view. On 29 August 1510, he sought an audience with the king but was unsuccessful because the king was sick and "was secluded with the queen" (*LC*, 1328). No one could be more sensitive than Niccolò to exigencies of the senses and the heart; he left king and queen in peace and moved to the house of the chancellor, where the Crown Council was assembled. Before the illustrious dignitaries, he explained that if the Florentine troops remained in Tuscany, they could do more to "restrain" the pope and thus do more good to the king's cause than if they were sent outside Tuscany. "Everyone listened carefully" and in the end agreed that he had spoken with great prudence. On 5 September, he could finally inform Florence that the king had decided the Florentine troops could stay in Tuscany and he would send his own soldiers to defend the Republic.

Machiavelli could do no more, and for the moment nothing remained to be done. He could return to Florence—on horseback, thanks to a loan from the Pistoian merchant Bartolomeo Panciatichi. If not for that loan, he had written to the Ten, he would have had to sell his horse and return on foot.

THIRTEEN

The Death of a Republic

Viewed from afar, the grand dramas of history—the death of a republic, or a people's loss of liberty, and the vast grief and suffering that such events entail—appear inevitable outcomes, necessities of their times. The protagonists seem to struggle in the skeins of a web woven by a greater power, a power we may choose to call Fortune, or Destiny, or Providence. As this power continues on its way, it takes care to draw a merciful veil over all the protagonists, be they great or small, noble or vile, wise or foolish, brave or cowardly.

Viewed up close, on the other hand, these same events appear results of chance, determined by opportunities variously taken or let slip, products of the purest happenstance. The overarching drama breaks down into individual stories: a ruler's lack of judgment, one man's courage or another man's fear, the tension in one individual between opposing passions. It seems that the great river of history may at any moment meander first in one direction, then in another. The characters seem to come alive: we can picture their faces as if the story were being performed on a stage; we are drawn into their lives, we listen as they speak, we pray for one and detest another. In the end, we come to our own conclusions. Whatever our ultimate judgment, we learn a little more about a most important problem that history continues, stubbornly, to set before us, seemingly trying to hammer into our heads a lesson we are reluctant to learn, or keep trying to forget—how and why people lose their liberty and become slaves.

It was already late in October 1510 when Machiavelli returned to Florence from France. The Florentine countryside and the city itself must have offered an enchanting spectacle, lovely as only a Tuscan autumn can be. It is a pity that none of his writings hints at his thoughts or feelings about nature's spectacle. Yet we know he had a deep poetic appreciation of life as well as an acute sensibility for beauty. Perhaps he never had the time; he was endlessly galloping off somewhere, always in a hurry, constantly trying to keep pace with a succession of political events that rapidly outstripped both his and the Republic's meager resources, events careening toward an outcome that promised to be grim. Or perhaps his gaze never veered from the world of mankind, with its vast store of misery and its scant offerings of greatness.

We do know he was happy to be reunited with his wife, Marietta, and his children at the country house in Percussina, just outside Florence. While in France, he had pestered the Chancery for news of his family, finally growing angry at his friends' and colleagues' failure to reply. When at last Marcello Adriani wrote, he took the opportunity to tease the anxious husband and father: "Your wife is here, and still lives; your children toddle to and fro; your house still stands; there will be a meager harvest in the Percussina this year" (L, 339). Admittedly, Machiavelli had found pleasant companionship in France, a certain Jeanne or Gianna or Janna, who doubtless helped him stave off loneliness better than the old hag in Verona. All the same, he had not forgotten his wife and children. He was bighearted—there was room in his soul for many loves and many passions.

The Florence to which he returned was more deeply riven by

strife than when he had left it. The Medici faction, whose adherents were encouraged by the favors Giovanni Cardinal de' Medici was showering from Rome, grew daily, both in numbers and in its determination to rid the city of Pier Soderini. Gonfalonier Soderini also sensed increasing opposition among the Florentine nobility, who accused him of ignoring their concerns and denying them the preeminent role in public affairs that was their birthright. Machiavelli, keenly aware that the pope and the king of France would soon be at war, immediately understood that these conflicts and divisions sounded a death knell for the Republic. The odds lay against any republic, even a united one, in the face of open hostility from the pope and his allies. What chances were there for a divided Florentine Republic, where the wealthiest and most influential men anticipated the fall of popular government as a liberation?

Existing embankments had to be reinforced and new ones had to be built—in great haste—to protect against the flood that was about to burst upon the city. To follow the guiding principle of Florentine politics—time helps those who wait—would amount to suicide. Machiavelli was one of the very few who saw this clearly, but he was without power. Important decisions were in the hands of others. He was forced to restrict his activities to military affairs, to fortresses and soldiers. When he did so, it was with his customary tireless energy. He set out to inspect the fortresses of Pisa, Arezzo, and Poggio Imperiale, along the routes that the pope's armies would probably follow; he plunged into the project of recruiting a corps of light cavalry. He believed the strength of an army lay in the infantry, but he also understood that no victory could be complete without cavalry. He enlisted men in the Valdichiana, and on the Sunday after Easter he paraded his new cavalry corps through the streets of Florence. At last, the city had its own infantry and cavalry. But these were green recruits who had never seen battle. They had marched in a few parades and done a bare minimum of parade-ground drilling. They had no idea of what war was like. They had no experienced officers who could establish discipline, inspire courage in men, and command skillfully.

Given time, the Florentine rulers could have overcome this inexperience and lack of officers. The Republic's enemies, however, were not disposed to wait. The clash between the pope and the king of France had entered a decisive new phase. The two rivals were now fighting with spiritual as well as physical weapons. King Louis persuaded a few French and Spanish cardinals to proclaim a Universal Ecclesiastical Council, to be held in Pisa in September 1511, there to condemn Pope Julius's conduct and call for reforms in the Church. The pope responded by excommunicating the rebellious cardinals and proclaiming a new council, to be held in Rome in May 1512.

The pope emerged the victor in this spiritual war, as might easily have been foreseen. Although the rebellious cardinals proclaimed that they were motivated by a desire to reform the Church, they deceived no one: it was all too clear that beneath the trappings of a noble desire to institute reforms, the cardinals were simply executing the political designs of the king of France and were driven by naked personal ambition. It was equally evident, in the words of Guicciardini, that "should any of them ever become pope, they would be in as sore need of reform as those whom they now proposed to reform" (G, X, 7).

While not too harmful to the pope, the prospect of the Council of Pisa damaged Florence greatly. Because Pisa was under Florentine jurisdiction, Pope Julius leveled an interdict against Florence, an ecclesiastical punishment that prohibited the performance there of any holy office, religious burials, and certain sacraments. This was not the first time the city had been subjected to an interdict; it was all the same a serious inconvenience to its government. The real issue was, however, political. By asking the Florentine Republic to host the Council of Pisa, the king of France was once again placing Florence between a rock and a hard place. If it refused, it angered its only ally; if it accepted, it would worsen—if that were possible—the pontiff's hatred.

It was necessary to persuade King Louis and his cardinals to give up the idea of the council entirely or to hold it somewhere else, or at the very least to put it off for a few months in hopes that a miracle of some sort—perhaps even the death of the pope—might come to the rescue of poor Florence. The Ten decided to entrust Niccolò Machiavelli with this challenging task and sent him along the road to Milan to meet with the cardinals: Bernardino Carvajal, titular of the Holy Cross in Jerusalem; Guillaume Briçonnet, archbishop of Narbonne; and Francisco Borgia, bishop of Cosenza, who were on their way south to Pisa. His instructions were then to continue into France to speak with the king. He met the three cardinals near Piacenza; with them was Federico Cardinal Sanseverino. We can imagine what a pleasure it was for him to negotiate with these characters, whom he would have been happy to see hurtling into Hell together with the pope; moreover, the cardinals left him to cool his heels for hours before responding to the proposals he had conveyed. We can also imagine his face as he listened to their self-important declamations justifying the council as an undertaking done for the good of all Christians that would be pleasing to God and as they tried to persuade him that for the love of Christ and the interests of the Church, the Republic of Florence ought willingly to take on the burden of playing host.

In any case, a makeshift solution was found. It is not clear whether the cardinals were intimidated by the hostility of the local populace and the Pisan clergy or persuaded by Machiavelli's eloquent arguments that it was in their own interest to move their "conventicle" elsewhere; in any case, in November, they gathered bag and baggage and trundled off to Milan, where they held a ghost council among general indifference.

It had been, however, nothing more than a makeshift solution. Having defeated the king of France in this spiritual duel, the diabolical pope was preparing to finish off his adversary by political and military means. In early October 1511, he established the Holy League—an alliance with Venice; the duke of Ferrara; and Ferdinand the Catholic, king of Aragon—in order to defend the unity of the Church, restore papal authority over Bologna, and expel from Italy anyone who might be opposed, namely the king of France. The viceroy of Naples, Raimondo di Cardona, was appointed commander of the army. On 17 November, a new member joined the Holy League, King Henry VIII of England; later, the emperor Maximilian became a de facto member as well. France stood alone and surrounded; Florence stood alone, surrounded, and defenseless.

Yet in military terms, the French had the upper hand, at least at first. Under the command of Gaston de Foix, a captain of great courage and skill who could inspire his men with words and by example, the French armies took Brescia and sacked it. On 1 April 1512, not far from Ravenna, they badly beat the Spanish and papal troops. It was a Pyrrhic victory, however; Gaston de Foix was killed as he charged on horseback against the retreating but orderly Spanish infantry. Its leader slain, the king's army fell into disarray. Instead of marching on toward Rome, it began a long retreat.

The army had been summoned home by none other than King Louis, frightened by the entry into the war of the feared Swiss infantry, who had finally agreed to an alliance with the pope. The Swiss were marching, as always, out of lust for money and loot but also out of hatred for the French monarch, who had used German soldiers instead of them. What finally turned the tide in the pope's favor were Maximilian's orders to those very same German soldiers to stop fighting for King Louis and to return home. The French were forced to cease hostilities. Milan fell to the Swiss troops, though it was officially taken by the Holy League; Bologna, Piacenza, and Parma surrendered to the pope; Genoa drove out the French garrison. Pope Julius II was the undisputed victor, and on 3 May he triumphantly inaugurated the Lateran Council. There were "lovely and sacred ceremonies," as Guicciardini recounts, "that would touch the cockles of the heart if one believed that the true thoughts and purposes of those who staged these events were consonant with the words they spoke" (G, X, 14).

All that remained was to settle the score with Florence. The city's fate was determined by the leaders of the Holy League in June, at a secret meeting in Mantua. They decided to force Pier Soderini to resign as gonfalonier, dissolve the republican government, and restore the Medici to power. The same Spanish troops that had miraculously survived the defeat of Ravenna began their march on the city under the command of Raimondo di Cardona; they crossed the Apennines and set up camp just north of Florence, at Barberino del Mugello. Soon they moved farther south, to Campi.

How things stood in Florence, with the Spanish troops only miles from the city walls, is clear from a letter Biagio Buonaccorsi wrote on 27 August to Machiavelli, who was with ordinance soldiers near Prato. Pier Soderini, wrote Biagio, "wants me to ask you to take steps there, because this arrival at Campi of the enemy displeases him greatly and astonishes him. Farewell. Do whatever good you are able, and let no time be lost with red tape" (LC, 353).

The chief authority of the Republic was astonished that the Spanish should have set up camp at Campi, as if he had no idea what the members of the Holy League had already decided for Florence's future! And he had the gall to ask Machiavelli to do something about it, as if, with no greater force than ordinance foot soldiers—little more than a crowd of farmers who had never seen combat, with neither officers nor artillery—he could work a miracle and save the Republic. Biagio understood this, even as he exhorted Machiavelli to do what he could. The "farewell" that concludes the letter foreshadows the death of the Republic and the tragedy that was to force the two friends to leave forever the halls of the Palazzo Vecchio, where for so many years they had worked, lived, suffered, and laughed together.

In the meantime, the viceroy Cardona, keenly aware of his army's weakness, offered a deal: We don't want to deprive Florence of its liberty, nor do we wish to change its form of government. All we ask is that Pier Soderini be dismissed and that the Medici be

allowed to return to Florence, to live as private citizens, subject to
the Republic's laws and magistrates like anyone else.

   This offer divided the Florentines. Some were in favor, arguing
that it was not fair for the whole city to be put at risk for the sake
of a single man, that if the Medici returned as private citizens they
could hardly constitute a threat to the people's liberty, and that Florence, abandoned by the king of France, was not strong enough to
withstand the Holy League. Those opposed to the offer replied
that it was ridiculous to think that the Spanish army had come all
this way just to depose Soderini and to bring back the Medici as
ordinary citizens. Once Soderini was removed from office, Florence would be like a flock without a shepherd; it would be a simple thing for the Medici, with the Spanish army's help, to lead the
enemies of the Republic, dissolve the Great Council, and destroy
Florence's liberty. The Spanish army had no artillery and was short
of food; if the city withstood the first assault, the viceroy would
come to easier terms. The wisest thing to do, then, was to reject the
ultimatum and prepare to defend the city's liberty.

   Soderini assembled the Great Council and delivered a memorable speech. This is Guicciardini's version of this signal address on
the destiny of Florence and the nature of Medici rule there—a
fine example of how a great historian *imagines* such a speech to
have been:

   If I thought that the Viceroy's demands concerned only my
   interests alone, I myself would have made the decision suitable to my proposal; since I have always been prepared to
   risk my life for your benefit, and it would be much easier to
   renounce the magistracy which you have given me, and so
   free myself of the troubles and dangers of war; especially
   since in all these years while I have held this position, my
   body and soul have been riven with toils and troubles. But
   insofar as something beyond my own interest is involved in
   this demand, it seemed to my honorable fellow counselors

and to me that matters which so concern the interests of all
should not be decided without public approval, and that
such a serious problem involving everyone should not be
deliberated upon by the usual number of citizens with
whom other matters are commonly discussed, but rather
with you who are the foundation of this city and who alone
have the right to deal with such a solemn decision. Nor do
I wish to influence you in any way; the recommendation
should be yours, the decision yours; I will accept and honor
whatever decision you come to. I offer you not only the
magistracy which belongs to you, but my person, my very
life; and I would consider myself singularly blessed if I
thought this might provide for your security. Examine what
the Viceroy's demands might mean with regard to your
freedom, and God give you grace of understanding that you
will come to the best decision. If the Medici were disposed
to live in this city as private citizens, patiently accepting the
decisions of the magistrates and your laws, their restitution
would be praiseworthy, in order that the commonweal
might be forged into a single body. But if their intentions
are otherwise, be aware of the danger facing you, and do
not let any expenses and difficulties seem too heavy to bear
when it is a question of maintaining your freedom; how
precious freedom is you will realize better, if fruitlessly (I
dread to say it), when you are deprived of it. Nor should
anyone delude himself that government by the Medici
would be the same as it was before they were exiled,
because the form and basis of things have changed: at that
time, raised amongst us almost like private citizens, [possess-
ing] the richest means in view of their position, harmed by
no one, they based their rule on the good will of the citizens, discussed public affairs with the outstanding men, and
made every effort to cover themselves with the cloak of
civic virtue as soon as their ambitions were revealed. But

now, having dwelt so many years outside of Florence, brought
up in foreign ways, and for this reason out of touch with
civic matters, remembering their exile and the harsh manner in which they had been treated, very reduced in means
and distrusted by so many families, aware that most, indeed,
almost the entire city abhors tyranny, they would not share
their counsels with any citizen; and forced by poverty and
suspicion, they would arrogate everything to themselves,
depending primarily not on good will and love but force
and arms, with the result that in a very short time this city
would become like Bologna at the time of the Bentivoglio,
or like Siena or Perugia. I wanted to say this to those who
preach about the time and rule of Lorenzo the Magnificent. For, although conditions were hard then and there was
a tyranny (although milder than many others), by comparison with this, Lorenzo's rule would be an age of gold. Now
it is your responsibility to deliberate wisely, in terms of the
security of your country; and it is my responsibility to give
up this magistracy with a resolved and joyous spirit; or
should you decide otherwise, honestly to attend to the
preservation and defense of your liberty. (G, XI, 3)

The Great Council decided to allow the Medici to return as private citizens but refused to remove Soderini from office as lifelong
gonfalonier; it further resolved to defend liberty and homeland
with every means possible, risking death if necessary. It was the
dying Republic's final burst of civic dignity.

Noble as the city's intentions may have been, they were not
matched by its political wisdom. Soderini concentrated most of his
troops in Florence—350 horsemen with heavy armament, 500
horsemen with crossbows and muskets (recruited by Machiavelli),
and 14,000 militia foot soldiers. To garrison Prato, which lay on
the Spanish marching route, he sent about 3,000 militia foot soldiers and 100 men-at-arms under the command of Luca Savello.

And in order to preserve the Republic from internal sedition, he ordered some thirty Medici supporters locked up in the Palazzo Vecchio.

On 29 August, the Spanish troops, with two hundred men-at-arms, five thousand foot soldiers, and two cannons, halted under the walls of Prato. Instead of immediately launching an assault, the viceroy—concerned about his troops' hunger and aware of the difficulty of storming a fortified city with only two cannons—offered Florence a new bargain: it was no longer necessary for Soderini to resign, only that the Medici be allowed to return as private citizens; for himself, he asked thirty thousand ducats. While the Florentines took time to consider this new offer, he requested bread for his starving troops. It was the opportunity of a lifetime: a last chance to save the Republic. But Soderini was opposed to the terms and dragged out negotiations; he refused to send bread to the Spanish troops, certain that they would decamp presently without it.

This was a serious error. On 30 August, desperate with hunger, the Spaniards began to fire at the walls of Prato with their scanty artillery. After many hours, they opened a breach some twenty feet across; they poured through the breach, filled with hatred and scorn for the farmers disguised as soldiers who were defending the town. Inside the walls, beneath the breach, a squadron of foot soldiers armed with small harquebuses and pikes awaited them with every intention of preventing them from climbing down the walls. That is not what happened. Panicking at the sight of the enemy, the Florentine infantry broke ranks, threw down their weapons, and took to their heels. The Spaniards literally chopped the Florentines to pieces as they begged for mercy. They broke into homes, raped, tortured, killed, looted, and burned.

More than four thousand people were slaughtered in the Sack of Prato. A chronicler of the time tells us that, so savage and cruel were the Spanish, "the bright sun covered its shining face" in horror. Machiavelli himself, writing to a noblewoman on 16 September, said that "better than four thousand men died there, and the rest were taken prisoner and forced in various ways to pay ransoms; nor did they spare virgins, enclosed in holy places, which were filled with rapes and sacrilege."

The Sack of Prato marked the end of the Florentine Republic. When the first survivors of the massacre reached Florence and recounted the horrors they had seen, the city was swept by panic. The very people who had promised Soderini their possessions and their lives in defense of liberty now accused him of being the cause of every evil turn of events. Soderini was forsaken, gripped by fear and guilt. His enemies understood this and went on the offensive. A number of young Medici supporters entered the Palazzo Vecchio and made their way, unhindered, to the gonfalonier's office. They ordered him to leave the palace, promising to let him live. Pier Soderini turned, for the last time, to Machiavelli, whom he sent to ask Francesco Vettori to stand surety for his safety. Vettori hurried to the Palazzo Vecchio, where he found the gonfalonier "alone and fearful." Vettori took Soderini to his home and that very night spirited him out of Florence, toward Siena. Now that the Republic was without a leader, it was ready to return in thrall to its former rulers.

FOURTEEN

Tragedy and Laughter

There are times when fortune inflicts wounds that simply won't heal, when the story of a life breaks into two distinct sections, a before and an after. Those who experience this sort of caesura discover that from a certain day on they are no longer the same person, they suffer an anguish they have never felt before, they discover personal resources they did not know existed, and they see the world and their fellow humans in a new and chilly light. They may find that they are stronger; they may find that they are more vulnerable; in any case, they find that they are different.

Tremendous grief is like a wind that sweeps away small things, leaving the soul capable of perceiving only the great, unless that wind withers up completely the very roots of life. Afterward, some still manage to smile, even though they have lost everything they held dear. This is a smile of determination and challenge; it dies on the lips without warming the soul, without loosening the grief that clamps tight to the heart.

Such was the smile of Machiavelli after that sad 7 November 1512 when the Signoria informed him, in a laconic memo, that he was no longer secretary of the Second Chancery or of the Ten of

Liberty and Peace. The same fate was visited upon Biagio Buonaccorsi. For both men, this was the end of an era, and with it their
friendship came to an end as well. Biagio continued to help Niccolò, copying out first *The Prince* and later *The Art of War* and
defending him from malicious accusations. But Niccolò never
mentioned Biagio again in his letters. I like to imagine that, as the
doors of the Palazzo Vecchio closed behind them, Niccolò found a
few words of gratitude and consolation for the man who had
helped him so often, in affairs of state and in family matters.

The decision to relieve Machiavelli was one of many measures
taken by the new political regime installed in Florence following
the expulsion of Pier Soderini. The Great Council elected to the
post of gonfalonier—for a term of fourteen months, no longer for
life—Giambattista Ridolfi, a man of great authority and once so
avid a supporter of Savonarola that Florentine historians of the
period considered him the chief of the friar's faction.

Yet Florentine politics was controlled not by Savonarola's followers but by the Medici, who had returned after eighteen years of
exile, though officially as nothing more than private citizens. They
certainly had no intention of remaining private citizens, just as Pier
Soderini had predicted in his last speech before the Great Council.
On 16 September, the Piazza della Signoria was crowded with
Medici supporters and with soldiers who clamored noisily for a
parlamento, that is, a general assembly of the people.

The assembly was agreed on, and the crowd approved the establishment of a parliament of roughly fifty citizens with full power
to reform the city's institutions. The citizens chosen—all Medici
supporters, or *palleschi,* as they were known—dismantled the foundations of Florentine republican liberty in the space of a few days.
On 18 September, they abolished the Nine Officials of the Ordinance and Militia and dissolved the ordinance that Machiavelli had
worked so hard and for so long to build. They then sentenced Pier
Soderini to political internment and dissolved the Great Council.

What Machiavelli experienced and felt in those September days
before he was expelled from the Palazzo Vecchio is easy to imag-

ine. Sitting at his desk with nothing to do, since the new rulers were not entrusting him with work, he must have thought back on the events that had led to the fall of the Republic and on the faults of the man who had led that Republic, the now-deposed gonfalonier Pier Soderini. Machiavelli's judgment of the man was harsh. After the Medici coup of 16 September, in the letter to a noblewoman mentioned earlier, he blamed Soderini for not having accepted the peace offer conveyed by the viceroy Raimondo di Cardona, who would gladly have settled for a cash payment. Soderini made the unfortunate decision to reject that offer, Machiavelli emphasized, because he was determined to follow the whim of the "multitude" instead of the advice of "wise men."

Passing years did nothing to soften his opinion. Soderini was unable to take the sort of extraordinary measure that the gravity of the situation demanded; what kept him from doing so was his kind heart and deep honesty. As a man, he deserved respect and admiration; as a politician, he merited the strictest condemnation, because the consequence of his decision was the collapse of the Republic. That is the judgment Machiavelli offers in a remarkable page in the *Discourses,* full of bitterness at the demise of the Florentine Republic:

> [Pier Soderini] believed he would overcome with his patience and goodness the appetite that was in the sons of Brutus for returning to another government, and [he] deceived himself. Although because of his prudence he recognized this necessity, and though fate and the ambition of those who struck him gave him the opportunity to eliminate them, nonetheless he never thought of doing this. For besides believing that he could extinguish ill humor with patience and goodness and wear away some of the enmity to himself with rewards, he judged (and often vouched for this with his friends) that if he wished to strike his opponents vigorously and to beat down his adversaries, he would have needed to take on an extraordinary authority and

destroy civil equality together with the laws . . . But his first
presumption was false: he did not know that malignity is not
tamed by time or appeased by any gift.

And so, because he would not take extraordinary measures against
the Republic's enemies, Soderini lost "not only his fatherland but
his state and his reputation" (*D*, III, 3).

Machiavelli blamed Soderini for his innocence, for his inability
to inflict the harm needed to save the Republic. He blamed him
for it again when Soderini died, on 13 June 1522, in verses that
became famous:

> *That night when Pier Soderini died,*
> *his spirit went to the mouth of Hell;*
> *Pluto roared, "Why to Hell? Silly spirit,*
> *go to Limbo with all the other babies."* (*SL*, 438)

It was a joke, a jest, and yet it clearly shows us that the fall of the
Republic had opened up a divide between the two men that was
not likely to disappear. It also shows us again that in Machiavelli's
view the proper place for real politicians, in the afterlife, was
Hell—as a reward, however, not as a punishment, because he
believed, or at least enjoyed saying, that Hell was much more interesting than Heaven.

In that autumn of 1512, however, he definitely did not feel like
joking about Heaven and Hell. He knew that everyone, aristocrats
first and foremost, considered him Soderini's tool and wanted to
expel him from the Palazzo Vecchio. His only hope was that the
Medici might afford him their protection, defending him from the
aristocrats' talons. For this to happen, however, he needed to persuade them he had something to offer: his experience in politics.
So he offered them the only thing he had, his wisdom as an adviser.
On 29 September, he wrote to Giovanni Cardinal de' Medici,
advising him to practice a policy of moderation and clemency in
the proceedings to recover the lands the Republic had confiscated

from the Medici in 1494. No sign of gratitude was forthcoming. He tried again in early November with a longer essay, which modern editors call *Ai palleschi* (*To the Mediceans*), in which he explained that it was not in the Medici's interest to demonize the name and deeds of Pier Soderini, since to do so only strengthened the "mighty" and undermined their own power.

This time a response arrived: it was the decision of 7 November to relieve him of the post of secretary; another one arrived on the tenth, enjoining him to remain within the dominions of Florence for a year and to pay a surety of one thousand florins; yet another, on the seventeenth, forbade him to enter the Palazzo Vecchio for a year. We do not know how carefully the dosage of these punishments was thought out and calibrated. Certainly, they could not have been more cruel: his work as secretary was what he loved most in life, and they took that away from him; he dearly loved to travel and to see new horizons, and they confined him to Florence; the Palazzo Vecchio was his true home, and they locked its doors against him.

Yet he would be summoned back there nonetheless—to account for his years of managing the huge sums intended to pay militia salaries. His onetime assistants from the Chancery, the same men he had so often reduced to helpless laughter with his letters and witticisms, now faced him and demanded he account for every last florin. With them was his successor, Niccolò Michelozzi, a faithful Medici servant, observing coldly so that he could report in detail to the city's new masters. The investigation went on from late November until 10 December. No evidence of malfeasance was found. Even though vast amounts of money had flowed through his hands, Niccolò had served the Republic with complete and impeccable honesty. In recognition of his work, he found himself, after fourteen years, poorer than ever. And worse was yet to come.

In a Florence roiling with resentment and suspicion, a plot against the Medici was uncovered. The ringleaders were Pietro Paolo Boscoli, Agostino Capponi, Niccolò Valori, and Giovanni Folchi. In a foolish move that tells us a lot about what lightweights these conspirators were, one of them—probably Boscoli—lost a

sheet of paper listing the names of twenty or so Medici opponents, among which was that of Machiavelli. The Otto di Guardia,
the magistracy that oversaw criminal justice, sent guards to seize
him at his home. Either because someone had warned him or by
pure chance, Machiavelli was not in. A decree was issued requiring
anyone who knew his whereabouts to report them within an hour,
under penalty of being outlawed as a rebel and having all property
confiscated.

Niccolò appeared before the Eight, the Otto di Guardia. They
sent him to prison. The prison was dark, dank, and chill; it stank of
human excrement, open wounds, oozing sores; there were lice, rats,
and clanking chains, prisoners with wrists bound in chains and feet
clapped in irons, screams of those being tortured. His life truly
hung by a thread. A single word from any of the other suspects
being interrogated and he might have been left to rot in prison forever; he might well have been beheaded. Giovanni Folchi declared
he had often spoken with Machiavelli about the gonfalonier Pier
Soderini's actions, but more about war than municipal affairs. He
added that Machiavelli had opined that the new regime would
struggle to survive because "there was no one at the helm of state"
and that the Holy League, which had brought the Medici back to
Florence, "was likely to dissolve someday."

These statements were not sufficient to prove that Machiavelli
had been directly involved in the conspiracy. So the interrogators
tried to extract a confession through torture. His hands were tied
behind his back, he was lifted on a pulley fastened to the ceiling, and
then dropped suddenly, stopping just short of the floor. This was the
so-called *strappado,* a torture designed to dislocate the joints. It was
administered six times, but he said nothing to incriminate himself.
In judicial proceedings of the period, confession was considered the
best form of evidence, even if obtained through torture. Without a
confession, the judges could not be certain of guilt.

Machiavelli knew better than anyone that new regimes are
unlikely to be delicate in dealing with conspiracies, whether real or

imagined. That the Medici regime was no exception was borne in upon him just before dawn on 23 February, when his cell was filled with the sound of funeral hymns being sung for Pietro Paolo Boscoli and Agostino Capponi as they went to the block.

Boscoli had spent the night in prayer, comforted by Luca Della Robbia (a nephew of the great sculptor and a distinguished classicist) and by Friar Cipriano of Pontassieve. He meant to die a good Christian and to repudiate the ideas about the nobility of tyrannicide that had led him to plan the conspiracy. Capponi committed his soul to God, proclaiming his innocence to the end. Then he and Boscoli were led before the executioner, accompanied by the funeral hymns of the Compagnia dei Neri, the charitable brothers who comforted prisoners sentenced to death. The headsman decapitated Boscoli at a single stroke; for Capponi, he had to take two.

Those hymns, and the thought of two young men being led off to die, did not inspire thoughts of piety in Machiavelli. Indeed, that night, or soon thereafter, he wrote some rather harsh words:

> *I was aroused (the dawn was peeping through)*
> *by voices singing, "We pray for you."*
> *In peace, oh, let them go . . . (SL, 424)*

Why did he write these cynical words, which have so horrified his biographers? When he wrote them, Machiavelli was a man who had descended within a few short months from the halls of government in the Palazzo Vecchio to a cell in the Bargello prison. His hands and feet were in chains, his bones racked by torture; he had no idea whether he would shortly meet the same fate as Boscoli and Capponi, or whether he would be locked up in some tower in a far corner of the Florentine dominions, as others implicated in the conspiracy had been. All this was the result of the foolishness of a few young men who had wanted to free Florence from tyranny and had been naive enough to write out a list of the potential conspirators' names. Their actions deserved absolutely no respect in his eyes. He cared nothing for their ideals or their feelings, still less for the destiny of their souls: that would be the concern of the friars and the members of the Compagnia dei Neri.

We must not forget that those chilling words—"In peace, oh, let them go . . ."—were part of a sonnet addressed to Giuliano de' Medici, composed to implore mercy and to persuade him to help Machiavelli. How could he ask mercy for himself and, at the same time, utter words of pity for those who had wanted to kill the man? The poem continues:

> But you, good father, do not refuse
> Your mercy, and soon break this evil noose.

Let Boscoli and Capponi go to their deaths, so long as your pity is accorded me. This was a man looking death in the face and making a desperate effort to save himself.

It may seem surprising that Machiavelli should have written two sonnets asking for mercy from the Medici. In prison, one writes to seek a meaning or reasons for one's punishment, or to rediscover oneself, or to search the depths of one's soul for the resources with which to resist. Above all, as was the case with Machiavelli, one writes to ask those who can help to do so, but then one does this with a serious letter, not with a sonnet making light of oneself, of the misery, the prison, and the torture.

Machiavelli wrote, "I have a set of fetters on my legs, and six jerks of the *strappado* on my shoulders," and I say nothing of "my other miseries": in short, this is no way to treat poets! On the walls of my cell, there are lice as big as butterflies; the stench is worse than on the corpse-strewn battlefield of Roncesvalles or on the bank of the river Arno where carrion is tossed to rot. To complete the irony, he speaks of his cell as a "dainty hospice" where he can hear the gloomy screech of keys and bolts and the screams of men being tortured.

He was begging for mercy, true, but with a smile on his lips, not with eyes glistening with tears. He was afraid, he was in pain, he was in grief, his heart was swollen with resentment, and yet he smiled. He was laughing first of all at himself and his condition; what else could he do? But he was also laughing at the powerful men who were treating him so savagely. He was not laughing openly, and he was not mocking them—he could not afford to do that. But he was laughing to show them that neither prison nor torture nor any other punishment had bent his will or made him humble, submissive, respectful—in a word, a different man. I am still the same man I was before, the sonnet says, I have not changed at all: I am still "Machia" the prankster, the irreverent and defiant man you all know. I am not "Dazzo"—that is, Andrea Dazzi, an untalented man of letters who was all the rage in Florence—he wrote in the second sonnet to Giuliano de' Medici. I am Niccolò Machiavelli, and for that reason I deserve to be set free. Those sonnets, if we read them carefully, were not so much invocations of mercy as requests proffered with a smile, from a man determined at all costs to remain himself.

The nightmare came to an end with an unexpected piece of good luck. After the death of the terrible pope Julius II on 11 March 1513, Giovanni Cardinal de' Medici was elected pope (Leo X). The Florentines went wild with joy, thinking primarily of the enormously profitable business they would soon be doing in Rome and the rich benefices the new pope would scatter high and low to his compatriots. In a day, everyone in Florence became an ardent Medici supporter. Secure now in their power, the Medici performed an act of clemency and pardoned all those sentenced in connection with the conspiracy except for Niccolò Valori and Giovanni Folchi, who remained locked up in the tower of Volterra.

Machiavelli was released on 11 or 12 March. A week later he wrote to Francesco Vettori saying that he had surprised himself by withstanding so much pain with a courageous spirit. He praised himself, without false modesty: "As for turning my face toward

Fortune, I should like you to get this pleasure from these troubles of mine, that I have borne them so straightforwardly that I am proud of myself for it and consider myself more of a man than I believed I was."

The man who left prison was still the same Machiavelli who had entered it—strengthened, even, by the terrible ordeal. Probably the friends who greeted him outside the prison were treated to his usual mocking smile, to reassure them he had not changed. That is, if any of his friends waited for him instead of singing hymns of welcome to the Medici, along with everyone else in Florence.

FIFTEEN

To Seem Alive

When Machiavelli left prison, he thought of himself as above all a man who had once been secretary of the Republic—"former secretary," as he signed a letter of April 1513. His new status clung like a second skin. It tormented him, and he yearned from the bottom of his heart for that intense excitement and pleasure in achieving great things that he had drawn from affairs of state. To some degree, he was to find both in writing—writing pages of infinite beauty. Before and even as he wrote those pages, though, a pain so powerful that it overcame his reluctance to reveal it prompted him from time to time to recount his feelings, his anguish, his passions. We are thus able to see, close up, the man who hid behind the secretary's mask, and, with his help, we are able better to decipher the enigma of his smile.

Newly released from prison, Machiavelli wanted to return to the Palazzo Vecchio. He confided this to his friend Francesco Vettori, in hopes he might persuade Pope Leo X to bestow on the former secretary some political office or other. He made the request in his distinctive way, wanting recognition of his ability, not asking for a favor. If these new masters of ours, he wrote to Vettori on 18

March 1513, see fit not to leave me lying on the ground, "I shall be happy," and I shall act so that they, too, will have reason to be proud of me; if, on the other hand, they decide to offer me nothing, I shall get on as I did when I first came into the world, because "I was born in poverty and at an early age learned how to endure hardship rather than flourish."

In the meantime, he did his best to enjoy life in the celebratory atmosphere that pervaded Florence. Each day, he and his friends would visit "some girl to recover our vigor," he says. He felt as if he were dreaming; after the horrors of prison, the pleasures of life were incredibly fine. But his friends had changed. The "gang," he wrote to Vettori on 16 April, "seems to be in confusion"; we no longer have a place to meet, and everyone's mood seems to have changed. Tommaso del Bene, for example, is "eccentric, churlish, irritating, shabby"—you will see when you return from Rome that he seems "a different person." He has become so stingy, Machiavelli reports, that to earn back the money he spent on seven pounds of veal, he begged his friends to dine with him at his house; prompted by pity, Machiavelli accepted the invitation—hardly the proper term—and went to dinner, along with two others. When the meal was over, Tommaso began to figure the bill. Each invitee owed fourteen soldi. Niccolò had only ten with him, and so he owed four. Tommaso badgers me daily for the four soldi, Niccolò told Vettori, and just yesterday confronted me about it on the Ponte Vecchio.

Then he told about a friend whose wife died, leaving him stunned as a trout; shortly thereafter, the bereft widower cheered up and decided to remarry. Another friend, Donato del Corno, has opened a new shop and spends his time shuttling from the old shop to the new one, generally behaving "like a dolt." Yet another one, Filippo Casavecchia, feuding with a fellow member of the gang, Giuliano Brancacci, is working to sabotage some of Giuliano's plans in Rome. Machiavelli tells these stories with a smile, because the human comedy, with its mingling of suffering and humor, has always amused him. Now that he has lost everything, these goings-on are a distraction.

But behind his smile he is weeping. He himself admits this, quoting—as a comment on his account of the latest squalid conflict between two friends—from a poem by Petrarch:

> So if at any time I laugh or sing,
> I do so for I have no way
> but this to hide my anguished tears.

He smiles, but his heart is twisted by grief, anger, hope, and fear. Tears would be more likely to assuage the suffering than laughter. He says this in some undated lines of verse that seem a natural extension of Petrarch's lines:

> I hope, and oh, to hope is to ache the more:
> I weep, and my tears feed my weary heart:
> I laugh, but there's no laugh I now can store:
> I burn, but no one sees my flaming smart:
> All that I hear and see I most deplore:
> And everything can a new grief impart:
> Thus hoping, I do burn and laugh and cry,
> And am afraid of both my ear and eye. (SL, 422)

A smile concealing a tear, without touching the heart. That is Machiavelli's smile: neither a grin nor a sneer; a mask, rather, to conceal inward weeping, a shield to protect against prying eyes, disconsolate and resigned before the world's squalor and malevolence. It is only a moment's pause, but it helps to get through the day.

When the smile is not enough, it is necessary to smother one's passions and desires. Niccolò learned this art in the first few months after his incarceration, as he tells Vettori in a letter of 9 April. I have accustomed myself, he writes, "to no longer desiring anything passionately," and if in the future I cannot obtain what I desire, "I shall not suffer for it." He was, in fact, quite right to desire nothing passionately. Vettori was unable to help Machiavelli or anyone else, in part because he was not a very skillful or enterprising diplomat, in part because of the objectively difficult conditions in which he was working.

Vettori may have assisted Niccolò unwittingly, however, by prompting him to consider the importance of keeping his remarkable mind active and continuing to think about affairs of state. There is some evidence of this in Machiavelli's response to a 30 March letter in which Vettori confessed that he was tired of "discussing things rationally," tired of making predictions and rational conjectures about political events, because too often the world then went off in a different direction, thumbing its nose at his theories. Niccolò replied: "If you find that commenting on events bores you because you realize that they frequently turn out differently from the opinions and ideas we have, you are right—for the same thing has happened to me. All the same, if I could talk to you, I could only fill your head with castles in the air, because Fortune has seen to it that since I do not know how to talk about either the silk or the wool trade, or profits or losses, I have to talk about politics. I need either to take a vow of silence or to discuss this" (*L*, 367).

Niccolò expressed his sorrow at being shut out of the world of politics and revealed—to Vettori and to us—the depth of his great passion for affairs of state. Yet he resisted his friend's urging and made no response to Vettori's reflections on the election of the new pope. He resisted because it pained him to speak of politics without being able to do anything, either in deed or in counsel. Still, he yielded to Vettori's second gambit, a request for an explanation of the king of Spain's decision on 1 April 1513 to call a truce with the king of France, a truce that at first glance gave Spain no advantage. He agreed to talk about politics once again because he could no longer remain silent. But he understood that for some time to come he could not hope to return to political work. He could no longer endure living in Florence under those circumstances, so he decided to move to the house his father, Bernardo, had left him in the country—in Sant'Andrea in Percussina—so that he could live "far from every human face." Despite having made this decision, he gathered his strength and responded to Vettori, "to seem alive and to obey your wishes."

In the letters in which he reasons about the purposes and consequences of the actions of princes, emperors, kings, popes, and peoples, Niccolò is still very much alive. The sentences come tumbling out: powerful, vital, angry, and rich in masterful observations that show us his mind at work. He never trusts appearances, still less anyone else's authority. He believes nothing but what he sees with his own eyes; he accepts only those opinions that seem based on solid reasoning. Vettori, trying to persuade him that there was nothing to fear from the power that the Swiss were acquiring in Italy since taking control of the duchy of Milan, cited Aristotle's *Politics,* the supreme work of political science. Niccolò replied that he did not know what Aristotle might have said about confederated republics and that he was interested only in "what might reasonably exist, what exists, and what has existed" (*L,* 417).

"What has existed" refers of course to the lessons of history. History teaches us, he explained to Vettori, that even federal republics are capable of enormous territorial expansion, as is shown by the example of the ancient Etruscans, who became masters of all Italy, as far north as the Alps. It also teaches us that only those republics and monarchs who arm their people achieve great things; and since the Swiss were fielding armies drawn directly from the people, it was only reasonable to expect that they would become more powerful than the Spanish and the Italians.

Although confident that he had both history and experience on his side, Machiavelli never dogmatically claimed to possess the truth. Vettori himself admitted that, even in the midst of their discussion of possible peace treaties among the various European powers, Machiavelli never insisted on a point obstinately but always listened to reason. This was not so much a character trait as a consequence of Machiavelli's awareness that anyone who thinks about political matters is inevitably guided or affected by personal passions. Therefore, in politics, judgments and predictions were not irrefutable truths but only more or less probable conjectures. To claim to know the truth is typical of those who, unlike Niccolò, study politics only in books.

In one sense, the political discussions with Vettori gave Machiavelli the illusion of still being close to the world of great events, and so they helped him to feel alive; in another sense, they accentuated the feeling that he was lost in the distance, trapped in the countryside of Sant'Andrea, and so they increased his suffering. "Physically, I feel well, but ill in every other respect," he wrote to his nephew Giovanni Vernacci, a merchant in the Levant. Marietta, that August, gave birth to a baby girl, but the infant died after just three days. Luck was definitely not with him.

In the letters they exchanged during that terrible year, 1513, Niccolò and Vettori wrote about politics, of course, but also about themselves and how they spent their days, one in Rome, the other in Sant'Andrea in Percussina. Vettori was bored, skeptical, disenchanted, and resigned. In politics, he saw only "empty ceremonies, lies, and tales" and wretchedness everywhere. At the papal court, he would say, at the most, twenty words to the pope, ten to Giulio Cardinal de' Medici, six to Giuliano de' Medici or Pietro Ardinghelli, the pope's private secretary. If he happened to meet an ambassador, he would exchange unimportant news. He would report to Florence, every four days, with some tidbit or minor development. This was a world away from the dispatches Machiavelli had sent to the Ten when he was on a mission.

Vettori was a religious man. On holidays, he wrote to Machiavelli on 23 November, "I go to Mass, unlike yourself, who sometimes cannot be bothered." He enjoyed reading ancient accounts of Roman history, especially tales of the horrors committed by emperors. These readings made him think about the countless miseries that Rome, a city that "once made the world tremble," had suffered over the ages. But they aroused in him neither indignation nor a desire to revive the greatness of ancient Rome.

Aside from reading, his distractions from the tedium of politics included riding horses in the countryside outside Rome, idle conversation with Giuliano Brancacci and Giovanbattista Nasi, and the company of the occasional courtesan—one in particular, "quite reasonably pretty, and pleasant in speech." I was accustomed to have a few, he told Machiavelli, but then, frightened by the unhealthy summer air of Rome, "I abstained." To tempt his friend to visit him in Rome, he mentioned that he had "a neighbor whom you would not find unattractive; and although she is of noble family, she does carry on some business."

The thought of the business being carried on by Vettori's attractive neighbor may have piqued Niccolò's interest, but the idea was too risky. In Rome, there were also Francesco and Pier Soderini, the latter having been entirely pardoned and rehabilitated. If Niccolò were to go to Rome, he would be obliged to call on them, and if he did so, he feared that on returning to Florence he might have to dismount not at home but at the Bargello prison, an experience he had already enjoyed. Even though the Medici regime was growing extremely strong, it was still new, hence suspicious. After what Niccolò had been through, he was very careful not to make any wrong moves.

So he declined his friend's invitation. He accepted, on the other hand, the implicit request in Vettori's letter to describe a typical day in Sant'Andrea. He did so in part to let his friend understand that his was a far drearier way of life—"If you would like to swap it for yours, I shall be happy to make the exchange"—but also to rail against his bad luck and to let his friend see that his mind was entirely bent on affairs of state and that he was ready to resume his role on the great stage of politics.

And so he describes his day, and the contrast with Vettori's is striking. Vettori's day unfolds in a setting of wealth and prestige, but it is filled with boredom, predictability, and an outward respect for convention; Niccolò's day takes place in a setting of rustic poverty, of loneliness and defeat, and yet it is brimming with powerful feelings, big thoughts, a determination to achieve, and a determination to challenge commonplaces and wretchedness. Vettori's account is a monotonous dirge composed in minor keys; Machiavelli's begins at a slow tempo, with a description of the start of the day in the woods and of the humble family meal, snaps and sizzles when he recounts games at the inn, and concludes majestically with an evocation of the evening spent communing about affairs of state with the great men of antiquity, the only ones with whom he can truly speak, the only ones who truly understand him.

"I am living on my farm" are the words with which Niccolò begins his account. For other Florentines of his and earlier times, to live "on the farm" meant getting away from the business and noise of city life, finding peace in study, thought, and rustic pastimes. For Niccolò, it was a forced renunciation of the life he loved best. Literary leisure, philosophical and religious meditation, rural peace were of no interest to him; he loved the city, with its streets, squares, porticoes, and benches; he enjoyed being in company, laughing at the happenings of everyday life, and taking part in the great affairs of state.

To convey to his friend how little country life suited him, he writes that for a while he amused himself by "snaring thrushes with my own hands," the technique being to spread birdlime on elm switches, where, once having lit on them, the birds were trapped, for the more they struggled to escape, the more they were caught: "I would get up before daybreak," he writes, "prepare the birdlime, and go out with such a bundle of birdcages on my back that I looked like Geta when he came back from the harbor with Amphitryon's books." Machiavelli, until recently a secretary of the Florentine Republic, leaving his house before sunrise to catch thrushes, so loaded down with birdcages that he is like Geta, Amphitryon's servant in a fifteenth-century novella—one would be hard-pressed to imagine anything at once so absurd and heartbreaking. Machiavelli describes the pastime as beneath his dignity and strange for him, alien, not his calling. And yet, though the

activity was "contemptible and foreign," he confesses to Vettori
that he misses it once the migration of thrushes has passed. Even so
slight a game, so little suited to his nature, now has a value in his
everyday life. This was the best way of telling his friend—and himself, and us—that his days were basically made up of nothing.

Alongside that nothing was the wretchedness of humanity,
which had so bothered him when he was secretary and continued
to afflict him here in the country. Now that I no longer catch
thrushes, Niccolò wrote, "I get up in the morning with the sun and
go into one of my forests that I am having cut down." Here he
must inspect the work done the day before and waste time with
the woodcutters discussing their seemingly incessant disputes and
fights among themselves or with others working nearby. Niccolò is
having the wood cut for his own use but above all to sell. And here
there are even worse problems and annoyances. Frosino da Pan-
zano, Niccolò reports, sent for "some loads without saying a word
to me; when it came time to settle, he wanted to withhold ten lire
he said he had won off me four years ago when he beat me at *cricca*
at Antonio Guicciardini's house." Stingier still was Tommaso del
Bene, who ordered a load of firewood when the north wind
started up in Florence; as soon as he had it, he set about arranging
it in stacks that would take up less space, then claimed it was worth
only half the price Niccolò was asking. To stack the wood, Niccolò writes, Tommaso set his "wife, children, and servants" to work
so hard that "they looked like Gabburra [a well-known butcher in
Florence] on Thursdays, when he and his crew flay an ox." When
he realized he was losing rather than making money selling firewood, Niccolò gave up that line of business, telling everyone he
had no more wood to sell.

Leaving the forest, the letter continues, "I go to a spring" and
from there to one of the places where he catches thrushes when
they are in season. Fed up with the disputes among the woodcutters and with the friends who want to buy firewood, he takes
refuge in an isolated spot to read a book, which he must have car-

ried with him when he left the house that morning: Dante,
Petrarch, or the Latin poets—Tibullus, Ovid, or some such. "I read
about their amorous passions and their loves, remember my own,
and these reflections make me happy for a while," he explains. His
consolation, his enjoyment, then, is to read love poems and to think
of his own love affairs. Which ones? We know about a lady who
lived near the Ponte delle Grazie; we know of the Jeanne or
Gianna or Janna whom he met in Lyons; and we know about
Lucrezia, called La Riccia. But none of them seems to have been a
true love. Perhaps there were others of whom no trace now sur-
vives, but that seems unlikely; perhaps the passage of time intensi-
fied the memory of loves that had been less than soul-shaking. But
there was also a new love that blossomed in his exile at his house in
the Percussina, the Albergaccio, about which I shall say more
presently.

Now we must return to the rest of the letter, keeping in mind
that here Niccolò shows us an important aspect of his personality:
for him, love—experienced as a passion that shakes the soul and
commands the heart, not as some literary conceit—was an antidote
to the misery of life and the evil of men. Machiavelli has been
described as having a soul of ice, sealed with an inscrutable sneer;
but here we see him finding joy, in the darkest days of his life, in
thinking back on his love affairs and reading about those of the
great poets.

The next scene in the letter takes place at the inn, to which he
is driven by his insatiable curiosity, but first he describes his walk
there: "Then I make my way along the road toward the inn, I chat
with passersby, I ask for their local news, I learn about various matters, I observe mankind: the variety of its taste, the diversity of its
fancies." The scene is familiar; when he had traveled in the great
world, he had done the same thing, watching the world, so varied
and unpredictable, in quest of knowledge, understanding, and
diversion.

Then he returns home to have lunch with his wife and chil-

dren, his "gang," as he refers to them; interestingly, he uses the same
word for his family—"gang"—as he used for his friends in the
Chancery. It is almost as if he is saying that his family is more a
small band of friends united by poverty and hardship than a hierar-
chically ranked group. Unfortunately, he tells us no more about his
meals than that the table is set with foods that "this poor farm and
my minuscule patrimony" yield. We shall have to wait a few more
years for a glimpse of Machiavelli as father.

After lunch, he returns to the inn, this time to play *triche-tach,* a
game similar to backgammon, with the innkeeper, the butcher, the
miller, and two kiln workers. The scene is tasty: Machiavelli at the
gaming table caught up in "thousands of squabbles and countless
vituperative spites" with the other players; they compete for a
penny a point, and yet they yell so loudly they can be heard, in the
quiet winter afternoons, two miles away at San Casciano. Enjoyable
to imagine, less enjoyable to experience. True, by playing and quarreling, he gets "the mold out of my brain" and forgets his worries;
but it lowers him and makes him brutish. To describe how he feels,
he even invents a verb, *m'ingaglioffo,* which means to become a
gaglioffo, a good-for-nothing, to sink into the muck of the everyday. He does it to let out the rage he feels at his fate. He wants to
see whether Fortune, satisfied at having spun him so low, will
finally feel shame and turn his wheel more favorably.

Evening falls around the inn; it is time to go home. But let us
hear it in Niccolò's own words:

When evening comes, I return home and enter my study;
on the threshold, I take off my workday clothes, covered
with mud and dirt, and put on the garments of court and
palace. Fitted out appropriately, I step inside the venerable
courts of the ancients, where, solicitously received by them,
I nourish myself on that food that *alone* is mine and for
which I was born; where I am unashamed to converse with
them and to question them about the motives for their

actions, and they, out of their human kindness, answer me. And for four hours at a time, I feel no boredom, I forget all my troubles, I do not dread poverty, and I am not terrified by death. I absorb myself into them completely.

In these remarkably beautiful lines, Machiavelli reveals his soul, displays all his inner grandeur. When, before going into his study, he takes off the work clothes in which he has walked through the woods and gone to the tavern, he also strips away the mask he has been forced to wear by Fortune when he is no longer allowed to be himself, when he must be poor and ordinary, when he can only hope that the savage goddess will tire of her cruel game. But the man in his study, dressed in the "garments of court and palace," the clothes he wore to meet kings, princes, emperors, and popes, is another man: this is the real Niccolò, who can on his own reason about his art, about the art of founding, preserving, and rescuing states.

At his desk, conversing with the great statesmen of antiquity—or, rather, analyzing what historians have written about those statesmen's decisions and deeds—Machiavelli finds his true self. He has left the world behind to enter, with the help of fantasy and imagination, the realm of poetry. Boredom, worry, poverty, even death are minor in comparison with the greatness of the men with whom he can now commune, and as they recede into the distance, they no longer frighten him, no longer hurt him. What Niccolò describes in his letter is a form of imaginative magic that one finds only in great men. Through this magic, he can enjoy four hours of true peace, peace with himself, in the nighttime silence of the wintry countryside, a fire crackling on the hearth behind him. Let us leave him be in this peace. He needs it.

sixteen

The Prince and Niccolò's Love Affairs

It is commonly thought that great political works are the products of detachment and the cold light of reason, unaffected by human feelings. This piece of foolishness is the invention, pure and simple, of professors. Truly great works, and they are few and far between, are the products of a pain distilled into pages of pure power and vitality, shattering conventions and crossing the boundaries set up by mediocre minds. These works are great because the author infuses them with all the intensity of a life he feels slipping from his grasp. Reason is involved, too, of course, but it is a reason given a steely edge by emotions, which not only sharpen the analysis but enrich the literary quality of the work, filling it with images, metaphors, and exhortations that capture the reader's heart and mind, piercing the soul and remaining firmly lodged there.

Such a work is *The Prince,* but perhaps it would be best to introduce it with its full name—*Dei principati (De principatibus),* literally, *Of Principalities,* as Machiavelli himself called the booklet that he wrote in the solitude of his house in Percussina, the Albergaccio. In this brief work are contained the results of his studies of

ancient history and everything he learned during his years as secretary of the Florentine Republic, when he had been able to observe
politics from a privileged vantage point. If anyone were to read it,
he wrote at the end of a letter to Vettori of 10 December 1513, "it
would be evident that during the fifteen years I have been studying
the art of the state I have been neither asleep nor fooling around,
and anybody ought to be happy to utilize someone who has had so
much experience at the expense of others."

Above all, he wished that his short work might be read and
understood by the Medici, lords of Rome through Pope Leo X
and lords of Florence through Lorenzo and, especially, Giuliano,
who was then at the papal court (and to whom Machiavelli
planned to dedicate the work). He hoped that if they read it, they
would realize that he knew better than anyone else what a prince
should do to consolidate power, especially a prince who was
"new"—as were the Medici in 1513. He hoped, in short, that they
would entrust him with an office, even the lowliest office, even
"having me roll along a stone."

He was unsure whether it would be better to go to Rome to
present the booklet to Giuliano in person or send it to him
through Vettori. Once again, he asked for advice and help from the
latter, who in Rome was close to both the pope and Giuliano. Asking for a favor cost him enormous effort, but circumstances
required it. His enforced inactivity was wearing on him; he feared
that poverty would make him despicable to himself and to others
and that he would become a burden, rather than a source of support, to his family.

Vettori, as was customary with him, gave a vague response—not
because he was mean-spirited but because he was not good at
resisting powerful men and he was unwilling to risk his own reputation to help a friend. He did not answer Machiavelli until 24
December: "You write to me . . . that you have composed a work
about states. I shall be grateful if you would send it to me" and I
shall judge its quality, even if I am not an authority; as for present-

ing it to Giuliano, we shall see. His appraisal came in a letter of 18 January 1514: "I have seen the chapters of your work, and I like them immeasurably. But since I do not have the entire work, I do not want to make a definitive judgment."

With these few chilly and formal words, Francesco Vettori made the first known comment on one of the greatest political masterpieces ever written. Of course, he was careful not to show the work to either Giuliano or the pope; there is no record of his mentioning *The Prince* again. When Niccolò came to understand that his efforts had been in vain and that no door was likely to open for him in Rome or Florence or anywhere else, he poured out his despair and bitterness in a letter to Vettori of 10 June 1514, an effort not to evoke pity but to bury hope once and for all:

> So I am going to stay just as I am, amid my lice, unable to find any man who recalls my service or believes I might be good for anything. But I cannot possibly go on like this for long, because I am rotting away and I can see that if God does not show a more favorable face to me, one day I shall be forced to leave home and to place myself as tutor or secretary to a governor, if I cannot do otherwise, or to stick myself in some deserted spot to teach children to read and leave my family here to count me dead; they will do much better without me because I am causing them expenses, since I am used to spending and cannot do without spending. I am writing this to you not because I want you to go to any trouble for me or to worry about me but simply to get it off my chest and not to write anymore about this matter, since it is as odious a subject as can be.

When *The Prince* began to circulate in handwritten copies, and again when it was first printed, it found very few discerning readers who understood its value. At the same time, it found a host of enemies who saw it as an evil work, inspired directly by the devil,

in which a malevolent author teaches a prince how to win and
keep power through avarice, cruelty, and falseness, making cynical
use of religion as a tool to keep the populace docile. There were
others who saw the work as a satire whose author pretended to
teach a prince how to defend his state while actually showing the
people that the prince's power was based on force, cruelty, and
deception and thus exhorting them to hate their ruler. But this last
view was rare; for most people, *The Prince* was a work of evil and its
author, as one of the more obtuse critics wrote, a "master of evil."

What had Machiavelli written to stir up such indignation? He
had explained that the ideas set forth by thinkers who had written
advice books for princes before him were simply wrong, even
though they were considered great experts; if not wrong, their
ideas were relevant to certain circumstances but not to others.
These writers maintained that a prince who wishes to keep power
and win glory must always follow the path of virtue—must be
prudent, just, strong, and moderate—and must possess those qualities proper to princes, specifically mercy, generosity, and fairness.

Machiavelli, in contrast, stated that a prince who followed such
advice in *all* circumstances not only would not conserve his power
but would surely lose it and be scorned and soon forgotten. He
knew he was going against a centuries-old school of thought, long
endorsed by illustrious writers. I hope I shall not be considered
"presumptuous," he writes in chapter XV, if I abandon the ideas of
the many writers who have preceded me in treating this subject.
My purpose, he adds, is "to write something useful to whomever
understands it"; I must, therefore, offer advice based on reality, not
imagination. Those who have written about the qualities a prince
must possess have imagined "republics and principalities that have
never been seen or been known to exist in truth" and have insisted
on teaching princes how to be good in their actions, forgetting that
a prince who is always and unfailingly good amid "so many who
are not good" will inevitably lose his realm. The conclusion of his
reasoning is persuasive: "it is necessary" for a prince, if he wants to

maintain his realm, "to learn to be able not to be good" and to use or not use this, "according to necessity."

Having set forth the general thesis, Machiavelli, with the courage and irreverence that only great thinkers possess, demolishes conventional wisdom brick by brick. A good prince, it has been said for centuries, repeating ancient precepts, should emulate neither the lion, fierce and brutal, nor the fox, cunning and deceptive, but rather should govern with virtue; he should try not to instill fear in but to win the love of his subjects: no prince, in conclusion, is more secure on his throne than one surrounded by loving subjects. Subverting this conventional wisdom, Machiavelli argues that a prince, especially one who has not yet consolidated his power, should "know well how to use the beast and the man." Of the beasts, he should follow the examples of "the fox and the lion, because the lion does not defend itself from snares and the fox does not defend itself from wolves"; and so "one needs to be a fox to recognize snares and a lion to frighten wolves" (*P,* XVIII). This was just the opposite of what was said by writers who took their inspiration from the ancients, especially Cicero.

With similar daring, he discarded the second doctrine, that a good prince must be generous, lavishing gifts and favors on his friends, and himself live in luxury. A prince who follows that advice, seeking to win a reputation for "liberality," will succeed only in flattering a few hangers-on and bankrupting his estate. To preserve his reputation, he will have to burden the people with taxes (literally, "be fiscal"). These taxes will engender hatred and disrespect and greatly endanger the prince's power. It is therefore far wiser, he concludes, to maintain "a name for meanness," which begets infamy without hatred, than "to be under a necessity, because one wants to have a name for liberality, to incur a name for rapacity, which begets infamy with hatred" (*P,* XVI).

Machiavelli treats the question of cruelty analogously. A prince should certainly hope to be considered merciful and kind, as classical doctrine teaches, but he must "take care not to use this mercy

badly." Out of fear of being considered cruel, for instance, the Florentines allowed factions to destroy Pistoia; Cesare Borgia, in contrast, was considered cruel but used that cruelty to bring order to
Romagna, making it peaceful and united. A prince, and especially
a new prince, must therefore be willing to be called cruel, if necessary, as long as he wins the respect of his subjects and keeps them
united (*P,* XVII).

As further confirmation of how radical Machiavelli's critique
of the classical doctrine of the good prince was, suffice it to say
that Cicero had written—and in the centuries that followed,
countless writers had repeated in many different ways—that "no
cruelty can be expedient" (*De officiis,* III, XI, 4). Let us distinguish,
shot back the impertinent Machiavelli, between cruelty "badly
used" and cruelty "well used." "Those [cruelties] can be called well
used," he explained, "(if it is permissible to speak well of evil) that
are done at a stroke, out of the necessity to secure oneself, and
then are not persisted in but are turned to as much utility for the
subjects as one can. Those cruelties are badly used which, though
few in the beginning, rather grow with time than are eliminated"
(*P,* VIII).

Cicero and the humanists wrote that nothing is more effective
"in defending and maintaining power than being loved" and nothing "more harmful than being feared." Machiavelli replied: "One
would want to be both one and the other," but because it is difficult to be loved and feared at the same time, "it is much safer to be
feared than loved, if one has to lack one of the two" (*P,* XVII). A
similar consideration applies, finally, to honesty and fairness. No
one denies, Machiavelli wrote, that it would be praiseworthy for a
prince to keep his faith "and to live with honesty and not with
astuteness." Nonetheless, the experience of the present day shows
that princes who have readily broken their word and who "have
known how to get around men's brains with their astuteness" have
"done great things" and have triumphed over princes who have kept
their word (*P,* XVIII).

In pages bursting with life, energetic strength, and a wealth of historical detail, Machiavelli delineates the features of the new prince, who must be able "not to depart from good, when possible, but to know how to enter into evil, when forced by necessity," and explains the basis of statecraft, the art he knew so well. Any prince who wished to achieve greatness had to be able to fight both lions, such as Julius II, and foxes, such as Ferdinand the Catholic of Spain, or even princes who knew how to be both one and the other, such as Cesare Borgia. In short, he wants a prince who knows how to win, not another Pier Soderini, who lost state and fatherland out of fear of being considered cruel.

Machiavelli explained why his prince had to learn to win, in the last chapter, "Exhortation to Seize Italy and Free Her from the Barbarians," which is wrongly considered an extraneous addition by the many readers who have failed to understand *The Prince*. The prince of whom Machiavelli dreamed was a rare and marvelous figure, capable of redeeming Italy from "barbarous cruelties and insults," that is, from foreign domination. Like the great redeemers of old, first and foremost Moses, he could count on God's help. If he must enter the realm of evil in order to win, God would stand by his side and remain his friend, because He would know that his work was righteous. Machiavelli never taught that the end justifies the means or that a statesman is allowed to do what is forbidden to others; he taught, rather, that if someone is determined to achieve a great purpose—free a people, found a state, enforce the law, and create peace where anarchy and despotism reign—then he must not fear being thought cruel or stingy but must simply do what is necessary in order to achieve the goal. That is what great men do, and that is what Machiavelli wanted his new prince to do.

At first, Machiavelli had planned to dedicate *The Prince* to Giuliano de' Medici, as I have said. Instead, he dedicated it to Lorenzo, Pope Leo X's nephew, who had become the operative chief of the Medici government in Florence in August 1513. Even in his dedication, written sometime between September 1515 and September

1516, he emphasized that the core of his book was concerned with the deeds of great men: "I have found nothing in my belongings that I care so much for and esteem so greatly as the knowledge of the actions of great men, learned by me from long experience with modern things and a continuous reading of ancient ones." Whoever reads this little book, he added, can learn "in a very short time" what I spent many years learning, "and with so many hardships and dangers for myself." He warned, all the same, that he has not filled the book with spectacular phrases and literary conceits, because the subject matter is grave and the style should be equally grave and clear.

Machiavelli knew that Lorenzo, like the other Medici, mistrusted him deeply, in part because he was a commoner while they were aristocrats, in part because he had served as secretary under Soderini and was accused, moreover, of a role in the Boscoli and Capponi conspiracy. He used his mastery of words to eliminate the first cause of suspicion: "Just as those who sketch landscapes place themselves down in the plain to consider the nature of mountains and high places and to consider the nature of low places place themselves high atop mountains, similarly, to know well the nature of peoples one needs to be a prince, and to know well the nature of princes one needs to be of the people." To assuage political suspicion, he proclaimed his desire that Lorenzo should "arrive at the greatness that fortune and your other qualities promise you."

When Francesco Vettori, who had become Lorenzo's most authoritative adviser, presented Lorenzo with Niccolò's masterpiece, Lorenzo barely glanced at it, showing much more interest in two stud dogs that someone had sent him. He had absolutely no interest in reading a work like *The Prince,* and if he had read it, he would not have understood it. Another harsh blow to Niccolò's hopes of finding a new political office, the lack of which was a disappointment that would torment Machiavelli for years. We can see signs of this disappointment in his dedicating the *Discourses,* written a few years later, to his friends Zanobi Buondelmonti and

Cosimo Rucellai. This time, he wrote, bitterly but firmly, I dedicate my new work not to a prince but rather to people who, for their many excellent qualities, "deserve to be" princes. If men wish to judge properly, they should "esteem . . . those who know, not those who can govern a kingdom without knowing." The problem, then as today, is that thrones and executive chairs are occupied almost exclusively by those who do not know, while those who do know are either ignored or mocked.

In the midst of so much sorrow, Niccolò found a source of consolation as unexpected as it was beneficial. It was neither a new job nor recognition for his *Prince*; instead, it was a great love. We know, and Vettori wrote in a letter of 18 January 1514, that Machiavelli was not new to falling in love: "I have seen you in love a few times and heard how much suffering you have borne." Until now, however, not a word slips out in any of the letters, aside from a reference to the mysterious Jeanne (or Gianna or Janna) and another nameless lover mentioned only in letters written by others. The only woman Niccolò himself mentions is Lucrezia, known as La Riccia, with whom he had an affair that lasted at least ten years. He was seeing her as early as 1510, when he was at the height of his glory, as documented by a letter from Roberto Acciaiuoli of 7 October of that year; and he must have been at least on good terms with her as late as 1520, when he was already in his fifties and no longer had either money or glory, for Filippo de' Nerli assured him then that a certain Bastiano di Possente would give him good lodgings in Pistoia "for the sake of La Riccia and myself." La Riccia was a courtesan; and yet she continued, unlike so many men, to be a friend to Machiavelli when good luck had long since abandoned him.

Generous and faithful she may have been, but she also had a sharp tongue and could easily whip Niccolò into line. When I go to Florence, he wrote in a letter of 4 February 1514, I divide my time between Donato del Corno's shop and La Riccia's house, but "I think I am getting on both their nerves because he calls me 'Shop Pest' and she calls me 'House Pest.' " Poor Niccolò! Penniless, unemployed, chilled to the bone, and they call him such names: "For the penniless there are no loans," as an old Romagna saying goes.

To maintain Donato's hospitality and La Riccia's favors, Niccolò did his best to earn the gratitude of each as an "adviser." For a while, everything worked out well: Donato "lets me warm myself by his fire," and La Riccia "sometimes lets me kiss her on the sly." But then things became even worse than they had been when he was an adviser to princes, and because of certain tidbits of advice that didn't pan out, La Riccia said to him—pretending to be conversing with her maid—"Wise men, oh these wise men, I don't know what they have upstairs; it seems to me they turn everything topsy-turvy."

Buck up, don't take it to heart, Vettori consoles him in a letter of 9 February 1514. Her sharp comment on wise men was uttered in a moment of anger, "but I do not think for this reason that she does not bear love toward you and that she will not open to you when you want; because I would consider her ungrateful, whereas up to now I have judged her humane and kind." Even if she now has a lover of the caliber of Anton Francesco degli Albizzi, Vettori continues, she has certainly not become proud or conceited.

And indeed La Riccia had a generous heart. Nearly a year later, Vettori wrote, "But you tell me something that astonishes me: you have found so much faith and so much compassion in La Riccia that, I swear to you, I was partial to her for your sake, but now I have become her slave, because most of the time women are wont to love Fortune and not men and, when Fortune changes, to change as well" (L, 487).

At this point, we should bid a reluctant farewell to La Riccia, noting that this generous, easygoing, and independent courtesan played an important role in Niccolò's life and hoping that one day new documents may surface to tell us a little more about her. But I cannot overlook one slightly more lurid episode which involved Niccolò and La Riccia and has been completely ignored by Machiavelli's biographers. It concerns an anonymous accusation of sodomy submitted to the Otto di Guardia, the magistracy that oversaw criminal justice, on 27 May 1510. Let me quote the text of the accusation: "Lords of the Eight, you are hereby informed that Nicholò [*sic*], son of Bernardo Machiavelli, screws Lucretia, known as La Riccia, in the ass. Interrogate her, and you will learn the truth."

Certainly, La Riccia was not responsible for this accusation, since she continued her relations with Niccolò for years and remained his friend. Without a doubt, this was the word of a malicious enemy. How serious an accusation was it? At the time, sodomy was a crime punished with fines, public humiliation, and a prison term; until 1502, there even existed a special office, the Ufficiali di Notte e Conservatori dei Monasteri, for the repression of so-called unnatural sexual acts. In practice, sodomy was tolerated, however, and the accusation against Niccolò remained a dead letter. It was a minor episode, then, but it confirms an important aspect of Machiavelli's personality, namely, that where passions, desires, and pleasures were concerned, he listened only to nature, his own nature, and paid no attention to the views of moralists and prudes. Just as he was strict and demanding in his respect for the law in public life and politics, so was he playful and indulgent in sex and love.

Did Niccolò engage in homosexual relations? I ask the question here because two significant documents concerning it also relate, in some sense, to La Riccia. The first is a sentence in a letter Machiavelli wrote to Vettori on 19 December 1513. After describing a terrifying sermon preached by one Fra Francesco da Montepulciano, he continued: "These activities demoralized me so much yesterday that when I was supposed to go this morning to see La Riccia, I did not go; I am not at all sure whether, had I been

supposed to go see Riccio, I would have been concerned." The
second is a passage in Vettori's letter of 9 February 1514 quoted
earlier. If La Riccia should slam her door in your face, Vettori
advised him, "stick to Riccio di Donato, who does not change
with fortune, but has sinew and backbone, and stays with friends
more when they are down than when they are up."

Riccio was a young fop who frequented Machiavelli's homosexual friends. The two letters might seem at first to be evidence
that Niccolò, too, appreciated his charms; but in fact, they suggest
the opposite: Vettori was making a joke designed to raise Niccolò's
spirits, since his friend feared losing access to La Riccia's favors.
The same is true of Machiavelli's own little comment, with its two
obvious untruths that Vettori would quickly detect: that the friar's
sermon had frightened him (if he listened to it at all, he certainly
laughed at it); and that if he had been intending to see Riccio, the
gloomy friar's sermon might have stopped him.

Yet if we read the letter Machiavelli wrote to Vettori carefully,
we have to acknowledge that Machiavelli, by his own admission,
engaged in homosexual relations with young men, as was common
practice in Florence at that time. In another passage, he wrote: "If
I—*who handle and care about women* [my italics]—had chanced to
enter the room, as soon as I had gotten the drift of the situation I
would have said, 'Ambassador, you are going to be ill; I don't think
you're allowing yourself any diversion; there aren't any boys here,
there aren't any girls here; what kind of a fucking house is this
anyway?' " As Mario Martelli has shown in his important 1998
essay on Machiavelli, the Italian verb translated here as "handle,"
toccare, in fact had the idiomatic meaning of having sexual relations
with young men, and therefore the phrase may be translated as: "I,
who have sexual relations with both men and women . . ."

The problem, or the wonderful thing, was that when Machiavelli fell in love he abandoned himself entirely to his passions of
love. The beauty of woman enveloped him, enchained him, and
transported him to a world as familiar to him as politics and state-

craft: the world of poetry. By an odd twist of fate, Niccolò experienced the most important love affair of his life just when his heart was swollen with bitterness. He met the woman in the summer of 1514, as he himself wrote in a letter of 3 August, less than two months after the 10 June letter in which he told Vettori he was so miserable that he considered leaving home and allowing his family to think he was dead.

The woman with whom he fell in love was, in all likelihood, Niccolò Tafani's sister, who lived not far from the Albergaccio and had been brutally forsaken by her husband, one Giovanni, who had left for Rome. Having noted these details, let us listen to Niccolò's account of his new love: "while in the country I have met a creature so gracious, so refined, so noble—both in nature and in circumstance—that never could either my praise or my love for her be as much as she deserves." He would like to tell us about

> how this love began, how Love ensnared me with his nets, where he spread them, and what they were like; you would realize that, spread among the flowers, these were nets of gold woven by Venus, so soft and gentle that even though an insensitive heart could have severed them, nevertheless I declined to do so. For a while I reveled within them, until the tender threads hardened, and were pinned down with knots impossible to loosen.

This time he was not afraid to reveal—indeed, he opened—his soul. It is a rare moment: "I nevertheless feel so great a sweetness, both because of the delight that rare and gentle countenance brings me and because I have laid aside all memory of my sorrows, that not for anything in the world would I desire my freedom—even if I could have it." The beauty of the woman, her "rare and gentle countenance," magically cast out of Niccolò's soul all his fear, sorrows, and grief, just as another kind of beauty—that of the deeds of great men of the past and of ancient history—had once done, for a few hours, every evening at the Albergaccio. His love for this woman, even more powerful than his passion for politics, made him forget about his troubles and made him forget about politics, too: "I have renounced, then, thoughts about matters great and grave. No longer do I delight in reading about the deeds of the ancients or in discussing those of the moderns: everything has been transformed into tender thoughts, for which I thank Venus and all of Cyprus."

At the time, Niccolò was forty-five years old, though he liked to say he was "approaching his fiftieth year." He knew that Love is a young boy and therefore fickle and that he "gouges out . . . eyes, livers, and hearts"; he knew that limitless sweetness could quickly turn into bitter tears. Yet at least at first he was unafraid. On the contrary, he felt a new strength. In order to visit the lovely lady, he had to walk many miles on "rough roads" under the August Tuscan sun or in the dark of a country night, yet everything seemed to him easy and "smooth."

His affair with La Tafani was, however, neither easy nor smooth, at least to judge from some poems probably written during those months of 1514. In the long "Serenade," he describes a woman—a "rare example of created grace," a "perfect soul in which all beauty hides and shows its ways"—who wages "wrathful war" against her beloved with her eyes. Her lover, in order to melt the beautiful woman's heart, which has been hardened by the fear that "some man might do her violence," tells her of the ancient myth of Anaxarete, a princess who is turned to stone for allowing a commoner, Iphis, to die of love. "And thus Pomona, out of fear a bit,/And a bit moved by such a radiant face,/Was no more stubborn, harsh, and obstinate" but, like the "pomes" that ripen in the August sun, from which she took her name, melts finally into the arms of her lover (SL, 428–35).

In one sonnet, Niccolò described a grief, a pointless and disconsolate weeping, and drew a parallel between the tragedies of states and realms and the grief of love that afflicts men, a parallel reminiscent of that between the pleasures that accrue from thinking about great affairs of state and contemplating the sweetness of love. Once again, a woman's eyes are the source of all this pain:

> *If you believed me, I would gladly feed*
> *On the despair that from your eyes I draw;*
> *Only these woods believe me, tired to heed*
> *My lamentation, oh, no longer new. (SL, 427)*

Neither grief nor tears, not even the fear of being enslaved by those irresistible eyes, discouraged Niccolò. A letter from Vettori of 15 December tells us that Niccolò had asked his friend to find him "blue woolen yarn for a pair of hose" in Rome. That old fox Vettori immediately understood what lay behind the request, partly because he had received another letter from Niccolò begging him to intervene in favor of the Tafani family; what a coincidence. Gentleman that he is, Vettori promises to send the yarn the next day, "without inquiring for whom you want it," he assures his friend, "because I shall be satisfied with making you happy."

Quite incapable of helping Niccolò in political matters, Vettori was at least eager to lend his friend a hand in affairs of the heart. Yet the two men had radically different attitudes toward love, to judge from their letters. On 9 February 1514, Vettori wrote of the torment he was experiencing over the lovely daughter of a neighbor. He was powerfully attracted to the young woman but assailed by doubts and fears. I am forty, he explained to his friend, I have a wife, and

> I have married and marriageable daughters; therefore I do not have anything to throw away; but it would be reasonable for me to keep everything that I can save for my daughters; and what a base thing it is to let oneself be overcome by sensuality—and she lived nearby, and I would spend money on her, and every day I would get a thousand annoyances from it; in addition, since she is beautiful, young, and graceful, I had to realize that since I liked her, others of a differ-

ent rank than I would also like her, so that I would not be
able to enjoy her much and would be subject to constant
jealousy.

Vettori decided to abandon his passion for the young woman.
He held out for two full days. On the third day, the mother visited
him and left her daughter alone with him, next to the fireplace. All
his good resolutions vanished like mist in the morning sun, he
wrote to Machiavelli, "and I decided to offer myself as prey to her
and that she should rule and guide me as she saw fit." At the time,
he was pleased that he had given in to his desires—"I do not wish
to tell you what happened then: suffice it to say that it happened to
me and I no longer thought about annoyances and jealousy"—but
then he was overwhelmed with distress. At a loss, he discreetly
asked his friend for advice.

Niccolò had no doubts:

> I have no response to your letter, except that you should
> give your love full rein and that whatever pleasure you seize
> today may not be there for you to seize tomorrow; if things
> still stand as they did when you wrote, I envy you more than
> the king of England. I beg you to follow your star . . .
> because I believe now, I have always believed, and I shall
> continue to believe that what Boccaccio says is true: it is
> better to act and repent than not to act and regret.

In these few words—"it is better to act and repent than not to act
and regret"—lies Niccolò's wisdom. In the presence of a woman's
beauty, much as in the presence of great statesmanship, he is not
hindered by the fear of suffering or loss; he allows himself to be
taken by passion, and he follows his great dreams.

His approach to love as escape and dream emerges as well in
another exchange of letters with Vettori. On 16 January 1515, Vettori returned to the theme of his dull days in Rome:

I cannot read much, by reason of my eyesight, which has been diminished by age. I cannot go out and enjoy myself unless I am accompanied, and this cannot always be done: I do not have so much authority or such resources as to be sought out; if I spend my time in thought, this mostly brings me melancholy, which I try my best to flee; of necessity one must endeavor to think of pleasant things, but I know of nothing that gives more delight to think about and to do than fucking. Every man may philosophize all he wants, but this is the utter truth, which many people understand but few will say.

Niccolò answered him with a sonnet on the irresistible strength of Love. The fetters with which Love has bound me, he tells his friend who has sung the praises of fucking, are so strong that I am in absolute despair of my liberty; but even if I could, I am not sure that I would want to get free from those fetters—"now sweet, now light, now heavy"—which create such a tangle of feelings that "I believe I cannot live happily without this kind of life." He adds that he wished Vettori was in Florence so that he could laugh at Niccolò's laughter and tears. Without him, he takes consolation in telling his troubles and joys to Donato del Corno and to La Riccia, the "woman about whom I wrote you earlier."

Niccolò found in women captivating beauty, limitless sweetness, playfulness, and desire; but he also found in them friends with whom he could share his most intimate joys and sorrows. And to think that people have written that Machiavelli hated women and scorned them, that he considered them servants and never wanted the same one twice, that he abhorred love and never wanted to be a slave to passion! We can only laugh, as Niccolò might have laughed, in the face of such appalling ignorance.

seventeen

The Comedy of Life

We are now somewhat more familiar with the meaning of Niccolò's smile. We know it is a smile that dies on his lips and conceals his pain. Machiavelli smiled at mankind, at the constant to-and-fro of men driven by passions and unaware of how ridiculous they were. He felt neither detached from nor superior to this but instead part of the human comedy. And so he could laugh at himself, at his laughter and his tears, with his men and his women friends.

Thus did he find the strength to survive each day, to withstand human malevolence, to continue to live with great feeling, and to turn his mind to affairs of state. He amused himself by watching the comedy of life go by, but he was always and irresistibly attracted to the great dramas of politics. He laughed at one and was passionately absorbed by the other, striving to understand how events would develop and what intentions lay hidden in the minds of princes and kings.

He liked life to consist of grave matters and lighter things. He thought there should be room for both. In this, he believed he was imitating nature, and he cared nothing for the opinions of moralists and bores who thought life should always be devoted to important and serious matters. In a letter of 31 January 1515, he said to Vettori:

> Anyone who might see our letters, honorable *compare,* and see their variety, would be greatly astonished, because at first it would seem that we were serious men completely directed toward weighty matters and no thought could cascade through our heads that did not have probity and magnitude. But later, upon turning the page, it would seem to the reader that we—still the very same selves—were petty, fickle, lascivious, and directed toward chimerical matters. If to some this behavior seems contemptible, to me it seems laudable because we are imitating nature, which is changeable; whoever imitates nature cannot be censured.

Without claiming to reveal any great truth and without treating the matter as important, Niccolò offers a wise philosophy of life in this letter. It is worth noting because everyone who has read his work recognizes his greatness as a political thinker, but very few, over the centuries, have viewed him as a great moral philosopher who taught, with a smile on his lips, that individuals should follow their own nature without concern for the opinions of others. In this world, Machiavelli explained to Vettori, there are "nothing but crazies," and "whoever seeks to act according to others will accomplish nothing because no two men who think alike can be found." Anyone who truly understands the world knows that when a man is considered worthy and respectable, whatever he does "to refresh his spirit and live happily" brings him honor and not criticism (*L,* 437).

Appreciating the variety of life also means accepting that there are different ways of living. Niccolò said as much in a letter in which he tried to reassure Vettori about criticisms made by their mutual friends Filippo Casavecchia and Giuliano Brancacci, who were guests at Vettori's home in Rome. Filippo was teasing Vettori because "I take a bit of pleasure in women, more to stay and chat with them than for any other reason, because I am now so far gone that there is little else I can do than talk" (we can imagine Niccolò laughing when he read these fibs). Giuliano, on the other hand, reproved him for his poor taste in receiving in his home a certain Sano, a notorious homosexual, whose company Filippo welcomed. Asked which of the two had better cause to criticize him, Niccolò answered that both were wrong and that Vettori would be even more in the wrong if he turned away from his door either courtesans or homosexuals.

Even though he was far away, in his mind's eye Machiavelli could see the scene unfolding that evening in Vettori's home. The story of the three men, Filippo, Giuliano, and Francesco, each driven by different passions, seemed to him worthy of inclusion in an "Annals of Modern Times," alongside accounts of political and military affairs, and might fairly be recounted to a prince (*L,* 442). He imagined the expressions on their faces, their movements, their words. In his imagination, a scene from a comedy begins to take shape.

He imagines Giuliano "sitting low in a chair," the better to observe the lovely visitor, Costanza, and "with words and gestures, with poses and pleasant expressions, with fidgeting movements of mouth and eye" showing that he dotes on her words, breath, gaze, perfume, and "receptive feminine ways." Then he imagines Filippo: he is standing, shifting his weight first to one hip, then the other, the better to listen to the shy, uncertain speech of Costanza's son. Vettori, landlord and host, is entertaining his guests but secretly lusts for Costanza's pretty daughter, and so he keeps one eye on the boy "and the other one on that young girl," one ear attentive to the widow's words and the other monitoring Filippo and Giuliano. He follows their conversation distractedly, limiting himself to answering his guests' questions and comments.

The faces and gestures of men in the throes of passion enchanted Machiavelli. If I knew how to paint, he wrote Vettori, I would send you a portrait of Filippo, because certain unmistakable actions of his, that way he has of glancing sidelong and his disdainful poses, "can in no way be rendered in prose." More than anything else, however, he was fascinated by the power of love. He imagined Vettori, sitting with his friends at a cheerful dinner table, consumed by a passion that burns all the more brightly—like flames that can set fire to green wood—because it has had to overcome bitter resistance. He knew his friend's heart was tormented: he was held back by duty, financial considerations, fear of pain; but at the same time he was yearning to give in to the passion of love. You would like, he wrote to Vettori, "to turn into a swan so you could lay an egg in her lap, now turn into gold so she could carry you in her pocket, now into one animal, and now another," as long as you never had to be separated from her.

While smiling at the comedy of life and abandoning himself to the beauty of love, Niccolò also experienced—between the end of 1514 and the beginning of 1516—days of pain and sorrow. He wrote about this to his nephew Giovanni Vernacci, a merchant in the Levant, in a series of unassuming, straightforward letters that more than any others reveal the most intimate depths of his heart. It is difficult to say why Niccolò spoke so sincerely about himself only to Vernacci. Certainly, he could confide in his nephew without fear that his despairing words might be interpreted as a request for help. Vernacci was not Vettori. He could do nothing to help Machiavelli in any way; indeed, it was more likely to be the other way around, though Niccolò could offer him, at best, only advice.

Niccolò confided in Vernacci because he thought of him as a son, as family, and especially as a friend, and he respected him. Fortune, he wrote on 19 November 1515, "has left me nothing but my family and my friends," and I consider them precious, especially "those who are closest to me, as you are." Two years later, to reassure Vernacci despite a long silence, he wrote that his respect and affection had not altered over time: indeed, since "men are respected according to their worth and since you have proved that you are a man of worth and ability," it is fair that I should love you even more than I once did. Niccolò had raised this nephew, and, poor though he might be, he had offered the youth his "humble and wretched house." He considered him good-hearted, capable of gratitude. He hoped that if Vernacci had business successes in the future, he would help Niccolò's sons. In the meantime, he would ask for a few small favors, such as sending, for Marietta, a swatch of camel-hair fabric and some sewing needles of damascene steel, making sure they were of good quality.

Because he trusted and respected Giovanni, Niccolò confided that his days were so difficult and sorrowful that he often forgot himself entirely. He wrote this once in a letter of 18 August 1515: these times are such "that they have made me forget even myself." And he repeated it almost two years later on 8 June 1517: I have come back to life in the countryside because of reverses I have experienced, and "I sometimes go for a month at a time without thinking about myself." The life he was leading was so far removed from his nature, his dreams, and his temperament that he felt distanced from his very self.

Indeed he was no longer himself. He had said for years in the Chancery offices, and had written many times in letters and poetry, that it is a mistake to wait for time to bring relief from the ills that afflict us, because time brings both evil and good. Now he wrote that he was biding "my time so that I may be ready to seize good Fortune should she come; should she not come, I am ready to be patient."

He was not laughing or concealing his sadness and desperation behind a laughing mask. He was baring his soul to his young friend and perhaps to La Riccia as well. He would have been glad if the intensity of the pain had not impelled him to acknowledge it, but the few lines in his letters to Giovanni clearly convey how much of an effort it took to smile. Yet when he succeeded, he rediscovered himself; he became once again, for himself even more than for his friends, Niccolò, "il Machia."

What had driven Machiavelli to the point of forgetting himself was the succession of hopes and disappointments that had tormented him since his release from prison. He had hoped that *The Prince* might reopen the doors of politics to him but had had nothing but words, and cold words at that. He had hoped that Vettori

would help in the court at Rome but had had only "a lot of talk
from me for quite a while without corresponding results" (L, 466),
as Vettori himself recognized.

Then the final bitter pill. In December 1514, Paolo Vettori,
Francesco's brother and a frequent visitor to the Roman court,
spoke to Machiavelli of a plan to give Giuliano de' Medici a vast
state that would include Parma, Piacenza, Modena, and Reggio
and intimated that if the plan were successful, Giuliano would
entrust Paolo with the position of governor. It went without saying that, once governor, Paolo would lift Niccolò from the moldy
idleness of Sant'Andrea and restore him to the great stage of politics. Niccolò, of course, began to think about this possibility; he
offered advice to show he was well acquainted with the requirements for governing a state of that kind, and he wrote to Francesco
to apprise him of the project and to urge him finally to do something to "pave the way" for the enterprise.

Nothing came of it, in part because of opposition from the
duke of Milan, the Swiss, and King François, and in part because of
Pope Leo's lack of enthusiasm. But even if the plan had been successful, Niccolò would have been left out in the cold. A few words
were enough to bury his hopes, words heavy as tombstones from
the powerful Pietro Ardinghelli in a letter to Giuliano de' Medici:

> [Giulio] Cardinal de' Medici questioned me yesterday very
> closely if I knew whether Your Excellency had taken into
> his service Niccolò Machiavelli, and as I replied that I knew
> nothing of it nor believed it, His Lordship said to me these
> words: "I do not believe it either, but as there has been word
> of it from Florence, I would remind him that it is not to his
> profit or to ours. This must be an invention of Paolo Vet-
> tori's; . . . write to him on my behalf that I advise him not
> to have anything to do with Niccolò." (R, 253)

Yet just a few months before, Cardinal de' Medici had praised
Machiavelli's political acuity in the presence of Francesco Vettori

and had expressed admiration for his mind, a veritable chorus of praise in which the pope and Bernardo Cardinal Dovizi of Bibbiena had joined. Once again, words and nothing more. Vettori told him, on 30 December 1514, that bad luck was to blame, that he, Vettori, was not a man who knew how to help his friends, and that in the end the good opinion of powerful men might help Niccolò one day. How much the praise of powerful men helped Machiavelli we have just seen. And we have also seen the effect on his soul of the dwindling of this last hope for recognition of his remarkable political skills.

"Remarkable" may seem an exaggerated term, but in this case, I think it is entirely appropriate. The cause of the praise showered so liberally in the court of Rome was a pair of letters from Machiavelli offering the pope valuable advice on what to do if the king of France were to march into Italy to retake the duchy of Milan, still held by the Swiss. Francesco Vettori, in a letter of 3 December, had asked his views on this delicate matter. In the eventuality that Venice chose to side with France and opposing them should be the emperor, the king of Spain, and the Swiss, Vettori explained, the question is whether it is best for the pope to side with the former, the latter, or remain neutral. Examine the question, he added: "I know that you have such intelligence" that even though two years have passed since "you left the shop, I do not think you have forgotten the craft" (L, 467).

Machiavelli certainly had not forgotten the craft; indeed, he had much refined it with his reading and reflection during the long days and nights at Sant'Andrea. The proof is in the quality of the counsel he offered Vettori in a letter of 10 December 1514. He remarked, I think it very likely that France will emerge victorious from this clash, and if the pope should take its side, victory is almost guaranteed. A French victory, moreover, is far better for the pope than a victory of the opposing side, while a French defeat would not have disastrous consequences and would be far more tolerable than a defeat in alliance with the king of Spain and the emperor. The best policy, then, is to set aside any temptation to remain neutral and to side resolutely with France, unless Venice should enter the fray on the side of Spain and the emperor.

Ten days later, on 20 December, he wrote to Vettori again, the better to explain his reasons for opposing a policy of neutrality. In this letter, he summarized ideas he had already set forth in *The Prince*—as if to say to his friend and to the "great men" of Rome that if they had read his book they would have found in it the wisdom they were now desperately seeking. I know that many say a policy of neutrality is the safest option, Machiavelli wrote. I believe, to the contrary, that neutrality is an exceedingly dangerous path, that it leads to certain defeat, and that both ancient history and my own experience of political affairs prove the correctness of my ideas. You know, he continued, that the first duty of every prince is "to keep himself from being hated and despised" by both his subjects and his allies. If a prince remains neutral when two others are fighting, he allows himself to be hated and despised: hated by the combatant who believes the prince (in this case the pope) is obliged to side with him—in the name of an old friendship or in return for favors recently granted or performed; and despised by the other combatant, who will consider him timid and indecisive, and therefore an "ineffective ally" and an enemy not to be feared.

To those who argue that rules applying to other princes do not apply to the pope, because the pope can always rely on the reverence generally felt for his person and for the authority of the Church, Machiavelli's answer was that in the past, and in times when the spiritual power of the Church was stronger than it is today, popes had been driven into exile, persecuted, forced to flee, and even killed. Things that happened in the past, he warned, can certainly happen again in the future.

Lastly, let the pope consider the fact that, if he sided against France and France should win, he would be forced to take refuge in Switzerland, where he would "starve," or Germany, where he would live in despair, or Spain, where he would be swindled and betrayed; if he sided with France and France should lose, he can stay safely at home, preserve his own state, and enjoy the friendship of a king who can "arise again in a thousand ways, thanks to either a treaty or a war." The truly wise are those who, confronted with two paths, choose the one that promises the least harm if things go badly.

That this was masterful advice was revealed by events later in the new year of 1515. In August, King François crossed the Alps and on 13–14 September decisively defeated the Swiss in the Battle of Marignano, forcing them to abandon to him the duchy of Milan. The pope had formed an alliance with Spain, however, though he had at least refrained from sending troops to fight against the French. And so he avoided paying the highest possible price, but he also lost the opportunity that Machiavelli had pointed out to him to reinforce the power of the Church.

We have seen how Machiavelli was rewarded for his advice. We can certainly understand why, after this latest disappointment, he might have lost the will to fight and might have given in to angry resignation, even though he had always urged the opposite, to be hopeful about better times. As he waited for Fortune to lessen her hostility, he thought about his fate and man's fate in general, and he committed his thoughts to poetry, writing "The Ass," a little poem that reveals a great deal about how he looked at life and the world.

Man, run the verses, is the only animal that comes defenseless into the world and begins his life in tears:

> But man is born defenseless, and his fate
> Is to be stripped of all—no hide, no quills,
> No feathers, fur, or bristles as his plate.
> He enters into life with tears of fright
> And his first word is but a sound of pain—
> He is indeed a most pitiful sight.

His life is short, afflicted with countless ills caused by ambition and greed, tormented by disappointments brought about by Fortune promising and then withholding miracles. Man is more obsessed with living than any other creature, but at the same time no creature on earth is so "confused with terror" and afflicted by "rancor."

He is also far and away the cruelest creature: "But men/Rob, crucify, and murder one another." Man believes he is godlike and considers himself the lord of creation, but in reality he is unhappier than all the other animals.

In Niccolò's despairing view, the course of human events follows an inexorable cycle. It is not a progression toward happiness or salvation but an alternating succession of order and disorder, virtue and vice, good and evil. Nothing stays the same; there is nothing constant under the sun: "So things go, always have, always will/Ill follows good, and good follows ill," and one is always the cause of the other. This is as true for states as for peoples and individuals. Niccolò sought in this iron rule the explanation of his own suffering. He knew that he had experienced the pain of ingratitude more than most, and he blamed adverse fortune, against which all resistance is vain. Happier times would return only when the heavens became benevolent again. One had to know how to wait and adapt to the moment; during times of bitterness, pain, and anguish, it was vitally important to have a stalwart soul. Niccolò did not want to weep, "because weeping is unbecoming of a man,/To the harsh blows of fortune/He must turn his face dry of tears," and if possible present a smile that masks, protects, and offers a moment of relief.

Perhaps the key to understanding the significance of Niccolò's smile is in the conception of life he set forth in "The Ass." We already know that his smile was a mask born of pain, but we do not yet know why he was so determined to conceal that pain. In "The Ass," he gives us the answer. He does not wish to show men and Fortune a face marked by tears and grief partly because he knows they would only take greater pleasure in making him suffer. When he can no longer endure it, he seeks solitude, as we have seen: I have "withdrawn to my farm, far from every human face" (L, 383); "one day I shall be forced to . . . stick myself in some deserted spot" (L, 462). He confides his sorrow in a male or, better yet, female friend, such as La Riccia, and it is worth noting that the figure of the woman friend reappears in "The Ass": "And still, after a while, she and I/Together spoke of many matters,/As one man would converse with another in friendship."

When possible, though, the best thing is to laugh at people's comic behavior, at their passions and their baseness, at their dreams and the bizarre variety of their ideas and ways of life—laugh at the comedy of life. And when the human comedy is not sufficiently funny, then it is time to write comedies of one's own.

At the same writing desk where he had composed his most serious works, Machiavelli now wrote—between 1517 and 1519—two comedies, first the *Andria*, or *Woman of Andros*, a translation and adaptation of a work by Terence, and then *The Mandrake*. In the latter comedy, his theatrical masterpiece, he included characters he found especially funny: an old and not very intelligent doctor of law who wants to become a father at all costs (Nicia); a "wretched swain" who is on the verge of dying from either joy or fear (Callimaco); a lovely woman and virtuous whiner who is ready to do whatever husband, mother, or father confessor tells her to do (Lucrezia); a "venal" monk who is as willing to traffic in sin as in virtue, so long as he can make a little money on the side (Fra Timoteo); a mother who sowed plenty of wild oats in her youth (Sostrata); a hanger-on or parasite who knows how to take advantage of human frailties and manages to achieve his grand scheme of persuading Lucrezia's husband to introduce the delighted Callimaco into the bed of his lovely young bride (Ligurio).

Machiavelli wrote *The Mandrake* to make audiences laugh loud and long. If you do not laugh, promises the prologue, I will "treat you to a flask of wine." The first to laugh was Niccolò, to stave off sadness: thus I try, he explained in the prologue, to make my "time of grief a little easier." Comedy was the only "thing to which he could turn" now that cruel fate had kept him from bending his thoughts to matters worthy of a "serious and wise man." If he did not turn his face to comedy and laughter, he would give way to sorrow and weeping, and he was determined to give that satisfaction neither to Fortune nor to anyone.

EIGHTEEN

The Flavor of History

Those with great souls can bring to life in their imaginations the events, people, and words of the past; they find comfort in history, especially when ambition and mean-spiritedness loom everywhere in the present and the future promises nothing but storm clouds. Viewed with the inward eyes of the imagination, the deeds of great men of the past take on a light that intensifies their beauty and their worth and prompts a desire to imitate them. Often, however, conditions of the present day make it impossible to follow their examples, and those who choose history as teacher and source of wisdom may commit errors of judgment. Despite this danger, those who know to search through history can find ideas and possibilities for action that most people don't notice, and when they tell us what they have found, they do so in words that go straight to the heart and mind. But teaching and lessons aside, history allows us to stay in contact with great deeds. When we tire of the dramas and comedies of life, it is time for history; passing from one to the other is an excellent way to live.

Only a very few know how to do this without losing their way

or muddling things up. Niccolò, however, was a master of the art.
While he was putting the final touches on *The Mandrake*—performed to great acclaim in Florence during the Carnival of 1520
and perhaps even earlier, and then in Rome in 1520 as well, in
Venice in 1522, in Florence in 1525, and again in Venice in 1526—
he was completing, if he had not already completed, the *Discourses.*
The subject of this work is history, specifically the history of
republican Rome as told by Livy.

Livy's work describes Roman political institutions and decisions in times of peace and times of war and recounts the deeds of
the lawmakers, consuls, and generals who made Rome great. From
its pages, Machiavelli derived principles of political action to apply
to the present, but it would be a mistake to think that his work was
simply an assessment of ancient Rome's political principles and
institutions. Machiavelli did take lessons from Livy, but his chief
goal was to persuade his readers of the political *wisdom* of the
Romans and move his readers to imitate them. To achieve this, to
give the reader a new understanding of the meaning of history
and a new enjoyment of its flavor, he used not just reason but his
finest literary style and a passionate power in composition.

He could not understand why his contemporaries did not
appreciate the greatness of Roman history and why they mostly
read stories of antiquity out of mere curiosity, attracted by the
variety of human experiences there, without wishing to follow in
the footsteps of these great men. He was astonished and aggrieved
to see that, while the artists of his time imitated classical art, while
jurists and lawmakers relied on the principles of Roman law and
medical doctors based their diagnoses and prescriptions on the
learning of ancient physicians, neither princes nor republics followed the classical examples "in ordering republics, maintaining
states, governing kingdoms, ordering the military and adminstering
war, judging subjects, and increasing empire" (*D,* I, Preface).

The causes of this sad state of affairs included the poor education
encouraged by the Christian religion, which counseled humility and

resignation, and the corrupt peace that had settled over so many nations for so long. Far more important, though, was that people did not understand history. The *Discourses* represents an effort to remove at least this last cause of modern wretchedness.

Machiavelli wrote with a special view to the young men of his time and those of generations to come. In the summer of 1517, he had started to frequent gatherings in the Orti Oricellari, the gardens of a palazzo belonging to Bernardo Rucellai. There young men from the best families of Florence would meet regularly to discuss poetry and philosophy, history and statecraft. By the time Machiavelli joined this group, Rucellai had died (in 1514), and his nephew Cosimo Rucellai had taken over as official host. Other regulars were the poet Luigi Alamanni; the philosopher Francesco da Diacceto; Francesco da Diacceto il Nero; Iacopo da Diacceto, nicknamed the Diaccetino; the historians Jacopo Nardi and Filippo de' Nerli; Battista della Palla; Zanobi Buondelmonti; Anton Francesco degli Albizzi; and Antonio Brucioli, the author of a major political work that featured Machiavelli himself as a voice in a dialogue.

They were all younger than Machiavelli, and they loved to listen to the veteran secretary talk about statecraft and the military techniques of classical Rome. Many of them became opponents of the Medici and partisans of the Republic. For Machiavelli, those conversations were a way of coming back to life. He was almost fifty years old; he had long since given up hope of returning to politics. Talking with these young men, teaching them everything he had learned, as they discussed ancient history and modern politics—this made him feel he still served some purpose, that he might leave behind a legacy, something that might live on after his death. These young men belonged to the Florentine aristocracy, and in teaching them, he was educating men who might have a chance to accomplish the great things that had been denied him. These thoughts and sentiments energized him and led him to accentuate the contrast between the greatness of the ancients and the misery of the moderns, so that "the spirits of youths who may read these writings of mine can flee the latter and prepare themselves to imitate the former," when fortune might offer them the opportunity (*D*, II, Preface).

He was prompted to write, as always, by passion and by a wish to occupy his mind with great matters, but also, this time, by a sense of duty. The words in which he tells us what this duty was, steeped in sad dignity, are some of the best in the *Discourses*: "It is the duty of a good man to teach others the good, which, because of the malignity of the times and of fortune, you could not achieve, so that when many are capable of it, one of them more loved by heaven may be able to achieve it" (*D*, II, Preface).

For his friends at the Orti Oricellari, he wrote that above all else they must despise tyrants. As worthy of praise as founders of republics or realms might be, equally deserving of scorn and condemnation were those who have imposed tyranny, as he wrote in chapter 10 of book I of the *Discourses,* one of the work's most passionate chapters—it almost seems to have been written to be declaimed rather than read silently. In it, he masterfully depicts the contrast between the reigns of good emperors and bad:

> In those governed by the good, he will see a secure prince in the midst of his secure citizens, and the world full of peace and justice; he will see the Senate with its authority, the magistrates with their honors, the rich citizens enjoying their riches, nobility and virtue exalted; he will see all quiet and all good, and, on the other side, all rancor, all license, corruption, and ambition eliminated. He will see golden times when each person can hold and defend the opinion he wishes. He will see the world in triumph, in sum, the prince full of reverence and glory, the peoples full of love and security.

The reader should then reflect on the times when bad emperors dominated in Rome, times that were atrocious . . .

because of wars, discordant because of seditions, cruel in peace and in war; so many princes killed with steel, so many civil wars, so many external ones; Italy afflicted and full of new misfortunes, its cities ruined and sacked. He will see Rome burning, the Capitol taken down by its own citizens, the ancient temples desolate, ceremonies corrupt, the cities full of adulterers. He will see the sea full of exiles, the shores full of blood. He will see innumerable cruelties follow in Rome, and nobility, riches, past honors, and, above all, virtue imputed as capital sins. He will see calumniators rewarded, slaves corrupted against their master, freedmen against their patron, and those who lacked enemies oppressed by friends. And he will then know very well how many obligations Rome, Italy, and the world owe to Caesar.

Whoever considers all this cannot but feel a profound hatred for tyranny and a powerful wish to emulate good rulers, wrote Machiavelli. In fact, whoever seeks true glory should hope to live in a corrupt city—not that he might bring yet greater ruin upon it, as Caesar did, but that he might bring it a new order, as did Romulus.

He then explained that republics, where the people are sovereign, are superior to principalities and kingdoms, because the people are wiser and more stable than a prince can ever be. As an example, he indicated the Roman people, who, as long as their republic endured uncorrupted, "never served humbly nor dominated proudly"; honorably preserved their standing in social and political life; obeyed when obedience was in order, and when it was necessary to resist and mobilize against a powerful individual did so; selected their magistrates wisely; and, when called on to deliberate public matters, showed remarkable prudence in foreseeing their own good and evil fortune (D, I, 58).

Only in republics was the "common good" observed. Sovereign citizens have the power to encourage the common interest, even where that interest may run counter to the interest of one private citizen or another; they can prevent powerful and arrogant individuals from imposing their private interests, and thus defend the liberty of one and all. From "living free," as Machiavelli described republics, as opposed to "living in servility," countless benefits ensue: the population grows because citizens are eager to bring children into the world, confident that they can feed and keep them, that they will be "born free and not slaves," and that if they are good citizens and distinguish themselves by their virtues, they may hope for election to the highest honors of the republic. Wealth mounts up, both that created by agriculture and that from trade and the arts, because all the people work harder in the knowledge that the fruits of their labor are safe from depredation. Liberty, then, increases both public and private benefits "marvelously" (D, II, 2).

The young men from the Orti Oricellari knew that republics could be governed by popular rule, as Florence had been when Machiavelli was secretary, or by an aristocracy, as Venice was. They must certainly have urged Machiavelli to share his thoughts on this important and controversial issue. In Machiavelli's opinion, it was much safer—as he writes in chapter 5 of book I—to entrust the defense of liberty to the people rather than to the aristrocracy, because the nobles "desire to dominate" while the common people desire only "not to be dominated" and, consequently, to "live free." A people's republic, therefore, is better suited to protect liberty than an aristocratic republic.

Of course, Machiavelli had to explain the success of Venice, the aristocratic republic par excellence, which not only defended its liberty much longer than Rome but enjoyed an enviable degree of domestic peace. Venice, said Machiavelli, owes its long-standing liberty to its geographic setting, which makes it difficult to attack. As for the idea, commonly held at the time, that Venice was preferable to ancient Rome because it had always been tranquil whereas Rome had been riven by struggles between plebeians and nobles, he met it with one of those decisive phrases he often used to demolish deeply held beliefs: "The disunion of the Plebs and the

Roman Senate" was precisely what made Rome's republic "free and powerful"; indeed, the longsighted way in which crises were generally solved was the "first cause of keeping Rome free" (*D*, I, 4).

Even when commenting on ancient history and making general observations, Machiavelli inevitably turned his thoughts to the history of Florence and the political errors that led to the demise of its republican government. In chapters devoted to the question of expansion, for instance, he noted how throughout history republics have enlarged their territories: by forming federations of several cities with equal authority, as the Etruscans did in ancient times and the Swiss in modern times; by establishing alliances in which one republic kept the central power and exercised authority over others, as was the case with ancient Rome; or by straightforward conquest and domination of subject peoples, as with Athens and Sparta in antiquity and Florence in modern times. Of these three means of expansion, Machiavelli observed, the best is the Roman way, the worst is that used by Athens, Sparta, and Florence, because to rule a city through violence, especially one accustomed to living in liberty, "is a difficult and exhausting undertaking." The Florentine policy must be abandoned entirely. If it was too difficult to imitate the Romans, then Florence must follow the ancient Etruscans and form federations and establish alliances with other Tuscan cities.

The problem that concerned Machiavelli most was political corruption. A people that lives under the rule of a prince for many years becomes accustomed to serving and seeking favors and forgets how to deliberate public matters. Not only that, but a free republican government established in a corrupt state must struggle against hostile factions without the support of the people, at least at first. Those who benefited from the tyranny or enriched themselves from the wealth of the prince will immediately become mortal enemies of the republic. Yet a free government cannot offer favors, because its fundamental rule must be to give public honors and recognition only for "honest and specific" reasons and, aside from those instances, honor or enrich no one. Nor can a free government rely much on the love of newly reconquered liberty, because citizens will not readily appreciate the "common benefit derived from a free government"—being able "freely to enjoy one's possessions without worry," not fearing for the honor of one's women and children, not living in fear. Liberty is like health: when we have it we fail to appreciate it, and only when it's gone do we regret its loss.

To preserve or found or restore a republic in a corrupt city, one must rely not on constitutional laws and regulations but on the virtue of a redeemer or founder who can give new power to those laws and regulations. That is why it is necessary, Machiavelli explained, for a republic being founded or refounded to be closer to "monarchical" than to "popular" government, so that "the men who cannot be corrected by the laws because of their insolence should be checked in some mode by an almost kingly power" (D, I, 18).

These and countless other treasures of political wisdom were Machiavelli's gifts to his young friends from the Orti Oricellari. After his death, the Discourses became an intellectual and political guide for all those who embraced the ideals of republican liberty and sought, in Florence and other places in Europe and the Americas, to replace the rule of princes and kings with free republics. But while he lived, Machiavelli received little or no recognition for the Discourses. He must have been used to this sort of treatment, yet it still hurt, for he cared deeply about being respected and appreciated. (We see this from a letter he wrote on 17 December 1517 to Luigi Alamanni, one of the Orti Oricellari regulars to whom he must have felt close, since he confided that he was hurt to read that Ludovico Ariosto, in Orlando Furioso, had not mentioned him in his list of poets.)

He took consolation, with his few remaining friends in Florence, poor unfortunates like him, "dying of cold and lack of sleep," in dreaming of traveling to Flanders. They talked about it so often and so much, and dreamed of it so fervently, he wrote in the same letter, that "we think we are already on the road" and have already devoured half the pleasures of the journey. It was lucky he had at least his imagination, which allowed him to travel to distant countries and faraway lands, protecting him to some extent from disappointments, boredom, and the winter chill!

If his imagination was a comfort, so was his "gang," or family. He kept an eye on his sons Bernardo and Lodovico, "growing up to be men," and tried to educate them. On 5 January 1518, Machiavelli wrote to Giovanni Vernacci explaining that Bernardo and Lodovico were sending him a little letter they had written themselves, asking him for "some fables or others." With his love of stories, it is likely that if those fables from the Levant ever arrived, Machiavelli read them aloud to his children himself. He was also doing everything he could to help Vernacci, first advising him to take a wife, and then doing his best to assist him when Giovanni's business ventures collapsed. Even though he had no business of his own, he must have become something of a bankruptcy expert by this point. In fact, in late March and early April 1518, he had gone to Genoa to defend the interests of some Florentine merchants who had been caught up in the bankruptcy of one Davide Lomellini.

Even if he was neither an accountant nor a lawyer, he was an expert negotiator. And he must not have been entirely ignorant of legal matters, since his father had been a lawyer, he wrote knowledgeably here and there about legal issues, and for his nephew he once wrote, or rewrote, a power of attorney "as it ought to be." Negotiating with merchants over bankruptcies was hardly a great satisfaction for him; but he accepted out of his constant yearning to mount his horse and ride, to have something to do, and maybe to make a little money.

Between business trips and holiday travels with friends, things began to look a little sunnier for Machiavelli. Fortune had finally tired of treating him harshly and had slowly set about improving his conditions. On 4 May 1519, Lorenzo de' Medici died. Lorenzo had ruled Florence more in the style of prince than citizen and had taken the title, beginning in June 1516, of duke of Urbino. But with his death, the Medici dynasty found itself without direct male heirs to govern Florence. Cardinal de' Medici came up from Rome to take the situation in hand. More human than his nephew Lorenzo, less foolish than Pope Leo X, he brought a breath of fresh air to Florence. Lorenzo Strozzi and others from the Orti Oricellari now asked him to intercede on behalf of the former secretary, and the meeting that Niccolò Machiavelli had been awaiting for eight long years finally took place in mid-March 1520: it soon yielded fruit.

Battista della Palla, another friend from the Orti, wrote to him from Rome on 26 April reporting that he had spoken extensively with the pope about Machiavelli's situation, that he had found him "very well disposed toward you," and that the pope had entrusted him to convey to Cardinal de' Medici that the time had come to do something good for Machiavelli. They are considering commissioning you to do some "writing or something else," he explained. The excellent Battista had persuaded the pope by lavishly praising Machiavelli, on his own behalf and on that of others from the Orti, and he skillfully tickled the pope's frivolous side by mentioning *The Mandrake*. That which Vettori had been unable to do was being accomplished by younger friends willing to take risks; the doors that had not been opened by *The Prince*, Machiavelli's most serious work, were opened by a comedy written out of a sheer sense of fun.

Before commissioning him to write, Cardinal de' Medici and the Signoria charged Machiavelli to oversee a bankruptcy case, that of Michele Guinigi, a merchant in Lucca who had lost everything by gambling, causing grave concern among Florentine merchants, who feared they would be unable to collect their debts. Actually, these merchants had entrusted Machiavelli with the mission, but the cardinal was behind them, writing directly to the Anziani Lucchesi, the Signoria's counterpart, as did the Signoria itself. Machiavelli set out for Lucca on 9 July 1520 to negotiate with its political authorities—that is, he would not be picking through accounting ledgers. The job was certainly better than nothing, though he enjoyed none of the honors that had accrued when he had traveled as secretary. We can see the change in his status in the Signoria's letters to the Anziani, which speak of "a citizen of our city, Niccolò Machiavelli" (*LC*, 1520). He is no longer noble or honored, only "a citizen of our city."

He had reached the twilight of his life and had learned to deal with the humiliation of doing tasks that offended both his intelligence and his self-esteem. He had knocked on the door for years and been left out in the cold; now they had opened the door a crack and were looking out at him with a half smile. To enter, however, he would have to bow and scrape, thank them politely. Being left out in the cold saddened him; being allowed in on those terms offended him. He had withstood sadness with his imagination, with thoughts of greatness, with his loves, with his comedies; now he would have to gird up his loins with patience and hope and try to make the best of the situation. He was not the sort of man to bear a grudge for affronts to his pride; he did not want to wallow in depression, the subtle punishment that afflicted so many in Florence.

To ennoble his time in Lucca, he studied the political institutions of its republic and put down the results of his observations, as he had been accustomed to do when he was secretary. The result, *Sommario delle cose della città di Lucca (Summary of the Civic Affairs of Lucca)*, contains some truly notable political thoughts. His reading and thinking during the years of forced idleness had clearly refined his views. One praiseworthy aspect of Lucca's institutions, he noted, is that its Signoria (the Anziani) and gonfalonier of justice, though central to the city government, have no direct authority over individual citizens, meaning they cannot make decisions concerning citizens' lives or property. This arrangement is good, Machiavelli explained, because those who hold the highest governing authority in a republic already have great power, and if they also had direct authority over the citizenry, they would have too much, with disastrous consequences for the city (O, 718–19).

Less laudable was that the Anziani had no majesty. Since one held office in that institution for only two months, and officeholders were then banned from reelection for two years, citizens with the highest reputation and prestige stayed away; as a result, the city's most important magistracy lacked majesty and wisdom, which instead one could find in abundance in the houses of private citizens. Lastly, the way in which the republic of Lucca distributed honors and offices was "good, civil, and well thought out," even if it differed from the model of classical Rome, which Machiavelli continued to prefer, whereby the greatest number (the people) distributed honors and offices, a middle number (the senate) gave advice, and the smallest number (the consuls) executed the laws.

In Lucca, Machiavelli received a letter from his son Bernardo, now seventeen, written in haste "by lantern light" with a malfunctioning pen. Bernardo told his father that bad weather had interfered with the harvest and that they could only barter for other wine the wine Machiavelli had told them to sell. The tone of this letter confirms my impression that Niccolò, either because he was goodhearted or because he was poor, or both, was not dictatorial with his children. Bernardo also added a few words from his mother: Marietta "reminds you to come back soon" and to bring something for her when you come. These were almost the same words Marietta had written him in her own hand nearly twenty years before, when Niccolò had been in Rome negotiating with the pope. Despite his affairs and his love for other women, he still knew how to win Marietta's love.

He also received a letter from Filippo de' Nerli, one of his "noontime friends" from the Orti Oricellari. Nerli informed him, among other things, that Zanobi Buondelmonti had had a son and commented on this happy event in words of profound political significance: the more sons we have, Nerli observed, the more soldiers we shall have to defend against the Turks. You care little about the Turks, but you are mistaken; you should warn the people of Lucca and exhort them to "make sure and screw a great deal, to make infantry," which will be more useful to them than moats and big towers.

Niccolò surely must have been tempted to convey Filippo's noble exhortation to the people of Lucca, but he did not fear a Turkish invasion. We know this from *The Mandrake,* written before Filippo's letter and when fear of the Turks had reached a fever pitch. Note this dialogue between a woman of the people and Brother Timoteo:

WOMAN: Take this florin, then, and you're to say the requiem mass every Monday for two months for the soul of my late husband. Even though he was a terrible man, still, flesh is flesh; I can't help feeling that whenever I remember him. But do you think he is really in Purgatory?

TIMOTEO: Absolutely!

WOMAN: I just don't know about that. You remember what he used to do to me sometimes. Oh, how I complained to you about it! I tried to stay away from him as much as I could, but he was so insistent! Ugh! Good Lord!

TIMOTEO: Don't worry, God's mercy is great. If a man doesn't lack the will, he never lacks time to repent.

WOMAN: Do you think the Turks will penetrate into Italy this year?

TIMOTEO: They will if you don't offer prayers.

WOMAN: Heavens! God help us, with those devilish brutes! I'm so terrified of that impalement business . . .

If Machiavelli wrote dialogue in this tone, we can imagine what he said to his friends about the Turkish incursions. Filippo's letter shows every sign of being responsive to who knows what obscene cracks that Niccolò spun out during afternoons spent in the Orti or on the *pancacce,* the stone benches of Florence.

His friends were beneficiaries of still other products of Machiavelli's creativity and imagination. Zanobi Buondelmonti and Luigi Alamanni received from Lucca *Vita di Castruccio Castracani,* or *Life of Castruccio Castracani,* about a Lucca-born condottiere (1218–1328). More than a history or biography, this was a keenly imagined portrait of a man who rose from lowly birth through his qualities and skills to achieve "very great things" and become a prince. Machiavelli's Castracani was exemplary, then, and to be emulated. Not surprisingly, Machiavelli fictionalized aspects of the condottiere's life: to enhance his humble birth, he had the infant discovered by the sister of a priest "under a vine among the foliage"; Castracani on his deathbed delivers a speech that smacks of Machiavelli's ideas on how to preserve states; and a long list of memorable sayings are attributed to him even though they were taken from the works of Diogenes Laertius.

Machiavelli wrote this essay in part to show his friends—who were encouraging Cardinal de' Medici to commission him to write a history—that he had mastered the rhetorical style of humanist historiography. In this respect, the *Life of Castruccio Castracani* was a success. Buondelmonti, in fact, on 6 September—addressing him as "my very honored *compare* Niccolò Machiavelli, Secretary" (!)— informed him that he, Luigi Alamanni, Francesco Guidetti, Iacopo da Diacceto, Anton Francesco degli Albizzi, Jacopo Nardi, Battista della Palla, and many others had read his work and everyone agreed it was "a good thing and well written." Note: "well written," as an oration should be, and not necessarily "accurate" or "true," as a work of historical scholarship should be. They had noticed, of course, that many of the sayings attributed to Castracani were taken from the mouths of "ancient and modern" sages. But that wasn't the point; the important thing was the quality of the "apothegms," the rhetorical clichés, and the "liveliness" and "grandeur" of the writing. The most successful part, he thought—and his judgment gets to the heart of *Life of Castruccio Castracani*—was Castracani's deathbed speech, the most exquisitely rhetorical section of the work.

The time had come to undertake a major historical work, and Machiavelli was encouraged by his friends' advice: "It seems to everyone that you ought to set yourself to writing this history with all diligence. I desire it above all others, . . . I feel that this model of a history of yours delights me." So he decided to return to Florence, because, among other reasons, Battista della Palla had just arrived from Rome and urgently needed to speak with him about plans for a new history of Florence to be funded by the Medici. When he mounted his horse to ride back to the city, Machiavelli may have felt more lighthearted. When he arrived, he found that everything was ready for the formal decision to hire him to write the history of Florence. He himself prepared the wording of the contract: "He is to be hired for _____ years at a salary of _____ per year with the condition that he must be, and is to be, held to write the annals or else the history of the things done by the state and city of Florence, from whatever time may seem to him most appropriate, and in whatever language—either Latin or Tuscan—may seem best to him" (*L,* 513).

The commission was approved on 8 November 1520, and the payment was set at one hundred small florins, little more than half of his old salary as secretary. Still, there was the honor of the thing. Historians of Florence before him had been great humanists, among them chancellors of the Republic: Leonardo Bruni, Poggio Bracciolini, and Bartolomeo Scala. So he was in good company, and the new post was much better than so many others he had held in the past.

nineteen

Stories of Monks, Hell, and Devils

Fortune often amuses herself by thrusting people into situations in which they never expected to find themselves. Some are bewildered and perplexed, and lose their spirits; others take offense and rail against the cruel whims of destiny; others rise to the challenge and respond to the playfulness of the blindfolded goddess with games of their own, and rather than falling into a funk or knitting their brows, they enjoy the new turn of affairs and even manage to laugh at fate. When this happens, days that might easily have been filled with boredom and misery become memorable.

Something of the sort happened to Niccolò in the spring of 1521, when he was sent to Carpi to a general meeting of the Franciscan brothers who had a large monastery there. Heightening the comic side of the adventure, Fortune gave him an exceptional straight man, the great, cold, and powerful Francesco Guicciardini, then governor of Modena. The result was one of the most remarkable episodes in Machiavelli's life, one that shows the character of the man better than many others.

But let us proceed in an orderly manner, without hastening to tell the tale of Niccolò's mission among the Franciscans, or, to use his phrase, in the Republic of Clogs. When he returned to Florence from Lucca, Niccolò had to tend to another important matter. Cardinal de' Medici asked him to draw up plans for a reformation of Florence's political institutions to be presented to Pope Leo X. Both pope and cardinal were concerned about the future of the Medici regime: not only was Lorenzo dead, but his princely ways had created a diffuse sense of discontent that seemed to foreshadow the end of his family's reign. There were those who advised the cardinal to restore a regime like that of Cosimo the Elder, who drew his power from a cunning policy of favors and a general respect of "civil ways"; others argued for reviving a "broad-based" republican government like that in which Soderini had served. Given such an array of opinions, the Medici wanted to hear the views of the former secretary whom they had just hired.

Naturally, Machiavelli accepted the new assignment with alacrity. As was his habit, he did not limit his suggestions to details but presented a plan for a transition based on a sweeping analysis of Florentine history and society. In *Discourse on Florentine Affairs after the Death of Lorenzo,* he showed first that it was not possible to return to Cosimo's methods because in his day the Medici had been loved by the populace, whereas now they were hated; then Florence had been capable of defending itself against any other state in Italy, now it could not do so, with France and Spain involved in Italian affairs; then the citizens paid their taxes without protest, now they had lost this habit, and to attempt to force them to return to the old method "would be dangerous and would arouse their hatred." Lastly, the Medici in Cosimo's day had behaved "with so much familiarity" that the citizens gladly accepted them; now they had "grown so grand" that they had "lost all sense of their common citizenship" and could not comport themselves in the manner that the Florentines had loved.

If it was unlikely that Cosimo's regime could be restored, it was out of the question to consider establishing a full-fledged principality in Florence. A principality can be established and thrive only when there is also an aristocracy with castles and armed men to shield the prince from the populace and to help him to govern the state. In Florence, there was nothing of the sort, and therefore founding a principality would be "difficult, inhuman, and unworthy for anyone who wants to be thought good and merciful" (O, 736–38).

The only remaining possibility was to return to a republican form of government, because the intermediate forms between principality and republic—"middle states," Machiavelli called them—are all highly unstable. Not a republic like that under Soderini, but a republic that would ensure all three classes of citizen—"upper, middle, and lower"—adequate representation in public institutions. One had to have the courage, Machiavelli explained, to make far-reaching changes if necessary. He implored the cardinal not to judge his proposal before reading it in its entirety and asked him not to be alarmed; he then set forth a complex reform plan for a transition to a "well-ordered republic" that would at the same time safeguard the Medici's power and their protégés' privileges, at least for the lifetime of Pope Leo and Cardinal de' Medici.

The hardest thing would be to persuade the Medici to undertake a political transition leading—albeit with countless precautions—to a return of the detested republican government that eight years before they had snuffed out with the help of foreign armies. To win them over, Machiavelli availed himself of all the rhetorical arms at his disposal. He tried to make them understand that in Florence "no stable republic was ever set up that did not satisfy the people" and that for the people to be satisfied, the hall of the Great Council had to be reopened. He added that the Medici would show great wisdom if they did this voluntarily, in ways and forms that would protect their self-interest, rather than being forced to it by their enemies (O, 741).

As in The Prince, Machiavelli imagined he was writing for a

prince who wanted to achieve great things and eternal glory and who was therefore willing to hearken to his words. As in the exhortation that concludes the *Discourses,* here we can clearly sense his admiration for the great statesmen who gave the rule of law to republics and kingdoms and for the great philosophers who also did so, if only in writing:

> I believe the greatest honor men can receive is one that is given voluntarily by their country. And I believe the greatest good one can do, and the most acceptable to God, is the good one does for one's country. Apart from this, no man is as ennobled in any of his actions as those who with laws and institutions have reformed republics and kingdoms. After those who have become gods, they are the first to be praised. Because only a few have had the opportunity to do this, and very few the ability, only a very small number have actually achieved it. This achievement has been much admired by men who were never interested in anything but glory and, if they could not create a republic in fact, created one in writing: like Aristotle, Plato, and many others, who wanted to show the world that while they could not found a society like Solon or Lycurgus, it was not because of ignorance but because they were powerless to bring it into being. (*O,* 744)

The problem was that Cardinal de' Medici had no interest in glory, only in saving the Medici regime with the smallest possible changes. To him, Machiavelli's words seemed too elevated and his suggestions for reform too peculiar and distant from the Medici style of politics. Once again, then, Machiavelli's attempt to educate, or perhaps I should say to shape, a great prince had come to nothing. Yet his essay contains some real gems of political thought—such as the idea that a republic can be stable only if its constitution assigns a proper role to each component of the society and "everyone has a hand in it, when everyone knows what he must do"

(*O*, 745). Like so many of Machiavelli's ideas, these would have to await better times, better conditions, and, above all, better politicians before they could be understood and bear fruit.

As a consolation, Machiavelli had the history of Florence to write, and he set to work happily on it in the winter of 1520–1521. A distraction came in the spring when a letter arrived from Pier Soderini, his old political mentor, who offered him a chance to become an adviser to the very influential nobleman Prospero Colonna in Rome, at the fabulous salary of two hundred gold ducats, plus expenses. This was unquestionably a tempting offer, yet Machiavelli turned it down. He had never wished to serve as the adviser to just any prince, merely for love of power and money, especially if it meant he would have to live at a court. His greatest hope was to achieve something important for Florence and to be honored for that achievement, to be remembered by the Florentines, and if possible to earn a little money so that he could buy what he wished, live decently, and assure a future free from want for his sons and daughters. His sentence "I believe the greatest honor men can receive is one that is given voluntarily by their country" was rhetorical, but it mirrored his own profound beliefs. He ignored the gold ducats and chose to stay in Florence.

As Machiavelli sat leafing through his papers, he was asked by the Eight of the Pratica, the council that oversaw Florence's foreign affairs, to go on a mission to Carpi, where the general assembly of the Franciscans had its headquarters, to negotiate matters of jurisdiction with the monks regarding their monasteries in Florentine territory. At first this seemed a joke, and a clever one. But it was deadly serious—not only a decision of the Republic's magistrates but a suggestion that came from Cardinal de' Medici himself, with the benediction of Pope Leo. Niccolò, who responded to the jokes that life played on him with even better jokes of his own, accepted the mission, mounted his horse, and set off on 11 or 12 May 1521. Along the way, he stopped at Modena to make the acquaintance of Francesco Guicciardini, who was governing its territories on behalf of the pope. Although the two had met before, they had not yet had a chance to spend much time together. They were as different as could be in social origin, temperament, and lifestyle. Guicciardini belonged to one of the noblest and wealthiest families in Florence; he was a master of calculation, caution, and reserve in word and deed; he was so skilled at masking his true feelings that various popes had awarded him posts of great prestige even though he scorned and utterly despised all priests; he was exceedingly ambitious and greedy for money and power; he had never known failure. Niccolò was a commoner and a misfit; he was fanciful, reckless, free with his opinions and, even more, in his way of life; he liked money, but only to amuse himself and enjoy life; he loved power, but as a tool with which to achieve great things, not as an end in itself; he had experienced a few moments of glory but for the most part had suffered only defeat and disappointment.

Yet Niccolò felt no envy toward this man—who was fourteen years younger than he and enjoyed so many things he had never had and would never have. Instead, he admired Guicciardini's political skills and uncommon intelligence. Guicciardini, in turn, admired Machiavelli and was captivated by his remarkable ability to analyze political matters and even rather warmed by his humanity; for once, Guicciardini indulged in jesting and laughter. His smile was one of measured amusement about matters that distracted him only briefly from the great public affairs that preoccupied him; here, too, he was unlike Niccolò, whose laugh was hearty and for whom public affairs had largely turned out to exist only in his imagination and in ancient history.

Machiavelli reached Carpi on 16 May, before vespers, as he had been ordered to do by a certain Friar Ilarione, who wanted to establish immediate control over the situation. He took lodging at the home of Sigismondo Santi, chancellor to Bishop Teodoro Pio, the city's governor. He found a letter waiting for him from the consuls of Florence's Wool Guild, entrusting him with a task even more bizarre than the one with which the Eight had charged him:

now he was asked to persuade one Friar Giovanni Gualberto, called Rovaio, to preach in the cathedral of Santa Maria del Fiore during the next Lent. Was it possible that the Wool Guild consuls did not know how Machiavelli felt about friars? In *The Mandrake,* he had ridiculed them mercilessly for their malice, their lust, and their greed. He never listened to sermons, he never paid heed to preachers, and he said so openly: "I myself did not hear the sermon, for I do not observe such practices," he had written to Vettori on 19 December 1513. When he had gone to hear the great Savonarola—and he had gone for purely political reasons—he had tucked himself away in a corner of the church and had laughed at the friar's many falsehoods.

He had laughed even more at the devil and Hell. In a poem of uncertain date, "Canto di Romiti," he wrote that a man who actually sees the devil "sees him with fewer horns and not so black." In a charming tale in which a demon takes a wife, probably written in these same years, it amused him to present Pluto, god of the underworld, as an excellent prince, prudent and fair. Just read this handsome speech that he attributes to the prince of darkness:

> My dear friends, even though I possess this kingdom by Heaven's decrees and by decision of Fate, entirely beyond repeal, and though I cannot be under obligation to any judgment, either heavenly or earthly, yet, since it is the highest prudence for those who are most powerful to be most subject to the law and most to esteem the judgment of others, I have determined, in a matter that may result in some shame to our empire, to obtain your advice on how I ought to conduct myself. Because, since the souls of all the men who come to our kingdom say that their wives are to blame and this seems to us impossible, we fear that if we pronounce judgment in accord with this tale, we shall be slandered as too credulous, and if we do not pronounce it, as not severe enough and hardly lovers of justice. (*SL*, 235–36)

Who would not live willingly under the rule of such a prince?

Machiavelli's irony on the subject of Hell was unbridled. Suffice it to mention the words of Callimaco in *The Mandrake*: "But then on the other hand, the worst that can happen to you is to die and go off to Hell. How many others have died! And how many excellent men have gone to Hell! Why should you be ashamed to go there too?" And when he spoke seriously of Christianity, his good-natured irony turned to scorn. The Christian religion, at least in its current interpretation, teaches men to be humble, to scorn earthly glory, and asks that "you . . . be capable more of suffering than of doing something strong." For that reason, it is responsible for having made the "world weak" and, therefore, easy prey for evil men (*D*, II, 2).

He recognized that men like Saint Francis and Saint Dominic had revived the original message of Christianity with their exemplary charity and their lives of poverty. But, he wrote, their efforts actually gave priests a greater license for corruption, for they persuaded multitudes of the faithful that "it was evil to say evil of evil," that it was good to "live under obedience" to the Church, and that if priests did wrong they should be left "for God to punish." And so, the results of the saints' authentic faith and preaching were that the clergy "do the worst they can because they do not fear the punishment that they do not see and do not believe" (*D*, III, 1).

Concerning the papacy he was merciless. Thanks to the examples set by the pope and the court of Rome, Italy has lost all real devotion and any authentic religious feeling: "Thus we Italians owe it first to the church and its priests that we have become without religion and wicked." The Church's second gift was that it had kept Italy from being united under the rule of a prince or a republic, and therefore from being independent and secure (*D*, I, 12).

He did recognize that the fear of God had beneficial effects on the way people lived and could be a powerful tool to support the law and authority of a prince or a republic. He even went so far as to say that observance of divine worship was one source of a republic's greatness, just as scorn for divine worship could lead to a republic's ruin, because where there is no fear of God it is necessary "either that the kingdom comes to ruin or that it is sustained by the fear of a prince, which supplies the defects of religion" (*D*, I, 10). But his god was a political god, a friend to princes who achieved great things (such as Castracani), or perhaps one should say a rhetorical god that he used to exhort princes to achieve great things. His god had very little in common with the Christian God, being neither a principle of faith nor a source of hope.

Such were the religious opinions of the man who was now in Carpi to negotiate about monasteries and preachers. The situation was so comical that not even the austere Guicciardini could resist being amused, and a brief letter he wrote to Niccolò gives us a lovely picture. My dearest Machiavelli, wrote Guicciardini, the Wool Guild consuls showed truly excellent judgment in giving you the task of finding a preacher; it is as if someone had entrusted Pacchierotto or Sano (two notorious homosexuals) with the task of "finding a beautiful and graceful wife for a friend." I am sure, he added mischievously, that you will prove yourself worthy of the trust the consuls have placed in you.

Even more mischievous was the spiritual advice that the sage Guicciardini imparted to his friend. Beware, he wrote, lest you fall into the temptation among so many monks to become a devout believer, because, since you have always lived in the opposite of devotion, people might well attribute it to "senility," not to goodness. Then he warned him of two serious perils: first, that the "holy friars" might infect him with the disease of hypocrisy; second, that the air of Carpi "might make you become a liar" because, he assured him as a connoisseur of the local towns, it has been well known for centuries that the air there has this effect. Moreover, if you should be given lodging in the home of a Carpi native, "your case would be without remedy."

A letter of this sort offered Niccolò the kind of opportunity he loved best. He replied on the same day, with the letter delivered by

a messenger on horseback. He was at the top of his form, irreverent and playful: "I was sitting on the toilet when your messenger
arrived, and just at that moment I was mulling over the absurdities
of this world." Because the world is absurd, one must respond with
even greater absurdities; he was a master of this art and would certainly have deployed it even without Guicciardini's encourage-
ment; in the august setting of Carpi, perfectly suited to this sort of
thinking, he was already dreaming up a good piece of fun. Once
he had read Guicciardini's letter, there was no stopping him.

First of all, he replied with aplomb to his friend's taunt at just
how he would serve the Republic: "And because never did I dis-
appoint that republic whenever I was able to help her out—if not
with deeds, then with words; if not with words, then with signs—
I have no intention of disappointing her now." Does Florence want
a preacher? It shall have one; but I shall seek out a friar who com-
bines all the shortcomings of the most renowned preachers ever to
work there: craftier than Domenico da Ponzo, more cunning than
Girolamo Savonarola, more hypocritical than Alberto da Orvieto.

Behind this noble intent was a more profound theological and
moral motivation: "I think it would be a fine thing—something
worthy of the goodness of these times—should everything we
have experienced with so many friars be experienced by just one
of them. For I believe that the following is the true way to paradise: learn the way to Hell in order to steer clear of it." Indeed, this
would be in keeping with the times: the Republic had sent him, in
violation of all reason and logic, to find a preacher, and he—who
truly wished to serve the Republic as it deserved—would find a
preacher quite unlike what it wanted. Was their instruction contrary to all reason and logic? He would repay them in the same
coin: they wanted a preacher "who would teach them the way to
paradise," and Niccolò planned to find one "who would teach
them the way to go to the devil."

"As for the lies of these citizens of Carpi," I am a far greater
liar than any of them could hope to be, Machiavelli wrote,
because "for some time now I have never said what I believe or

never believed what I said; and if I do sometimes tell the truth, I hide it behind so many lies that it is hard to find." He had already paid enough for having said the things he thought—out of bold-ness, not naïveté. And after all, what was the sense of telling the truth in a world where the meanings of words were inevitably twisted? Feigning and dissembling were now his most powerful weapons; he used them without shame but also without pride. He had often told the truth, and he would continue to tell the truth—not to monks or the people of Carpi, but to us, in his books and letters. For once, the passage of time has done us a good turn, because it has allowed us to know truths that Niccolò hid from his contemporaries amid his many deceptions and eva-sions.

Niccolò planned a masterful prank at the expense of the monks and notables of Carpi, foremost among them the chancellor Sigis-mondo Santi and Bishop Pio. His plan was to pit the monks against each other, "either here or somewhere else—[so that] they might start going after one another with their wooden clogs"; with this noble goal, he called on Guicciardini to help him with "some mas-ter stroke."

He had noticed that everyone in Carpi had been very impressed that the governor of Modena had sent him a letter by the hand of a mounted crossbowman, who had presented it with a bow "down to the ground." Niccolò took care of the rest by telling onlookers, gravely, that the letter contained priceless political information about the emperor, the Swiss, and the king of France.

The result was even better than he could have hoped for: Everyone, Niccolò wrote, "stood around with their mouths hang-ing open and with their caps in hand." Even as I write, "I have a circle of them about me; to see me write at length, they marvel" and watch me with wide-eyed astonishment. I, in turn, make them think I am writing things of enormous importance; I stop writing every now and again and puff up my chest by taking a deep breath; they drool with curiosity and admiration.

Niccolò had a plan: Send me another crossbowman tomorrow,

he wrote to Guicciardini, "let him gallop and get here covered in sweat," which will arouse general amazement. In this way, I shall acquire a reputation, and your crossbowmen and horses will get some exercise, which can only do them good, especially in spring-time. If Fortune and his fellow men were mocking him with this mission, Niccolò would respond tit for tat: it was the best retort to Guicciardini's taunts about the danger of senility.

Guicciardini was willing to play along with the game: the next day, 18 May, another crossbowman arrived from Modena, even more out of breath than the first; he told everyone who would lis-ten that Machiavelli was a very important individual whose busi-ness was much more serious than quarrels among friars. With a masterful touch, Guicciardini added to the bundle of letters, to give it more bulk, messages from Zurich, which Niccolò could brandish ostentatiously or hold secretively, whichever was more effective. He told Machiavelli he had written to the chancellor Santi to tell him that his guest was a "very exceptional person." When Santi, his suspicions aroused, "answered me, begging me to inform him in what your exceptionalness consisted," Guicciardini gave no answer, to stimulate his curiosity and induce him to scru-tinize Niccolò's every move. The letter ended with a moving exhortation to continue the task of sowing trouble among the monks: if you succeed, "it would be the most outstanding deed you ever accomplished," and it should not be difficult, given "their ambition and ill will."

Niccolò's situation among the monks seemed so absurd to Guicciardini that he returned to it again on the same day. Taking pen in hand, he drew a comparison that may have consoled Nic-colò but must have grieved him, too, because in the end it por-trayed his sad state and held up an unwelcome mirror: "My very dear Machiavelli, when I read your titles as ambassador of the Republic and of friars, and I consider how many kings, dukes, and princes you have negotiated with in the past, I am reminded of Lysander, to whom, after so many victories and trophies, was given the task of distributing meat to those very same soldiers whom he had so gloriously commanded . . ." (*L*, 524).

This comparison suggested to Guicciardini, subtle observer of the world that he was, a more general observation on the usefulness of history in understanding life and especially politics: "You see that, with only the faces of the men and the extrinsic colors changed, all the very same things return; and we do not see any incident that has not been seen in other times." Machiavelli was of the same opinion. He had written, in fact, in the *Discourses*: "Prudent men are accustomed to say, and not by chance or without merit, that whoever wishes to see what has to be considers what has been; for all worldly things in every time have their own counterpart in ancient times. That arises because these are the work of men, who have and always had the same passions, and they must of necessity result in the same effect" (*D*, III, 43).

All the same, Guicciardini added an important warning, fruit of his vast political experience: Since the names and appearances of things often change, even if a resemblance to past events remains, only the wisest men can recognize that what is taking place in front of their eyes once happened in the past as well. Therefore, great care must be taken in proposing solutions to present-day issues based on similarities with past situations and solutions, as Niccolò so often did, with his continuous exhortation to follow the example of the ancient Romans.

That Guicciardini wished to emphasize the difference between his own way of thinking about politics, which focused on concrete aspects and details, and Machiavelli's approach, which tended to develop models and proceed by general comparisons, can be seen in the next part of the letter. Guicciardini told his friend to take consolation from the thought that he could benefit from this absurd mission, if for no other reason than that in learning about the kind of state composed of and run by monks (the Republic of Clogs), he could make interesting comparisons with other abstract models of republic and principality; this interested Guicciardini little if at all, but Machiavelli had discussed it in depth in *The Prince* and the *Discourses*.

To sweeten his words, Guicciardini promised that the next messenger would bring not only the usual "exceedingly important" dispatches but also a lovely pie, to add flavor to their pranks with the Carpi monks. All the same, he worried that the crafty chancellor Santi, a "nasty" man, might discover their machinations and take revenge. It is up to you to keep him in suspense, he warned, and as long as you succeed, you can cadge rich meals.

Luckily for Niccolò, the trick continued to work. The arrival of another crossbowman with a bundle of letters made a tremendous impression on Sigismondo and all the neighbors, wrote Niccolò promptly. But he, too, was beginning to fear Sigismondo's suspicions. He had noticed that the Carpian was reserved and seemed to be wondering what could possibly prompt such lengthy dispatches in this "Arabian desert" where there were only monks. And he must have doubted that Machiavelli was truly an important man, since Niccolò did nothing but sleep, read, and relax in his house. Fortunately, the abundant meals continued to be served on time, and "I gobble up enough for six dogs and three wolves." Yet even as he enjoyed these memorable meals and giving tit for tat to the life that had played such evil tricks on him, he began to feel a slight twinge of remorse for the unlucky—though evil—Sigismondo, and he confessed to his accomplice that he felt rather grateful to his host: if Santi should ever come to Florence, "I shall make it up to him." Luckily, Santi never did come to Florence, or who can say how many dinners Machiavelli would have had to offer him.

Of course, Niccolò still had to resolve the apportioning of the monasteries and the matter of a preacher for Florence. On neither issue was much progress being made. That "traitor Rovaio," as Machiavelli called him, was acting coy, claiming he was reluctant to come to Florence because he didn't know what to preach there, was afraid of being thrown into prison and equally afraid he might not be taken seriously. The last time I went to Florence, Rovaio explained to Machiavelli, I had a law passed that obliged whores to wear yellow veils when they walked down the street. But now, he said in a voice breaking with indignation, I learn from my sister that the whores ignore my law entirely, that they walk the streets "as they please" and wiggle their tails more than ever!

One may imagine the expression on Machiavelli's face as he listened to this foolishness, he who was so respectful and fond of whores and courtesans. It must have been hard for him not to laugh or, worse, answer the priest with one of those lewd jokes for which he was renowned in Florence. Instead, he managed to placate the indignant monk with a masterpiece of dissembling: "I kept on confronting him by pointing out that he ought not to be surprised at this news because it was customary for great cities not to stand by a decision for any great length of time and to do one thing today and to undo it tomorrow; I brought up Rome and Athens." At these cunning words, the monk calmed down and almost promised to come to Florence. Only Machiavelli could have pulled this off.

Still, his and Guicciardini's fears were well founded. When the crossbowman arrived bearing the lovely pie, the diabolical Santi clearly showed he had tumbled to their game. Niccolò lost no time in telling Guicciardini: "Holy dick! We are going to have to go carefully with this fellow," for he is as crafty as thirty thousand devils. When the messenger came, Santi had exclaimed, "Look here, there must be something big going on; the messengers are coming thick and fast," and Machiavelli had told him he had left some dealings up in the air in Florence that concerned Guicciardini. Still, he worried that Santi might soon "take a broom and pack me off to the inn." It would be best to return to Florence before it was too late, even if he had not yet solved the question of apportioning the monasteries (though he had spoken with each of the monks, one by one, using all his negotiating skills) or the matter of the preacher.

Hardly the end of the world. In the meantime, he had enjoyed three days of "solid meals, splendid beds, and the like," which had allowed him to recover his strength. He had benefited physically, and he had also learned and observed. During this visit to the Republic of Clogs, he told Guicciardini with his distinctive irony in his last letter from Carpi, "I have found out about many of their regulations and their organizational arrangements, which have good things in them, and so at some point I think I may make use of them—especially in comparisons, because whenever I have to discuss silence, I shall be able to say, 'They are quieter than friars eating' " (L, 529).

The next day, 19 May, or at the very latest 20 May, taking advantage of Friar Ilarione's request that he return to Florence to deliver in person, posthaste, letters to the Eight of the Pratica, he leaped into the saddle and bade farewell to the Republic of Clogs. Friar Ilarione had enjoined him to do all he could to be in Florence before 22 May. But when he reached Modena, he thumbed his nose at the supposed urgency, claiming he was "indisposed" and could not ride quickly, and spent some time with Guicciardini. With his smile and his skill at adapting to even the most absurd situations, Machiavelli had for once outfoxed Fortune.

TWENTY

Niccolò's Last Loves

Niccolò's life was coming to an end. One clear sign that the conclusion was drawing near, clearer than the inexorable passage of the years, was the progressive waning of the chief passions that had animated him—his love of women and his desire to achieve great things for Florence and for Italy. Time, which often saps one's strength without dousing one's desire, made him set aside the former; the malevolence and mean-spiritedness of those who were unwilling to use or even consider his understanding of political matters kept him from developing the latter. His life was ending, like so many other lives, under the sign of bitterness and sadness— "Niccolò Machiavelli, Historian, Comic Author and Tragic Author," as he signed a letter in October 1525. He had certainly written histories and comedies but never a tragedy: the tragedy to which he referred was his own life, and he realized this only during the last act.

A few months after returning from his triumphant mission to Carpi, in August 1521 Niccolò had the satisfaction of seeing an important work he had written, *On the Art of War (Dell'arte della guerra)*, printed by the Florentine publisher Filippo di Giunta. He had written it, he explained in the preface, to keep from wallowing in the idleness to which circumstances confined him. This seems plausible; if there was anyone Machiavelli despised, it was the lazy and the idle, people who waste their lives doing nothing useful or important. "Infamous and detestable," he had written in a splendid page of the *Discourses,* are those men "who are . . . enemies of the virtues, of letters, and of every other art that brings utility and honor to the human race, as are the impious, the violent, the ignorant, the worthless, the idle, the cowardly" (*D*, I, 10). He had also written the new tract for his friends from the Orti Oricellari, who, like him, were fascinated with antiquity and especially with the legendary military organization of classical Rome.

He dedicated the new book to Lorenzo di Filippo Strozzi, who had helped him during the darkest years with occasional gifts and had caused him to be introduced to Giulio Cardinal de' Medici. Whether it was because writing about war and the militia made him feel he was still a secretary or because his young friends from the Orti Oricellari still considered him as such, he presented himself to his readers as "Niccolò Machiavelli, Florentine secretary and citizen."

Moreover, the ideas he advanced were the same ones he had defended and tried to implement, at least in part, when he was secretary, beginning with the book's basic premise: that the practice of the art of war is both the capstone and the foundation of civil life. Without military support, the good customs of civil life are, in fact, "vain" and destined to perish, like the rooms of a "splendid and kingly palace" that, "though ornamented with gems and gold," has no roof to keep out the rain (*O*, 530).

Nine years had passed since August 1512, when the Spanish infantry had trampled and destroyed, without even fighting, the militia that Machiavelli had conceived and built. Countless times, friends and enemies must have reminded him of that shameful defeat, to his face and behind his back. Now he could answer them all, stating loudly and clearly that a single defeat did not prove that the idea of the militia had been wrong. The armies of the Romans and of Hannibal had been defeated, and yet no one questioned the worth of Rome's or Carthage's military organization. The Florentine militia had been defeated at Prato because it was neither well commanded nor well trained, but that did not mean the idea of entrusting the defense of the Republic to a militia composed of citizens and subjects of the countryside—rather than to mercenary soldiers and generals—was a bad one. The ordinance should be improved, then, not abolished, and Machiavelli explained how to improve it, down to the smallest details.

The Art of War also contained important political lessons. Machiavelli explained that no well-governed kingdom or republic had ever allowed its subjects or citizens to use war as their own art, which is to say, to become professional soldiers; that the proper end of the art of war was not war itself but defense; and that in order to defend a kingdom's subjects or a republic's citizenry, a ruler must "love peace and know how to wage war." He praised military virtues, first and foremost courage, strength, and discipline, but he never praised war, either as a proof of power or as a grand and terrible event. He knew, from direct experience, that war was an appalling, filthy eruption of cruelty, especially harsh on noncombatants and on the helpless; he knew that the worst kind of war was waged by bands of mercenary soldiers, who fought without laws, discipline, or honor; and above all he knew that wars could be stopped not by prayers, pleas, or money but only by well-trained militias.

As in the *Discourses*, Machiavelli sometimes allowed himself to be overwhelmed by the splendor of classical Rome in comparison with the misery of modern Italy. He failed to realize that the introduction of movable artillery was changing the way wars were fought, though, admittedly, this change was just beginning to take effect; he never stated that artillery was unimportant, only that the "backbone" of warfare was still the infantry. For that matter, he truly believed it was possible to regain the majesty of antiquity: here resides all the strength and yet the weakness (a weakness more of detail than of substance) of his political thought. Precisely what it was he wished to revive from classical politics is stated more clearly in *The Art of War* than in any other of his works: "To honor and reward excellence, not to despise poverty, to esteem the methods and regulations of military discipline, to oblige the citizens to love one another, to live without factions, to esteem private less than public good, and other like things that could easily fit in with our times." He believed it would be easy to persuade people that such a model was far superior to the current way of life and that anyone could understand that a republic organized according to ancient principles would be like a great tree, and no one could live "more prosperously and more happily than beneath this shade" (*O*, 536).

With his *Art of War*, Machiavelli wished to give to younger readers and future generations the knowledge he had gathered through study and experience. He felt old by now and knew he would have no more opportunities to implement the wisdom of a lifetime, which he had hoped to translate into new ways of life for states and peoples. Most of all, he wanted to save his treasure of wisdom from the oblivion of death. It was for this reason, rather than literary vanity, which was after all a venial sin, that he had put it down on paper. His bequest was shot through with resentment of nature, which, he thought, either "should have made me such that I could not see this or should have given me the possibility for putting it into effect." And he was inspired by the thought that in Italy the true art of war might actually be revived, because "this land seems born to raise up dead things, as she has in poetry, in painting, and in sculpture" (*O*, 689).

The work was praised widely, and by important men. Giovanni Cardinal Salviati wrote to him on 6 September 1521 to say he had been very impressed by the book because "to the most perfect manner of warfare in antiquity" Machiavelli had coupled "everything that is good in modern warfare, and compounded an invincible army." If it achieves nothing else, the cardinal commented, your book will at least show that in the Italy of our times there was someone who knew "what is the true way of waging war."

Within a few years, the cardinal would see with his own eyes the bitter consequences, for the Church and for Italy, of keeping those who understood military art from practicing it and of having those who practiced it fail to understand it. The cardinal's words certainly pleased Machiavelli, and he would have been even more pleased to know that his work was reprinted seven times during the sixteenth century alone and translated into many European languages. The acclaim and renown did nothing, however, to lessen his disappointment at having been kept from politics, stuck in Sant'Andrea in Percussina, surrounded by garden warblers and chickens.

While his reputation as an expert in military affairs increased, Machiavelli continued to work on the *Florentine Histories,* commissioned by Pope Leo X and Giulio Cardinal de' Medici. Not that the pope cared much about it—and in any case, he did not live to read the product of Machiavelli's efforts, for he died on 1 December 1521, leaving the cardinal as sole arbiter of the government of Florence. As before, Giulio de' Medici was worried by the lack of direct Medici heirs, and once again he thought about reforming the city's constitution and allowing the return of some form of republican rule. Again, he asked for the opinions of Florentine experts on statecraft, among them Machiavelli, who responded with *A Discourse on Remodeling the Government of Florence,* as if the reform had already been decided on and remained only to be implemented.

As he had said in *Discourse on Florentine Affairs,* written for Pope Leo X in 1520, the solution to Florence's political problems was a peaceful restoration of republican government that would preserve Cardinal de' Medici's power and assure Ippolito and Alessandro de'

Medici (illegitimate sons of, respectively, Giuliano and Lorenzo) of
their property and prestige. It would be a transition controlled by
the Medici, but nonetheless a transition to a republic. A republic
meant a Great Council; it meant "restoring the venerable hall"
where the Great Council met. Machiavelli said all this outright;
therefore, it is surprising that scholars ever assert that Machiavelli,
during the last years of his life, abandoned his republican ideals.

Nothing came of this imagined transition to a republic, so
much like the one that had been bandied about in Pope Leo X's
time; one discouraging factor was the discovery in 1522 of a conspiracy to assassinate Cardinal de' Medici on Corpus Christi Day
(19 June). The leading conspirators were two of Machiavelli's
friends, Zanobi Buondelmonti and the poet Luigi Alamanni di
Piero; among those implicated were others who had frequented
the meetings at the Orti Oricellari, where Machiavelli had spoken
of tyrannicide. Even though in the *Discourses,* the book most
closely linked to the Orti Oricellari circle, Machiavelli argued that
it was difficult and dangerous to undertake a conspiracy against a
prince, there was plenty of reason to believe he had been involved
in or at the least helped to instigate the plot. There was a real danger he would once again be put through the horrors of prison and
torture, and this time he would surely not emerge alive.

Fortunately, he was left in peace, as far as we know. Less fortunate were Luigi Alamanni di Tommaso and Iacopo da Diacceto.
They were interrogated under torture, they confessed, and on 6
June they were beheaded. Buondelmonti and Alamanni di Piero
managed to save their lives by fleeing. This marked the end of the
Orti Oricellari group. Machiavelli owed much to those young
men, and he was tied to them by bonds of deep respect, gratitude,
and fondness. In the most difficult years of his life, their attention
and their interest in political affairs and ancient Rome had
prompted him to write many of his finest works. For him, they
were generous souls who, with their qualities and high social
standing, might accomplish some of the great things of which he

could only dream. Once execution and banishment emptied the Orti Oricellari, Niccolò again found himself alone and disconsolate.

Even more painful, in early June 1522 he received a letter from Roberto Pucci, gonfalonier of justice, with the news that his brother, Totto, who had become a priest in January 1510, was at death's door. Totto was a good, kind man who had been close to his wild brother even at the worst times. Niccolò appreciated good men and knew how to feel gratitude, and he loved his brother. He gave what little money he could to the chaplain, Vincenzo, to continue to say Mass in Totto's parish church so that the peasants there might take comfort.

A few months later, in October, he drew up a brief memoir for Raffaello Girolami, who was going to Madrid as ambassador to the emperor Charles V in Spain. It is easy to imagine his emotions as he wrote words of advice to a young man who had been chosen for a mission that he might especially have wanted for his own. He distilled into those few pages the best of the diplomatic wisdom he had accumulated when he had had the honor of representing the Republic in the great courts of Europe. *Advice to Raffaello Girolami When He Went as Ambassador to the Emperor* is of special importance to our story, since it allows us to understand Machiavelli's ideas about the diplomat's work and how he remembered his own experiences, now more than a decade in the past. Since these pages are like a small autobiography, they deserve special attention.

Advice to Raffaello Girolami begins with words both sincere and melancholy praising citizens who serve as ambassadors: "To be an ambassador is one of those civic functions which bring honor to a citizen; he cannot be called fit for government who is not fit to hold this rank." To do the job well, Machiavelli explained, an ambassador must especially have a "reputation," showing with his behavior that he is an "able man," generous, a man of integrity, "not stingy and two-faced," and he must not be considered a man who "believes one thing and says another." Ambassadors who

behave with duplicity lose the trust of the princes in whose courts
they are received; they cannot then negotiate effectively.

An ambassador, of course, cannot always tell the truth. There
are times when "you need to conceal a fact with words." A good
ambassador must be capable of dissembling, and when found doing
so, he must have a rapid and ready explanation. But the true challenge lies in being well informed about "things decided and finished" and in understanding the "things being negotiated" and
"things to be done." While it is relatively easy to gather accurate
information about things decided and finished (except in the case
of secret agreements), it is very difficult to grasp the developments
of negotiations that are under way and to know princes' plans, for
the obvious reason that princes always try to dissemble and conceal
their true intentions.

To do this part of his job successfully, the experienced Machiavelli advised, an ambassador should use "judgment" and "infer-
ence"; that is, he should make accurate analyses and conjectures
based in fact. He should also be skilled at gathering information
from the many "busybodies" around courts. The best way to get
information is to give it, because "a man who wants others to tell
him what they know must tell them what he knows." A good
ambassador, then, can understand things on his own and then
expand his knowledge by exchanging it for information held by
others.

Lastly, Machiavelli admonished, an ambassador must know how
to present his opinions to his ruler so that they appear not as personal evaluations but as objective analyses of the political and military situation. The artifice to use toward this end—and here we
see the veteran diplomat's years of experience—is a formula such
as the following: "Considering, then, everything about which I
have written, prudent men here judge that the outcome will be
such and such" (O, 729–31).

Once he had delivered this precious advice to Girolami, Machiavelli immersed himself in the composition of the *Florentine Histories*. We see this in a letter written on 26 September 1523 to

Francesco del Nero requesting payment of a promised salary; in turn, wrote Niccolò, to pay you back for the "trouble I am causing you," I shall "give your regards to the chickens." He couldn't do better than that at Sant'Andrea in Percussina. One year later, in late August 1524, he was still hard at work on the *Florentine Histories;* to Guicciardini he wrote, after complaining that there were no more garden warblers that year, that he was still absorbed in his work and would gladly pay ten soldi to consult with his prudent friend on how to handle delicate episodes in Florence's history without, "in my exaggerating or understating the facts," offending living Florentines. He was striving "to arrange it so that—still telling the truth—no one will have anything to complain about," and he finally did find an ingenious stratagem. Because he could not openly say "in what manner and with what means" Cosimo de' Medici had amassed such great power in Florence, for example, since the Medici were paying him to write the book, he had Cosimo's adversaries say these things.

We owe this important piece of information about how Machiavelli wrote the *Florentine Histories* to Donato Giannotti, a lowborn young man, like Machiavelli, who was to distinguish himself in later years with a number of major political works, notably the dialogues *Della Repubblica Fiorentina* and *Della Repubblica de' Viniziani.* Giannotti was also secretary of the last Florentine Republic, crushed once again by foreign troops (in 1530). At the time Machiavelli confided to him this delicate secret about the composition of the *Florentine Histories,* he was a close friend.

The calm days of writing history were interrupted by surprising events. Machiavelli began to frequent the house of the wealthy Iacopo Falconetti, known as Fornaciaio, literally the Baker, who was confined for political reasons to a villa on one of his estates beyond the city gate called Porta San Frediano. Here he gave banquets and parties to which he invited men and women of the citizenry and nobility of Florence. Among the women was the young and lovely Barbara (also spelled Barbera) Salutati Raffacani, a singer and poet.

Niccolò met her in February 1524 and, without trying to defend himself or conceal his desire, was overwhelmed by her charms—so overwhelmed, in fact, that he offered an easy target for his friends' banter. Tell Machiavelli, Francesco Vettori wrote to Francesco del Nero, "I think it is much better to sup occasionally with Barbara at the expense of Fornaciaio than to be here standing by a door around supper time, which even after a long wait has still not opened" (R, 324). Far more biting were Filippo de' Nerli's words, also to Francesco del Nero, of 1 March 1525: since "Machia" is a relative of yours and a friend of mine, I have to tell you that here in Modena everyone is talking about him and about this "family man" falling head over heels in love with "someone whom I should prefer not to name" (L, 541). One year after meeting Barbara, then, "Machia" was securely bound by the chains of his new love.

He did not seem frightened or worried by the fact that Barbara was interested in the overtures of many men and offered her favors to others as well. Guicciardini pointed this out in a letter of August 1525: "You are used to your Barbara who strives, as does her kind, to please everyone and seeks rather to seem than to be." But Machiavelli knew all this; on 3 January 1526, in connection with a performance in Modena of *The Mandrake* (later canceled), he wrote to Guicciardini: "As for Barbara and the singers [to supply light songs and a chorus between acts], I believe I can bring her for fifteen soldi to the lira unless some other consideration holds you back. I mention this because she has certain lovers who might block the way; still, one might contrive to keep them quiet."

In any case, Niccolò was happy to fall in love with more than one woman if given the chance. The perceptive Guicciardini understood this: you "are a lover of all women," he wrote (L, 553). As passionately as Machiavelli felt about Barbara, he was not indifferent to the charms of one Maliscotta, whom he met in Faenza while on a mission to Guicciardini's court on behalf of the Florentine government in the summer of 1525. In fact, while preparing to go to Modena for the planned performance of *The Man-drake,* he asked Guicciardini to arrange lodging for Barbara (among the monks, which would drive them crazy: he could not resist playing a prank whenever he had dealings with monks) and at the same time asked him to give his fond regards to Maliscotta.

This is not to say that his feelings were superficial. He wrote about Barbara and Maliscotta in ways that indicate profound affection and attachment, reminiscent of what he had written years before about La Riccia. Indeed, he told Guicciardini that he had found in Barbara "such gentleness and mercy that she would season an entire city for you" (*L*, 552). To the extent he could, he tried to repay her kindness and courtesies with the occasional favor. When she went to Rome in the spring of 1526, Machiavelli wrote Guicciardini: "if you can do her any service, I commend her to you, for she gives me far more concern than does the emperor." Again to Guicciardini, on 3 August 1525, he wrote: I glory in being with Maliscotta "more than anything I have in this world."

At the age of fifty-six, neither wealthy nor powerful but still marked by the soul of a poet and with a capacity for passionate desires, Machiavelli esteemed a woman's love a precious gift that brought beauty and warmth to his life. He still knew how to make a woman love him. Maliscotta told Guicciardini she had appreciated Niccolò's "manners and conversation" during his time in Faenza, and Barbara went so far as to help him obtain the right—which he had never had—to be elected to public office. Moreover, in 1544, seventeen years after his death, she asked Lorenzo Ridolfi to extend protection to her in the name of the "love he bore to the memory of Niccolò Machiavelli," a sign that she gladly remembered, without regrets or recriminations, her affair with "Machia."

But his being fifty-six was a problem. He cared nothing about gossips like Filippo de' Nerli; all his life he had openly confessed his vices without fear, and he had always urged his friends who were concerned about their reputations to follow natural impulses—"it is better to act and repent than not to act and regret"—so he was unlikely to start worrying now about what people thought. Yet he

was deeply worried about being in love with a woman so much
younger than he. It was not like "Machia" to deny his feelings or
flee in the face of danger, so instead he responded in his own
way—laughing and making a comedy of the situation, with himself as the butt of the joke.

To please Fornaciaio and as a compliment to Barbara, he wrote
a new comedy to be performed at Fornaciaio's villa on 13 January
1525. He based it on a classical text, Plautus's *Casina,* adapting it
freely and entitling it *Clizia.* The main character is an "old man all
afire with love" for a young maiden; his name, coincidentally, is
Nicomaco. The whole comedy revolves around the way that this
man becomes ridiculous because of his passion: to see an old man
in love "is an exceedingly ugly thing," one of the characters says.
As if that were not enough, Machiavelli inserted a lovely but cruel
little song between the second and third acts; in all likelihood, it
was sung by Barbara herself:

> *How beautiful is love in youthful heart!*
> *And how incongruous*
> *In one who's long since passed life's flowering part.*
> *Love's power parallels declining years,*
> *And in our time of bloom evokes esteem,*
> *But with old age its honor disappears.*
> *And so, ye amorous old men, 'twould seem*
> *The better part of valor to leave wooing*
> *To ardent youths' pursuing,*
> *For they're a fitter butt for Cupid's dart. (SL, 197)*

Behind the laughter and jesting was a biting pain, for the real and
intense desire he felt for Barbara was not matched by his physical
vigor. This was the harsh sentence of time, and to complain about
it was pointless. He could blame no one but himself for not having
wished to resist—or succeeded in resisting—the attraction of such
a lovely woman. We already know how reluctant Niccolò was to

discuss his passions and especially his sorrows and how well he knew, as a character in *Clizia* says, "There are a lot of people who let you talk, as if they were sympathetic, and then snicker at you behind your back" (*SL,* 182). But this time he opened his heart, in verses that are a disconsolate farewell to his lifelong passion and fantasies. He wrote them for Barbara, but he was probably also thinking of other loves of the past:

> *If worthiness in me*
> *Were as immense as my desire,*
> *Pity, now still asleep, awake would be.*
> *But since desire and strength*
>
> *Do not go well together,*
> *Suffer I must the length*
> *Of all my woes, my lord.*
> *And you I do not blame—*
>
> *I blame myself for this:*
> *Great beauty finds its bliss—*
> *I see and I confess—*
> *In a much greener age.* (*SL,* 437)

In the meantime, Machiavelli completed the *Florentine Histories,* and in early March 1525 he was ready to present the work to Giulio Cardinal de' Medici, now Pope Clement VII, having been elected to the papal throne on 19 November 1523. Niccolò had worked hard, despite his old sorrows and the new passions of love. Indeed, it is perhaps more accurate to say that writing about history and statecraft softened his sorrows and gave him respite from the frenzy of love and that the harsher the sorrows and the more powerful the passions, the more beautiful and compelling his writing became.

All the same, he waited until the end of May before going to

Rome to present the *Florentine Histories.* Vettori advised him not to go in March; cautious as always, he pointed out that the times were not propitious for "reading and gifts." For once, Vettori was right. On 24 February, the armies of the emperor Charles V had defeated the troops of King François, with whom Pope Clement had established an alliance. That victory placed Italy at the mercy of the emperor, and the pope, thinking as always of his self-interest, tried to obtain a treaty that would safeguard the papal lands. But the emperor delayed in signing it, especially because of a clause that called for the transfer of Reggio from the duke of Ferrara to the pope. It was understandable, then, that the Curia should be occupied with other concerns than a new history of Florence.

At this juncture, Niccolò's life nearly took a glorious new change of direction. Worried by the emperor's hesitation, Pope Clement had decided to send a prestigious ambassador to Spain, Giovanni Cardinal Salviati, and seriously considered the idea (supported by Iacopo Salviati, Giovanni's father) of sending Machiavelli along; certainly no one was more qualified, in talent or experience, for the intricate task at hand. To go to the emperor's court with Cardinal Salviati! It would have rejuvenated Machiavelli by a good thirty years, and if the order had ever arrived in Sant'Andrea, we can only imagine the pages he would have written and how quickly he would have ridden off to Rome. Once again, however, Fortune turned her back on him at the last minute: "Niccolò Machiavelli," Iacopo Salviati wrote to his son on 24 May, "is no longer a candidate."

So when Machiavelli went to Rome, it was not in order to set off for Spain but to deliver his *Florentine Histories.* Still, his visit yielded 120 gold ducats, a gift the pope gave him out of his own purse. Most of the money went to the dowry of his daughter Bartolomea (known as Baccina); in time, she married Giovanni de' Ricci and gave birth to the Giuliano de' Ricci who lovingly gathered and preserved many of his grandfather's letters and papers that would otherwise have been lost forever. I do not wish to be irrev-

erent, but that gift of 120 ducats was probably the only thing Pope
Clement ever did right.

Machiavelli reciprocated with a piece of advice that only he
could have devised. If you wish to save the Church and Italy, you
must have the courage to take exceptional measures: arm the subjects of Romagna and use them to fight the emperor's armies. The
idea met with favor at court: Machiavelli was sent to Faenza to
present the plan to Guicciardini so that he might judge whether it
was feasible or not, since he was familiar with the places and people in question. He set out from Rome on 10 or 11 June, carrying
a papal brief written by Jacopo Sadoleto, the papal secretary, that
spoke of the need to consider "extreme remedies," since all ordinary solutions had proven inadequate; to listen to Machiavelli's plan
with great attention and to place complete faith in him; and to
report back quickly and confidentially as to the plan's feasibility.
This, wrote Sadoleto, is a matter of the greatest import; it may
determine the salvation of the papal states, Italy, and virtually all
Christendom.

Machiavelli arrived in Faenza on 21 June. On the twenty-
second, Guicciardini was already prepared to give his answer in a
letter to Cesare Colombo, his agent in the Roman court. The following day he completed his analysis with another letter, also
addressed to Colombo, accompanied by a request to show the letter to the pope, to observe closely "his demeanor and words," and
to inform him of everything; he was also to show the letter to the
pope's advisers.

The verdict was negative. To arm and organize the subjects of
Romagna in a militia, Guicciardini explained, would be "one of
the most useful and praiseworthy works that His Holiness could
undertake," if only it were possible. But in present conditions, it
would be very dangerous, because the people were torn by chronic
political hostilities and the Church had neither partisans nor
friends there: those who wished to live well and peacefully disliked
the Church because they wanted a government that would protect

them; troublemakers and evil men disliked the Church because they saw disorder and war as a chance to settle accounts and see to their own interests.

As for the idea of getting money from the people of Romagna to finance a militia, at least in part, as Machiavelli had suggested, Guicciardini thought the communities in question had already been bled white, and new funds could be obtained only by force; this made the likelihood of success even more remote. Finally, if the pope were to decide to undertake this project despite these many difficulties, he should commit to it fully and meet every setback with renewed optimism. For someone who, like Pope Clement, was chronically indecisive and timid, this last advice was tantamount to telling him to forget it (*LC*, 1568–72).

Machiavelli, too, wrote Sadoleto a letter to defend his point of view to the pope and his advisers. On 6 July, Sadoleto answered that the pope wanted "to think a little more about it." Machiavelli waited a few more days, enjoying abundant meals, the company of Maliscotta, and conversations with Guicciardini. On 26 July, when it was clear the idea of a militia in Romagna had been abandoned, he set off for Florence, certainly not in a happy frame of mind, but neither crushed nor angry. He had probably been persuaded by the more cautious Guicciardini's arguments and clearly bore his friend no resentment.

In fact, their friendship seems to have been strengthened by this episode. For example, we note Guicciardini asking his friend to look at two properties he had purchased sight unseen. Diligent as always, Niccolò reported back on 3 August in his unique style, with subtle jabs at a friend who bought property without looking at it first. For three miles around Finocchieto, he wrote, nothing can be seen "that is pleasing—Arabia Petraea is no different"; the house itself can't be called bad, but it isn't good either. I'd try to make some improvements and then sell it, he said, because in its current state you'll never sell it except to someone else who buys it sight unseen "like yourself."

Guicciardini took this news badly. Caring as much as he did about money, he was not happy to hear he had bought a pig in a poke, even less to be ribbed about it. At first, he tried to laugh it off and on 7 August in a polite note told Machiavelli to stop using high-flown titles (especially "illustrious") and to address him only by titles that "you would enjoy having given to you." On the same day, he sent him another, longer letter, in which he spoke in the offended voice of "Milady Property of Finocchieto," in which guise he answered his ill-mannered friend in kind, telling him that his affair with Barbara ought to have taught him not to judge by appearances. Like Barbara, whose name might seem to indicate "complete cruelty and ferocity" but who was sweet and kind, Finocchieto concealed "many good aspects," which deserved praise, not the slighting words that the overhasty Niccolò had used. Learn then to trust less to your quick judgment, concluded the offended Milady, because many excuses are admissible in others that "cannot be accepted" in someone of your wisdom and experience.

Deep down, Guicciardini was a very serious man, and the jests, however labored, could not mask his irritation. Still, the letters left no ill humor; Machiavelli reported to Guicciardini on 17 August that in a few days he would be setting out for Venice, to discuss a serious wrong committed by one Giovan Battista Donà against some Florentine merchants, and that on his way back he meant to stop over in Faenza to spend an evening with him and their friends.

About his mission in Venice we know something, for a letter written by Filippo de' Nerli on 6 September tells us that the Florentine merchants were complaining that Machiavelli was wasting time with writers instead of doing his work. We also know that his Florentine friends were saddened by the absence of "Machia," "the root of all evil," and they no longer got together as they had because "someone to bring the band together is always missing when you are not here." In Florence, a rumor spread—later proved false—that Machiavelli had won the lottery in Venice, pocketing two or three thousand ducats. If there were any thoughts that cheered him in those September days of 1525, they were of Maliscotta awaiting him in Faenza and Barbara in Florence. When these last loves dwindled and once he had finished writing the historical and political works he had undertaken, life began to lose its color, its beauty, and its dreams. All that remained was the spectacle of mankind's malevolence and stupidity, with popes, emperors, and kings leading the parade. Sadly, this was not a comedy—it was a tragedy.

TWENTY-ONE

In the Palazzo Vecchio and in the Field, for the Last Time

As their lives come to an end, many men begin to release their grip on the world. They let others make plans for the future, they put away their dreams and fantasies, they let their passions cool, they narrow their social circle to their family, especially their children, and above all else, they seek peace, as if preparing for the immobility, silence, and loneliness of eternity. Some, terrified by the thought of the timeless darkness, cold, and solitude that await them, seek comfort in hopes of light and warmth beyond the tomb, and they dream of being reunited with their loved ones.

In part because he was swept along by events, in part because it was in his nature, Niccolò spent the last few months of his life immersed in politics and war: he urged princes and army generals to make decisions to save Italy from the ultimate shame; he galloped from place to place; he reviewed troops, oversaw quartering and billeting, inspected and designed fortifications; he tried to train troops, though he was completely incompetent at it; he called for a commander who might raise a flag of battle and lead an insurrection to free Italy from the barbarians. He displayed a special tenderness toward Marietta, his children, and weak and defenseless creatures in general, but he did so while fully involved in great affairs of state. He set aside his last love affairs more out of necessity than out of a desire for solitude and meditation. Indeed, these last few months were a time of intense passions that translated into words of remarkable power, words that allow us to sense the almost palpable torment raging in his soul.

As we read his last letters, and as we watch him race against time to stop a horde of German and Spanish soldiers advancing into Italy, thirsting for pillage and plunder, we should think of him as a man whose face is marked by too much bitterness, his body bent by too many ordeals. But he was still Niccolò, even though "il Machia," prankster and scoundrel, had by now retreated to the background.

In the autumn of 1525, after returning from Venice, Machiavelli turned his hand once again to writing history, seeking to vent his frustration by accusing the princes who ruled Italy of pushing it to the brink of ruin. The first warning of impending tragedy came soon. Fernando de Ávalos, marquess of Pescara and general of the Spanish armies, ordered the arrest on 15 October of Girolamo Morone, secretary to Francesco Sforza, duke of Milan, for trying to persuade him to switch allegiance to the forces arrayed against the emperor. Seeing an opening, the Spanish took advantage of the chance to capture almost all the fortresses in the Milan region and were soon masters of the duchy. Morone was seized, Machiavelli commented, and "the duchy of Milan was done for"; the same fate would soon befall the other princes of Italy, "nor was any remedy now possible."

He had accurately predicted events, and if he was farsighted, it was partly because he had long understood that the Italian states, unarmed, divided, ruled by weak and unwise princes—and with the papal court, that den of moral and political corruption, at the heart of the peninsula—could hardly help falling into foreign hands. What sense was there in writing about history when he knew how things would end, and why? He had already placed Florentine events in the context of Italian history and had then explained that because of factions and civil strife, the Florentines had failed to "make themselves and their homeland great" and thus to become a decisive force for the salvation of Italy.

He had written the *Florentine Histories* to teach citizens who govern a republic a lesson on the terrible consequences of factionalism's pitiless strife. He felt certain that his work could persuade Florentines to be wiser in the future, because "if every example of a republic is moving, those one reads concerning one's own are much more so and much more useful" (*IF,* Preface).

To draw from his city's history all its "meaning" and "flavor," he had traced a parallel between social conflicts in ancient Rome and factional strife in Florence, demonstrating to even the most obtuse reader the reasons for Florence's political and military decline. In Rome, social conflicts had been resolved by discussion and by law; in Florence, social conflicts were resolved by open combat, with the banishment and death of many citizens. The effect of social conflict in Rome had been to increase military strength; in Florence, to diminish it.

The reason for such different effects lay in the nature of the conflicts. The Roman people had wanted to share public honors with the nobility; the Florentine people wished to govern on their own. The reasonable desires of the Roman people neither offended nor frightened the Roman nobles; the "injurious and unjust" desire of the Florentine people had driven the Florentine aristocracy to defend itself with every means at its disposal, including killing and banishment. When the people triumphed in Florence, they stripped the nobles of public honors; as a result, "the virtue in arms and the generosity of spirit that were in the nobility were eliminated, and in the people, where they never had been, they could not be rekindled," so Florence became ever more humble and abject (*IF,* III, 1).

Poorly ordered republics, he had explained, continually modify the form of their government. Still, they do not shift from liberty to tyranny, as many believe; rather, they drift from tyranny to license or excessive liberty. Both are unstable, because "the one state displeases good men, the other displeases the wise; the one can do evil easily, the other can do good only with difficulty; in the one, insolent men have too much authority, in the other, fools" (*IF,* IV, 1). This was a synthesis of Florentine political history and a portrait of many Italian principalities of Machiavelli's time; but it was also a prophecy of the nature of many future Italian governments—composed of insolent tyrants or of the cowardly servants of whichever major figure was swaggering and shouting at the time.

Machiavelli saw these old vices once again in his fellow Florentines during those weeks; every sign indicated that war was imminent, yet no one was willing to "do anything honorable and bold worth living or dying for," he wrote Guicciardini on 19 December 1525. The citizens show "much fear" and little determination to withstand the emperor who is about to devour them. The worst was Pope Clement VII, an alumnus of the Medici school, unfailingly indecisive, always ready to rely on a trick or seek refuge in delay, never realizing he was only giving "his enemy time." Guicciardini agreed, and wrote back on 26 December that he had never seen anyone who, "when he sees bad times coming, did not seek in some way to try to protect himself, except for us, who want to await them unprotected in the middle of the road."

While Pope Clement, reassured by the marquess of Pescara's death, stalled for time and looked for a deal, Machiavelli felt certain that war was inevitable and imminent, that one had to prepare and one had to make courageous, honorable decisions, rather than wait and worry: "For as long as I can remember, people have always been either making war or talking about going to war; it is now being talked about and in a short while it will be declared; when it is over, people will start talking about it again" (*L,* 575).

He wrote those words on 3 January 1526. On the fourteenth in Madrid, in order to gain his freedom, King François signed a treaty with the emperor Charles V, giving up his claims to Milan and Naples and surrendering his children as hostages. The Treaty of Madrid caught Machiavelli by surprise, for he never expected the emperor to make such a glaring mistake; he also erred in his predictions of King François's next moves, assuming the French king would observe the treaty's provisions once he was free. That is not how things went. Where Machiavelli was right was in predicting that war would ensue, and on a vast scale: "However matters turn out, I believe that war in Italy is inevitable—and at hand," he wrote to Guicciardini on 15 March.

Given that war was impending between, on the one hand, the Holy Roman Emperor Charles V and, on the other, the king of France and various states of Italy, Machiavelli proposed to Guicciardini—in hopes that he might speak of the idea to the pope—a venture that was at once audacious and strange, perhaps even ridiculous, but in keeping with the absurdity of the times. Why not secretly arm and finance Giovanni de' Medici, known as Giovanni delle Bande Nere, the son of the great Caterina Sforza? There was no military leader in Italy whom the troops would more willingly follow, none whom the Spanish more deeply feared and respected. Everyone agreed that Giovanni delle Bande Nere was "brave and impetuous," had "great ideas," and could make momentous decisions. Give him enough soldiers, and the Spanish will be so bewildered they will most likely give up their plan of ravaging Tuscany and the papal states, while the king of France would commit seriously to the Italians, once they stopped chattering and instead "showed him deeds."

This suggestion, too, was rejected. If the pope were to help Giovanni delle Bande Nere, Filippo Strozzi explained in a letter of 31 March, he would make an enemy of the emperor; he might as well do it openly. It was safer to depend on the French king's wisdom and hope that the emperor would fail to notice that he had a "fine and great opportunity" to make himself master of all Italy. This was tantamount to relying on luck, in the pope's classic style, champion of indecision and foolishness that he was. The pope did understand one basic fact: with war looming, it might be wise to reinforce Florence's fortifications. With that idea in mind, he sent to Florence Count Pedro Navarro, a Spanish deserter who was reputed to be a skilled military engineer, and asked Machiavelli, on the strength of the knowledge about military matters shown in *The Art of War,* to help.

Reinforcing Florence's walls and defenses so as to make the city able to withstand "any kind of serious and violent attack," as Machiavelli wrote to Guicciardini on 4 April, excited and absorbed him. He finally had an opportunity to do something useful for his homeland, something concrete and not bookish. He met with Navarro and immediately set off for Rome to present a fortification project: both the pope and Guicciardini were so pleased with the plan that they established a new magistracy, the Procuratori delle Mura, charged with overseeing the reinforcement of the ring of city walls. The new superintendent and chancellor of the Procuratori was, of course, Machiavelli. After fourteen years, he was once again working in the Palazzo Vecchio.

He must have felt as if he were a secretary once again. He threw himself into his new job heart and soul; he thought of nothing else: "my head is so full of ramparts that nothing else could enter it," he confessed to Guicciardini in a letter of 17 May. When he wasn't thinking about walls and fortifications, he was thinking about the danger posed by Charles V and his army, which now controlled Milan and might soon take all of Italy. When news arrived of the revolt of the Milanese people against the Spanish occupiers, he exhorted—indeed, pleaded with—Guicciardini not to miss this heaven-sent opportunity to strike the enemy hard, to be decisive, to show courage.

It is as if we were reading one of the many letters he wrote when secretary to persuade the Florentine rulers to abandon their pitiful policy of stalling for time: "You are aware of how many opportunities have been lost: do not lose this one or, putting yourself in the hands of Fortune and Time, trust in having it again, because Time does not always bring identical circumstances and Fortune is not always the same." These words are reminiscent of the remarkable "Exhortation to Seize Italy and Free Her from the Barbarians" with which he concluded *The Prince*: "Free Italy from long-lasting anxiety; eradicate those savage brutes, which have nothing human about them save their faces and voices." The passing years and the vicissitudes of life had done nothing to change him: he still felt the same anguish about Italy's troubles and miseries, the same intolerance for the idiocy and cowardice of princes, the same burning desire to see the barbarians driven far north of the Alps. He was still Machiavelli.

Guicciardini agreed, but he warned that when the powerful try to come to terms, matters proceed slowly. At last, on 22 May in Cognac (and thanks especially to Guicciardini's patient and determined diplomacy), the king of France, the pope, Florence, and Venice formed a Holy League against the emperor Charles V. Leading the Venetian troops was Francesco Maria della Rovere, duke of Urbino; Guido Rangoni commanded the papal soldiers; Vitello Vitelli commanded the Florentine forces; Giovanni delle Bande Nere was "captain general of the Italian infantry"; the lieutenant general was Francesco Guicciardini.

In theory, this army could defeat the imperial troops, especially if the commanders moved decisively and quickly to attack Milan. In practice, however, this army was split by rivalries and resentments. How could anyone expect the duke of Urbino to fight with real determination when the Treaty of Cognac stated that the fortress of San Leo, taken from him by Florence, would remain Florentine property? Another factor was the duke of Ferrara, who might easily have been a formidable obstacle to the imperial troops when they marched into Italy from Germany but who chose not to join the League because the pope insisted on taking back Reggiò and Rubiera. Italy was about to be swallowed whole, and everyone, the pope first of all, was concerned only with safeguarding his own interests.

That the Holy League's armies were ineffectual became clear as soon as war broke out in earnest. Without waiting for French reinforcements, which were uncertain in any case, they advanced toward Milan and on 24 June occupied Lodi, which had surrendered. On 7 July, the League's troops moved to attack Milan, but when they encountered Spanish resistance, the duke of Urbino, who had the final say in all tactical decisions, withdrew toward San Martino and Marignano: *veni, vidi, fugi*—I came, I saw, I fled, as Guicciardini wrote in his *History of Italy*.

Present at the camp at Marignano was Machiavelli. He had left his fortifications, after persuading the pope to ignore advice to expand the perimeter of the walls so as to enclose San Miniato; he now had another extremely important job (entrusted to him by either Guicciardini or the cardinal of Cortona, who was governing Florence on behalf of the pope): he was supposed to "reorder this militia," as Guicciardini wrote on 18 July to Roberto Acciaiuoli. As soon as he reached the camp, Machiavelli reported to Guicciardini: the level of corruption in the militia was unacceptably high, he realized, and he would have to give up the task; he would stand aside and "laugh at the errors of humanity, since it is impossible to correct them" (*L*, 593 n. 2).

Besides laughing at errors he could not correct, he thought about Barbara, who was not writing to him. He complained about this to Fornaciaio, who told him on 5 August that Barbara had assured him she had written to Niccolò and had been sullen only "to see if you love her." Now that she knows you are happy to receive her letters, she will write you every week, and she begs you not to be annoyed with her. Cautiously, he added: "Now, you know her better than I do: I do not know if she should be believed completely."

Machiavelli, when he wasn't mooning over Barbara, had tried to impose martial discipline on his troops. Once, he even tried to parade the soldiers of Giovanni delle Bande Nere, the commander he admired most, in accordance with the concepts he had described so well in *The Art of War,* concepts that seemed so solid and simple on paper, though on the field things went a little differently. Unfortunately for Machiavelli, one witness of the episode was Matteo Bandello, a monk, courtier, and renowned author of novellas; Bandello was merciless in recounting the ridiculous figure cut by our would-be commander. "Niccolò," wrote Bandello, "kept us under the hot sun for more than two hours that day while he tried to parade three thousand foot soldiers in the way he had described in writing, and he was having a very difficult time in so doing." Finally, Giovanni delle Bande Nere put an end to the farce, telling Machiavelli to step aside to see how it was done. In the "wink of an eye," to the beating of drums, Giovanni put the foot soldiers through their paces "to the immense admiration" of all the onlookers. This story shows, wrote Bandello cuttingly, "how great the difference is between someone who knows and who has not set in operation what he knows and someone who, as well as knowing, has often rolled up his sleeves and plunged in" (R, 357–58). For once, Niccolò had to submit to the shame of being the butt of a monk's laughter.

His reputation as a military and political expert was not, however, badly damaged by cutting such a poor figure at Marignano. The letters he sent during his time there concerning the state of the troops and political and diplomatic developments were read in Florence with great interest and admiration. "I desire your letters very deeply and . . . to me they have the value of oracles," Bartolomeo Cavalcanti wrote him on 11 August. Young Florentines like Cavalcanti cared deeply about their homeland and found in the venerable Machiavelli's letters an exemplary treatment of the "great matters" of politics, written with his special clarity and passion.

Meanwhile, the Holy League's military operations continued in their usual manner, which is to say, without strategy or order. After abandoning the idea of storming Milan, where Francesco Sforza had surrendered and handed over the castle to the Spanish occupiers, the duke of Urbino sent part of his army to lay siege to Cremona. The attack was beginning to look like another pointless waste of time and men. To prevent a fiasco like the retreat from Milan, Guicciardini sent Machiavelli to the siege camp; among so many arrogant, rancorous, and suspicious chiefs and commanders, he could rely only on Machiavelli.

His instructions were precise: Machiavelli was to persuade the Venetian plenipotentiary and the other commanders that unless Cremona fell within four or six days, they should break camp and march on Genoa, to prevent the arrival of Spanish reinforcements. He set off on 9 September, and on the thirteenth he took part in a council of war. He wrote a plan for the attack on Cremona, probably because no one else was willing to do it. The city surrendered on 23 September, but on terms, not by conquest. It was not a triumphant victory, but still, it was better than the shame endured beneath the walls of Milan.

If spirits had been ever so slightly cheered, a cold shower now arrived from Rome, a piece of news that seemed incredible: Pope Clement VII had signed a truce with the powerful Colonna family, and then released his soldiers from duty! The baronial Colonna family, in concert with the emperor's agent Hugo de Moncada, had sent their troops back into Rome during the night of 19–20 September and sacked the Vatican and Saint Peter's, forcing the pope to take refuge in the Castel Sant'Angelo. Even worse, the pope signed a four-month truce with Hugo de Moncada, with a clause promising the withdrawal of papal troops from Lombardy.

A war that seemed impossible to lose had been transformed into such a tangled welter that not even Jesus Christ would have been able to straighten it out, Machiavelli wrote to Bartolomeo Cavalcanti in early October. We have the pope to thank for this fine mess: first he refused to raise funds "with means that other popes have employed," and then he allowed himself to be captured "like a baby." Even worse, the "ambitious and insufferable" commanders had done their best to make the campaign fail, and now that the papal troops had departed, they were fighting like dogs; worst of all had been the duke of Urbino, who "against the will of us all was able to act badly; against the will of us all he was not able to act well" (*LC*, 616).

Despite Guicciardini's "promptness and conscientiousness," the war in Lombardy was ending in failure for the Holy League. Machiavelli could do nothing but return to Florence. Along the way, he stopped at Modena, where he made fun of Filippo de' Nerli and consulted a seer who claimed to have predicted the pope's flight and the campaign's failure and warned that "all bad times" were by no means ended and much suffering was still in store.

The seer was right; Niccolò would not pass the coming winter at all, pestering Donato del Corno's shop and smelling it up, as the evil-minded Filippo de' Nerli had written (in revenge for the ridicule Niccolò had heaped on him when passing through Modena).

TWENTY-TWO

To Love One's Native City
More Than One's Own Soul

With the failure of the campaign to expel the Spanish troops from Milan, the Italian states—Florence and the papal states in particular—were now exposed to the threat of an imperial army composed of Spanish infantry and German foot soldiers marching down the peninsula. Machiavelli knew better than anyone of what atrocities such a horde might be capable, and he had family in Florence; his children were in Florence. He felt a deep tenderness toward his family, and more strongly than ever he felt love for his homeland. His homeland was the free Republic of Florence, but it was also Italy. And now in just a few months, Italy was to experience the horror of the Sack of Rome, while Florence, refounded after the expulsion of the Medici once again, turned Machiavelli away.

If ever there was a propitious time for Niccolò to seek comfort in penitence and redemption, it was in the last few months of his life. I believe, all the same, that before he closed his eyes forever, Niccolò did not repent or ask God's forgiveness for having loved life, his homeland, and women too much. He may have hoped for redemption, not in the company of the saintly and the blessed, whom he disliked, but with the great statesmen, lawmakers, political philosophers, warriors, and heroes who had no need of God because they had transformed themselves into gods with the strength of their minds and hearts, men who lived in a world all their own, basking in the light of true glory.

Lansquenets commanded by Georg von Frundsberg concentrated in Bolzano in early November, whence they marched toward the river Po, encountering no resistance from the Venetians. The only commander to oppose them was, of course, Giovanni delle Bande Nere, at Borgoforte, near Mantua, on 25 November 1526. In the battle, Giovanni was wounded in the thigh by a musket ball; on 30 November, he died in Mantua. Giovanni's death was an excellent example of what Machiavelli had written: when Fortune wishes to inflict "great ruin" on a people, she places men in charge who will "aid in that ruin," and if there is anyone who might cause her plans to fail, "either she kills him or deprives him of all faculties of being able to work anything well" (D, II, 29).

With that resistance overcome, the German soldiers crossed the Po at Ostiglia on 28 November. Now the way was clear to Milan, or else toward Florence and Rome. The Florentine rulers wanted to know which way the terrifying human flood would turn and what the Spanish troops quartered in Milan intended to do next, and above all they had to find a way of stopping them. They needed someone to travel to Modena to discuss the matter with Guicciardini. The choice fell on the aged Machiavelli, who was instructed to say that the rulers despaired of saving Florence and were inclined to seek out "some agreement," entrusting Guicciardini with negotiations on behalf of the city "as circumstances seem to dictate" (LC, 1600).

Riding on horseback over the Apennines in the winter was no laughing matter for a man of fifty-eight. The wages, as usual, were scanty, and the honors even scantier. All the same, Machiavelli set out for Modena, arriving late in the day on 2 December. He

immediately met with Guicciardini and that evening wrote to let
Florence know Guicciardini's views on the military situation and
the possibility of reaching an agreement. Some say the Germans
number fifteen or sixteen thousand, he reported, others say no
more than ten thousand; and it seems they intend to march on
Milan to join forces with the Spanish. From there, they may move
either against Venice or against the papal lands in Romagna or else
move toward Tuscany. Behind them are the troops of the duke of
Urbino, who has no interest in attacking, even though Guicciardini
has "repeatedly urged [him] to do so." In all, the Holy League has
about twenty thousand troops. If they join into a single army and
if the pope's funds don't dry up, then we can feel confident,
according to Guicciardini. He hastens to point out, however, that as
long as the troops are divided and the commanders mistrust each
other, "little good can be expected."

As to how many could defend Florence, Machiavelli reported,
Guicciardini said he could safely offer only those "six or seven
thousand foot soldiers that the Church has here" and that he would
do everything in his power to unify the armies so as to help Florence more. The Florentines should therefore abandon the idea of
trying to start peace talks: there was no possibility of corrupting
the Germans or winning them away from the Spaniards, because
together they form "a single body." If the Florentines still wished
to try, however, they should begin in Rome, directly contacting the
viceroy of Naples, Charles de Lannoy, or else Hugo de Moncada.

In this letter from Modena, Machiavelli reported only what
Guicciardini had to say. No comments of his own, no exhortations. This time they were unnecessary, since he agreed word for
word with Guicciardini. The only thing he added was a strange little postscript: "Your Excellencies must have heard of the death of
Lord Giovanni, who died to the regret of one and all" (*LC*,
1601–3). Strange because there was no reason to tell the Florentines something they already knew. Those words were an outburst;
he could not accept that Fortune should have killed the only con-

dóttiere who might have changed the course of the war and staved off defeat.

He wrote again the following day, to report that the war was shifting toward Parma and Piacenza, that Guicciardini had gone to Parma, and to repeat—in case they had not grasped the idea—that suing for peace seemed to Guicciardini "an entirely vain undertaking, harmful and to no one's benefit." Once Guicciardini had left, there was nothing to do but mount his horse and ride back to Florence. He set off on 5 December and rode slowly, "as there was no need to wear himself out."

The terrible year of 1527 was now beginning, a year "full of atrocities and events unheard of for many centuries: overthrow of governments, wickedness of princes, most frightful sacks of cities, great famines, a most terrible plague almost everywhere in Italy; everything full of death, flight and rapine," as Guicciardini later wrote in his *History of Italy*. Guicciardini, one of the few who could see things as they were among so many who were blinded, warned the Florentines of the ills that lay in store for them. Many believe, he wrote on 31 January, that the imperial army will head for Tuscany; one can only "expect the worst," and it is especially necessary to take proper measures as "vigorously as possible" (*LC,* 1617).

To establish what vigorous steps the situation called for, the Eight of the Pratica sent Machiavelli to Parma to meet with Guicciardini. The latter had urged this, so that he would have at his side a trusted person who saw things as he did, an assistant in the difficult negotiations with the army commanders allied against the emperor. Machiavelli did not reach Parma until 7 February, partly because of hindrances created by enemy armies and partly because of poor traveling conditions during an unusually cold, rainy, and snowy winter.

He wrote to Florence that same evening to report that Guicciardini, too, wanted the troops of the duke of Urbino and the marquess of Saluzzo to march into Tuscany, positioning themselves in front of—not behind—the Germans and Spaniards. He also reported on a meeting with the duke of Urbino, held at Guicciardini's behest; despite all his efforts—and we know what a persuasive negotiator and speaker he was—the duke of Urbino was determined to persist in remaining behind and well away from the imperial troops. They were to meet again the following day, "with pen in hand," to establish plans and reciprocal commitments.

On 11 February, Machiavelli reported to the Florentines that the imperial army, short on money and supplies, could not remain united for much longer. The only strength it could count on was the allies' errors and indecision: "experts of warfare here agree that victory will be ours, unless bad advice or lack of money bring defeat." Three days later, he reported again that the imperial forces were "so short on supplies that if our people can stall them, it will be impossible for them to be victorious in this campaign." He urged the Florentines to prepare a stout defense and suggested they emulate the people of Lombardy, who had heard of the Spaniards' violent behavior in Milan and were now so frightened that they "would all sooner die" than have Spanish troops among them. He also gave them another, equally important piece of advice: to give back the cursed fortress of San Leo to the duke of Urbino, so that he might be encouraged to "fight willingly" and abandon his absurd tactic of always lagging far behind the imperial troops.

On the same day, Guicciardini wrote to Rome with the same advice, trying to make the pope listen to reason: "without the assistance of the Venetians our forces are not sufficient to defend us; unless the duke is satisfied, their help will be of little worth; I would like to know how much the weight of that fortress is holding him back, for by refusing to hand it over we are risking great ruin" (*LC*, 1611).

Neither Machiavelli's exhortations to Florence nor Guicciardini's to Rome attained the desired effects, because the pope was motivated more by a "long-standing and recently renewed hatred" for the duke of Urbino than by "reason." Hatred and rancor were also the prime forces driving the duke of Ferrara, who was supplying the imperial army with foodstuffs, gunpowder, and artillery, including the musket that had mortally wounded Giovanni delle Bande Nere. Not to mention the Sienese, who were ready to do the same once German and Spanish troops reached Tuscany. In such a situation, even a weaker force than the imperial army could easily bring the Italians to their knees.

Though lacking money and provisions, the emperor's army was nothing to scorn. From one moment to the next, it seemed about to dissolve, and yet it continued on. The commanders' determination to keep advancing into Italy "without money, without ammunitions, without sappers, and without an organization to provide victuals," in the midst of so many "hostile towns and cities and in the face of enemies who so greatly outnumbered them," surprised everyone, Guicciardini and Machiavelli included. They were even more surprised by the "determination of the Germans, who had set out from Germany with a ducat apiece, and after holding out in Italy for so long with no more than two or three ducats apiece in all that time, set themselves—in defiance of the customs of all soldiers and especially German soldiers—to march on, with no other rewards or assurances than their own hopes of victory" (G, XVIII,4).

The chief factor pushing the Germans forward was certainly the authority of their commander, Georg von Frundsberg, and the idea of taking Rome, as Guicciardini noted. Still, one should not forget that the troops were Lutherans, and driven though they might have been by a lust for plunder, they were also driven by a religious zeal to punish the corrupt papal court of Rome. Moreover, their distinctive organization made the troops relatively autonomous vis-à-vis their commanders. The importance of this factor became clear when Frundsberg had a stroke on 17 March and had to resign his command. Even then his army remained

intact, and his departure scarcely marked the beginning of "ruin" for
the imperial army, as Machiavelli predicted in a letter of 18 March
from Bologna, where he was enjoying the generous hospitality of
Innocenzo Cardinal Cybo in a city covered with snow "a yard
deep."

Frundsberg's departure did, however, make it that much harder
to come to an agreement with the imperial army. Negotiating with
the viceroy of Naples, Charles de Lannoy, or with the duke of
Bourbon, the emperor's lieutenant general who commanded the
imperial army, was an exercise in futility, since neither was powerful enough to make the soldiers accept a deal if they weren't satisfied with its terms. At this point, the only thing that would satisfy
them was the sack of either Florence or Rome. Pope Clement
learned this at his own expense; tired of the king of France's broken promises and the duke of Urbino's dithering, generally incapable of making a decision, as well as short on cash, he agreed on
16 March to an eight-month truce with the viceroy Charles de
Lannoy. The agreement stipulated that if the pope paid the imperial army 60,000 ducats, the troops would withdraw beyond the
river Po. Once the truce was signed, however, the duke of Bourbon marched on Florence and on 29 March told the pope that a
truce would cost 150,000 ducats.

To Machiavelli, who—in the *Discourses*—had extolled the
example of the Romans, since they "never made peace with
money, but always with the virtue of arms" (*D,* II, 30), it was obvious that safety lay in being well armed, not in treaties or truces, and
that money should be used to prepare for war, not paid to one's
enemies only to make them stronger. Once again, he and Guicciardini agreed. So, while Guicciardini wrote to Rome urging that all
negotiations be broken off, that new money be raised by appointing new cardinals, and that the viceroy be arrested, Machiavelli
wrote on 2 April from Imola to exhort the Florentines to prepare
fortifications and defenses rather than offer money to the imperial
troops to spare the city.

Machiavelli argued his case with all the passion and clarity he could muster. The imperial troops, he explained, have shown their "animus toward Italy, and especially toward this city," which they want to plunder. None of their commanders, not even the viceroy, had the authority to stop them. To keep them from attacking Florence and to force them to accept tolerable terms, one had to prepare for war: "because what sort of truce can you hope for from those enemies, if, with the Apennines still separating them from you and your troops standing ready, they demand 100,000 florins in three days, and 150,000 florins in ten days?" When they reach you, they will demand everything you have, because they are attracted only by "the lure of plundering you." The only solution is to force them to change their minds by using every means within your power before they cross the Apennines. Don't drown in a well after "safely crossing a tempest-tossed sea"; instead, make up your minds to spend 10 florins "to secure certain liberation" rather than 40 "so that they might seize you and destroy you" (*LC*, 1645–46).

That day he also wrote to his son Guido. The two letters give us the unique opportunity of seeing, at close quarters, the public Machiavelli and the private Machiavelli. The public letter shows us a man working with all his strength and cunning to save his homeland; the private one demonstrates how kind and tender he could be. The letter to Guido certainly has a special intensity due to his fear of the war moving ever closer to Florence, but this cannot be a onetime thing, for tenderness does not suddenly emerge. This letter more than any other shows us the face Niccolò concealed behind his smile.

Guido had just recovered from an illness and could finally go back to his studies, which he loved. Niccolò had great hopes for his son; he wanted to help the boy and let him feel his presence; he wanted to comfort and exhort him, with the voice not of a father but of a friend. He offered his own help and that of what friends he still had, but he wanted to teach Guido above all that the best way of distinguishing oneself is to learn and to do one's work well.

If God grants us life—and that was more than a mere expression, with German soldiers bearing down on Florence—

> I may make you a man of good standing, if you are willing to do your share . . . But you must study and, since you no longer have illness as an excuse, take pains to learn letters and music, for you are aware how much distinction is given me for what little ability I possess. Thus, my son, if you want to please me and to bring profit and honor to yourself, study, do well, and learn, because everyone will help you if you help yourself. (*L,* 624–25)

An even finer lesson was taught in connection with a young mule that little Guido loved and that had evidently gone mad. Guido feared the mule might be tied up or worse and had asked his father to intervene. Imagine his joy when he read these words:

> Since the young mule has gone mad, it must be treated in just the reverse of the way crazy people are: for they are tied up, and I want you to let it loose. Give it to Vangelo, and tell him to take it to Montepugliano and then take off its bridle and halter and let it go wherever it likes to regain its own way of life and work off its craziness. The village is big, the beast is small, it can't do any harm.

Guido's delighted reply came on 17 April: "The young mule has not yet been sent to Montepugliano, because the grass has not yet grown back; but, however the weather turns out, he will go there." It is hard to imagine a better way of teaching a child that liberty is good for the mind and even the weakest and most unfortunate creatures deserve our pity.

In his letters, Niccolò did his best to reassure Guido and the others. He promised Marietta he would be home "before any danger comes" and told her to "be of good cheer," whatever rumors might be circulating in Florence about the imminent arrival of the lansquenets. He meant it when he wrote that he had never yearned so much to be in Florence. Instead, he had to stay with Guicciardini and continue to monitor the progress of the war, to prevent the stupidity and miserliness of the pope and the princes from triggering a catastrophe whose first victims would be the very ones he held dearest in Florence. But his letters managed to reassure his "gang": since you have promised you will be with us, Guido wrote, "we are not worrying about the lansquenets anymore"; Marietta "is no longer worried," and little Baccina, now that she knows you bought her a "beautiful little chain," thinks about nothing else. To make Niccolò even happier, Guido wrote that he had begun to study participles and that when Niccolò returned he would recite for him the entire first book of Ovid's *Metamorphoses,* which he had learned by heart.

Meanwhile, the lansquenets continued to advance on Florence. That army, Machiavelli wrote to Francesco Vettori on 5 April, would never prevail if it encountered serious opposition, but there was a genuine risk that no Italian princes would oppose it, torn as they were between fighting and striking deals, while the imperial troops had only one thought: war. At this point, his letters were so many desperate invocations: if the duke of Bourbon moves his troops tomorrow, he wrote to Vettori on 16 April, then we must turn all our thoughts to war "and leave aside all thought of peace." It was too late to trudge along, one had to have "some recklessness." The enemy lacked artillery and was marching through hostile lands; let us gather "whatever little life remains," let us concentrate the Holy League's troops at one point, and once and for all let us force them either to turn back or to accept a reasonable agreement: "I love Francesco Guicciardini, I love my native city more than my own soul." Finally, the words he had hidden in his heart for so long pour out. True, in Florence, the phrase "to love one's native city more than one's own soul" was a manner of speech dating back to the fourteenth-century War of the Eight Saints. But

Machiavelli's words were much more than a manner of speech; they were the confession of a profound passion, of his pained grief at watching Italy ravaged when he couldn't do anything, though he knew what needed to be done. Hence that "I love Francesco Guicciardini": Guicciardini, too, in the past few months had understood what needed to be done and had done all he could to persuade the deaf, make the blind see, infuse a little courage in the hearts of so many cowards. Guicciardini alone had taken action and could do something for their shared homeland, which was why Machiavelli loved him. Those words were more than a banal patriotic expression; with them he was confiding to a friend the meaning and pain of his own life.

Finally, after endless explanations and harangues from Machiavelli and especially Guicciardini, the Holy League's troops concentrated near Florence to defend the city from the imperial forces. Even the duke of Urbino marched, having become active and quick once the Florentines restored San Leo to him. The duke of Bourbon understood that Florence, well defended, was too tough a nut to crack, and he marched off toward Rome.

Machiavelli returned to Florence on 22 April, after an absence of nearly three months. The city crackled with tension and hatred for the Medici, in the person of the cardinal of Cortona, still governing as regent for the two illegitimate Medici scions, Ippolito and Alessandro. On 26 April, a riot erupted, culminating in the occupation of the Palazzo Vecchio by Medici opponents, among them the cream of the Florentine nobility. The cardinal of Cortona, with the duke of Urbino's approval, threatened to use force to clear the building. A massacre of nearly all the city's aristocrats and the sack of Florence by the troops who had come to defend it were narrowly prevented through the authority and skill of Francesco Guicciardini. Even so, the cardinal of Cortona criticized Guicciardini for his actions that day, because he had kept Medici power from being secured for all time "with arms and the blood of the citizenry," while the rebels criticized him for having persuaded them to "surrender unnecessarily," to the advantage of the Medici (G, XVIII, 7).

No one, with the exception of Count Guido Rangoni, with five thousand infantry and one thousand cavalry, had bothered in the meantime to halt the imperial soldiers, now more a horde of desperadoes than an army, marching on Rome. No one seemed to realize that the soldiers' desperation meant they were now capable of anything. They reached the walls of Rome on 4 May. They stormed the city on the sixth, and they sacked it.

This truly was the moral demise of Italy, as is so often said. It was also the end of Medici rule in Florence. On 16 May, the cardinal of Cortona, more out of cowardice than out of necessity, allowed the Florentine citizenry to restore the Republic in exchange for assurances of safety for himself, his nephews, and the young Medici. Niccolò Capponi was elected gonfalonier of justice for a year, with the possibility of being reconfirmed for as long as three years. The following day, he assembled the Great Council and empowered it to pass laws and appoint all magistrates. After fifteen years, the "hall" was finally reopened, and Florence was once again free.

Meanwhile, Machiavelli had been working with Guicciardini to save Pope Clement VII, who in his stupidity had failed to stave off the tragic Sack of Rome. When he returned to Florence, he found the citizens rejoicing at their newfound freedom. If they rejoiced, so did he; indeed, his joy was greatest of all. He, too, was a republican: he had served the Republic for fifteen years with passion, intelligence, and impeccable honesty; when the Medici expelled him from the office of secretary, he had written the fundamental work on modern republican thought, the *Discourses,* a book inspired by his love for "living free"; after the *Discourses,* he had written *The Art of War* and the *Florentine Histories,* to teach once again that liberty is best defended by armies under the rule of law and by eliminating the plague of factionalism; he had offered

an education in republican ideals to many young Florentines who
were to be important players in that last Florentine Republic; and
at every opportunity, he had told the Medici that the only proper
government for Florence was a well-ordered republic founded on
the sovereignty of the Great Council.

It was natural that he should expect the revived Republic to
give him back his old post as secretary. Encouraging him in this
expectation were Zanobi Buondelmonti and Luigi Alamanni, his
two old friends from the Orti Oricellari. Instead, on 10 June, one
Francesco Tarugi got the job—he had been secretary to the Eight
of the Pratica since June 1525 and was therefore a Medici supporter.

One factor—which was unfair, wrongheaded, and, even worse,
ridiculous—weighing against Machiavelli in this decision was
certainly that he had served Pope Clement VII in the disastrous
war against the emperor. Even more important, however, was the
now widespread impression that Machiavelli was an evil man, a
heretic, and an adviser to tyrants. The common people, according
to a contemporary, "'hated him because of *The Prince*': the rich
thought his *Prince* was a document written to teach the duke 'how
to take away all their property, from the poor all their liberty;
the *piagnoni* [followers of Savonarola] regarded him as a heretic;
the good thought him sinful; the wicked thought him more
wicked or more capable than themselves—so they all hated him'"
(R, 388–89).

In naming another man secretary, the Florentines could not
have inflicted more pain on the aged Machiavelli. Over the course
of a month, Niccolò had swallowed the bitter pill of watching all
his efforts to free Italy from servitude foiled, then had to see himself kept away from the Palazzo Vecchio once again, this time not
by a Medici but by a republican government. Never before had he
so understood the words of Petrarch with which he concluded
"Exhortation to Penitence," written in that same period or slightly
earlier: "and my repentance, and the clear awareness/that worldly
joy is just a fleeting dream."

Giuliano de' Ricci, the son of Machiavelli's youngest daughter,

Baccina, recorded that his grandfather belonged to a number of lay confraternities, or brotherhoods, whose members gathered "in oratories throughout the city, to sing vespers and say matins, engage in religious discipline, and pursue other good works." Among the customs of these confraternities was that of assigning a lay brother to write an exhortation to penitence to be read during Lent. Since Machiavelli was a "fit and devout and religious person," he was assigned to write one, said de' Ricci.

It is difficult to believe these words. Concerned as he no doubt was with redeeming Machiavelli's reputation as an evil atheist, he presented him as a pious and devout man. But how can we believe in an image of Niccolò retreating to a cloister and exhorting his listeners to penitence, Niccolò who throughout his life followed the maxim "it is better to act and repent than not to act and regret"—certainly the most ferocious possible mockery of penitence? For that matter, "Exhortation to Penitence" is clearly patched together from homiletic commonplaces and paraphrases and quotations from the Psalms and Gospels. In short, it is a commissioned text, like so many other orations and poems Machiavelli wrote.

Machiavelli fell ill immediately after 10 June, apparently of acute peritonitis. On the twentieth, he took what may have been an overdose of the aloe-based pills he had long been using to treat his stomach and head pains. He died on 21 June, after confessing his sins to one Friar Matteo. He was buried on the twenty-second in the church of Santa Croce. During those days of sickness, he told his friends about the dream he had had, the dream with which I began this account of his life. As we have seen, he left the world saying that he preferred to go to Hell in the company of the great ancients to discuss politics, rather than to Heaven with the blessed and the saintly. It was his last joke, told to friends so that together they could laugh about Hell and Heaven, to show them he was still "il Machia" and not even death could remove his smile or freeze his face into a mask of fear.

That is how Niccolò Machiavelli died, with the same smile with which he had lived. We know now that he responded with that smile to the miseries of life, to keep from being overwhelmed by grief, outrage, and melancholy and to keep from giving men and Fortune the cruel satisfaction of seeing him weep. Still, the smile was more than just a defense against life; it was also his way of immersing himself in life. In his smile, there was love of liberty and civil equality, always a powerful force in him, for only among free equals—not among masters and servants—is laughter truly possible. Above all, there was a profound, sincere charity, a charity that made him love the variety of the world and that lay at the heart of his love for his homeland, a benevolent charity that "is not envious, is not perverse, does not show pride, is not ambitious, does not seek her own profit, does not get angry, meditates on the wicked man, does not delight in him, does not take pleasure in vanity, suffers everything, believes everything, hopes everything," as he wrote in "Exhortation to Penitence." These words, which Niccolò borrowed and made his own, are the final key, perhaps, to understanding the beauty of his smile and the wisdom of his life.

Suggested Reading

Albertini, Rudolph von. *Firenze dalla repubblica al principato.* Turin: Einaudi, 1970.

Baron, Hans. *The Crisis of the Early Italian Renaissance: Civic Humanism and Republican Liberty in an Age of Classicism and Tyranny.* Princeton, N.J.: Princeton University Press, 1966.

Berlin, Isaiah. "The Originality of Machiavelli." In *Against the Current,* 25–79. New York: The Viking Press, 1980.

Bock, Gisela, Quentin Skinner, and Maurizio Viroli, eds. *Machiavelli and Republicanism.* Cambridge, U.K.: Cambridge University Press, 1990. See especially Michael Mallett, "The Theory and Practice of Warfare in Machiavelli's Republic" and John Najemy, "The Controversy Surrounding Machiavelli's Service to the Republic."

Chabod, Federico. *Machiavelli and the Renaissance.* London: Bowes and Bowes, 1958.

Colish, Marcia L. "Cicero's *De officiis* and Machiavelli's *Prince.*" *Sixteenth Century Journal* 9 (1978): 81–93.

———. "The Idea of Liberty in Machiavelli." *Journal of the History of Ideas* 32 (1971): 323–50.

De Grazia, Sebastian. *Machiavelli in Hell.* Princeton, N.J.: Princeton University Press, 1993.

Dionisotti, Carlo. *Machiavellerie.* Turin: Einaudi, 1980.

Donaldson, Peter S. *Machiavelli and Mystery of State.* Cambridge, U.K.: Cambridge University Press, 1988.

Garin, Eugenio. *Dal Rinascimento all'Illuminismo.* Pisa: Nistri-Lischi, 1970.

Garver, Eugene. *Machiavelli and the History of Prudence.* Madison: University of Wisconsin Press, 1987.

Gilbert, Allan. *Machiavelli's "Prince" and Its Forerunners.* Durham, N.C.: Duke University Press, 1938.

Gilbert, Felix. *History, Choice, and Commitment.* Cambridge, Mass.: Harvard University Press, 1977.

———. *Machiavelli and Guicciardini: Politics and History in Sixteenth-Century Florence.* Princeton, N.J.: Princeton University Press, 1965.

Kahn, Victoria. *Machiavellian Rhetoric: From the Counter-Reformation to Milton.* Princeton, N.J.: Princeton University Press, 1994.

Mansfield, Harvey C. *Machiavelli's Virtue*. Chicago: University of Chicago Press, 1996.

Martelli, Mario. *Machiavelli e gli storici antichi*. Rome: Salerno, 1998.

———. "Machiavelli politico amante poeta." *Interpres* 17 (1998): 211–56.

Najemy, John M. *Between Friends: Discourses of Power and Desire in the Machiavelli-Vettori Letters of 1513–1515*. Princeton, N.J.: Princeton University Press, 1993.

Parel, Anthony J. *The Machiavellian Cosmos*. New Haven, Conn.: Yale University Press, 1992.

Pitkin, Hanna. *Fortune Is a Woman: Gender and Politics in the Thought of Niccolò Machiavelli*. Berkeley: University of California Press, 1984.

Pocock, J. A. G. *The Machiavellian Moment: Florentine Political Thought and the Atlantic Republican Tradition*. Princeton, N.J.: Princeton University Press, 1975.

Price, Russell. "The Theme of *Gloria* in Machiavelli." *Renaissance Quarterly* 30 (1977): 588–631.

Procacci, Giuliano. *Machiavelli nella cultura europea dell'età moderna*. Bari and Rome: Laterza, 1995.

Ridolfi, Roberto. *The Life of Niccolò Machiavelli*. Trans. Cecil Grayson. Chicago: University of Chicago Press, 1963.

Rubinstein, N. *The Government of Florence under the Medici, 1434–1494*. Oxford: Oxford University Press, 1966.

Sasso, Gennaro. *Machiavelli e gli antichi e altri saggi*. 3 vols. Milan and Naples: Riccardo Ricciardi, 1987.

———. *Niccolò Machiavelli*. 2 vols. Bologna: Il Mulino, 1993.

Skinner, Quentin. *The Foundations of Modern Political Thought: The Renaissance*. Vol. 1. Cambridge, U.K.: Cambridge University Press, 1978.

———. *Machiavelli*. Oxford: Oxford University Press, 1981.

———. "Machiavelli on the Maintenance of Liberty." *Politics* 18 (1983): 3–15.

Tinkler, John F. "Praise and Advice: Rhetorical Approaches in More's *Utopia* and Machiavelli's *The Prince*." *Sixteenth Century Journal* 19 (1988): 187–207.

Villari, Pasquale. *The Life and Times of Niccolò Machiavelli*. 1929. Reprint, Houston, Tex.: Scholarly Publications, 1972.

Viroli, Maurizio. *From Politics to Reason of State*. Cambridge, U.K.: Cambridge University Press, 1992.

———. *Machiavelli*. Oxford: Oxford University Press, 1998.

Index